A LEGAL THEORY OF STATE-OWNED ENTERPRISES

The privatization of state-owned enterprises (SOEs) can be better understood as a process of legalization rather than liberalization, given that the state often continues to regulate private enterprises even after privatization. This process requires clearly defining the boundaries between public power and private property, which entails significant social costs. The continued prevalence of SOEs in China is partly due to the difficulty of defining these boundaries, especially in sectors where safeguarding private property clashes with state priorities. Such sectors include water utilities, coal mining, commercial banking, and infrastructure, where competing state goals complicate the full privatization of the market. Therefore, it is essential to be cautious against the "legal centrist view" that assumes law is inherently superior to state ownership. Privatizing SOEs is not merely the transfer of equity – it demands the establishment of advanced legal and regulatory frameworks, making it a complex and gradual endeavor.

JAMES SI ZENG is an associate professor of Law at the University of Hong Kong (HKU). Prior to joining HKU, he served as an associate professor at the Chinese University of Hong Kong, holding a JSD from Yale Law School and dual degrees in Law and Economics from Peking University.

"*A Legal Theory of State-Owned Enterprises* provides an important new theoretical perspective on the development and persistence of Chinese SOEs, based on a wide-ranging analysis of the interplay between ownership costs and regulatory costs in China's distinctive political/legal system. But Professor Zeng's book is more than a theoretical exercise. It offers a nuanced, thoroughly researched account of China's public and private-sector commercial actors and a roadmap for their future reform. It should be read by anyone interested in Chinese economic and institutional development."

Curtis J. Milhaupt, William F. Baxter – Visa International Professor of Law, Stanford Law School

"Professor Zeng's insightful analysis of SOEs highlights the critical role that law and legal institutions can play in shaping state and private ownership. A particular contribution is his consideration of the under-explored concept of regulatory costs, demonstrating how contractual limitations and the incompleteness of the law, among other factors, can influence the choice between SOEs and private ownership. In doing so, Professor Zeng provides a nuanced framework in which to understand the trade-offs between state ownership and public regulation, and demonstrates that the choice between public and private ownership is often shaped by the structure and stability of the law and legal institutions. Professor Zeng's analysis is particularly compelling in its application to China, providing a sector-specific review of SOEs and offering new insight into why SOEs are dominant in some industries while private enterprise thrives in others. In the end, beyond SOEs, Professor Zeng's analysis is a prescription for what China must do to encourage further private ownership. As he explains, the cost of replacing state ownership with a formal legal and regulatory system may be substantial. Nevertheless, he provides a compelling argument for why China must commit to doing so if it chooses to promote further private investment."

Charles K. Whitehead, Myron C. Taylor Alumni Professor of Business Law, Cornell Law School

A LEGAL THEORY OF STATE-OWNED ENTERPRISES

The China Experience

JAMES SI ZENG
University of Hong Kong

CAMBRIDGE
UNIVERSITY PRESS

CAMBRIDGE
UNIVERSITY PRESS

Shaftesbury Road, Cambridge CB2 8EA, United Kingdom

One Liberty Plaza, 20th Floor, New York, NY 10006, USA

477 Williamstown Road, Port Melbourne, VIC 3207, Australia

314–321, 3rd Floor, Plot 3, Splendor Forum, Jasola District Centre, New Delhi – 110025, India

103 Penang Road, #05-06/07, Visioncrest Commercial, Singapore 238467

Cambridge University Press is part of Cambridge University Press & Assessment, a department of the University of Cambridge.

We share the University's mission to contribute to society through the pursuit of education, learning and research at the highest international levels of excellence.

www.cambridge.org
Information on this title: www.cambridge.org/9781009457682

DOI: 10.1017/9781009457736

When citing this work, please include a reference to the DOI 10.1017/9781009457736

First published 2026

Cover image: Shanghai Nanpu bridge at night / Yaorusheng / Moment / Getty Images

A catalogue record for this publication is available from the British Library

A Cataloging-in-Publication data record for this book is available from the Library of Congress

ISBN 978-1-009-45768-2 Hardback

CONTENTS

FIGURES

TABLES

ACKNOWLEDGMENTS

This book marks an important milestone in my academic journey. It has been with me since I first embarked on my scholarly career at Peking University. During this period, I began contemplating pursuing a doctoral program in the United States, and my interest in applying classical theories of law and economics to the study of Chinese state-owned enterprises began to take shape. I am immensely grateful to my mentor Yan Liu, as well as to Ruoying Chen, Feng Deng, Yunsong Ge, Jianbo Liu, Daxing Jiang, Bing Peng, Charles Whitehead, and Defeng Xu, whose perspectives profoundly fueled my academic curiosity. Additionally, I had the privilege of visiting Columbia Law School, where I drew inspiration from the insights of the faculty members – especially Ronald Gilson, Zohar Goshen, Curtis Milhaupt, and Thomas Merrill – whose work significantly influenced my early thoughts on this subject.

The book project formally began when I was pursuing a JSD degree at Yale Law School, where I had the great fortune of working under the supervision of Henry Hansmann. His invaluable guidance was critical in helping me develop and refine the central arguments of this work. I am deeply grateful for his mentorship, as well as the support I received from other distinguished faculty members, including Christine Jolls and Yair Listokin. At this stage, I particularly benefited from the insightful suggestions of Taisu Zhang, who helped correct the broader direction of my dissertation, and from Curtis Milhaupt, whose comments significantly strengthened my arguments. I also benefited from the thoughtful feedback offered by Ian Ayres, Alvin Klevorick, Daniel Markovits, Jonathan Macey, John Morley, Mariana Pargendler, Robert Post, Roberta Romano, Susan Rose-Ackerman, and Charles Sabel. This project was further enriched by the input of Yutian An, Donald Clarke, Boli Chen, Xiaodong Ding, Qinwei Gao, Jingwen Han, Yinzhi Miao, Xu Pang, Shitong Qiao, Zhiang Song, Yun Tang, Kate Tian, Andrew Verstein, Jingjian Wu, and Wenguang Yu, all of whom provided valuable comments and critiques. I am also grateful for the financial support from the Oscar M. Ruebhausen Fund at Yale Law School.

Following the completion of my doctoral studies, I joined the Chinese University of Hong Kong and continued to refine this research over the years. I am grateful for the comments from my colleagues and friends in Hong Kong, especially Anatole Boute, Ngoc Son Bui, David Donald, Robin Huang, Shixue Hu, Lauren Lin, Zhuang Liu, Noam Noked, Christopher Roberts, Samuli Seppänen, Chao Xi, Ying Xia, and Yuhong Zhao. Their perspectives and suggestions helped me further sharpen the arguments presented in this book.

Parts of this work were presented at various conferences in the past few years, including the annual conference of the American Law and Economics Association. I received constructive feedback from Omri Ben-Shahar, Ryan Bubb, Anthony Casey, Yun-Chien Chang, Kevin Davis, Li Guo, Haibo He, William Hubbard, Cree Jones, Keneeth Khoo, William Organek, Adriana Robertson, Holger Spamann, Yingmao Tang, Wenyu Wang, and Wenming Xu. Their expertise and insights were invaluable in sharpening my analysis and advancing the development of this project. Additionally, one of the articles that serve as a cornerstone for this project was honored with a nomination for the "2019 Masahiko Aoki Award for Economics Paper" at Tsinghua University. I am immensely grateful for the feedback provided by Shuo Chen, Barry Naughton, and Lan Xue during this process.

I also extend my heartfelt thanks to Joe Ng, the editor at Cambridge University Press, for his dedicated efforts, expertise, and patience throughout the publication process. Two anonymous reviewers invited by the press evaluated my book proposal and initial sample chapters. One of them provided particularly encouraging feedback that strengthened my resolve to pursue this project. Although I do not know their identities, I hope they will read this acknowledgment and know how much I appreciate their support.

Overall, this book benefited from the collective insights, critical feedback, and unwavering support I received from so many individuals across different institutions and stages of my academic career. I am profoundly thankful to all those who walked beside me during the various stages of my academic path, nurturing and shaping the ideas that have found a place in this book.

Some parts of this book draw on earlier articles of mine, including: "Competing with Leviathan: Law and Government Ownership in China's

Public-Private Partnership Market," *76 International Review of Law and Economics 106166* (2023); "Judicial Reform and Privatization of State-Owned Enterprises: Empirical Evidence from China's Public-Private Partnership Market," *European Business Organization Law Review* (2025); "Environmental Policy and Compensation in China: An Empirical Analysis of Article Eight of the Chinese Administrative License Law," *34 Journal of Environmental Law* (2022) 287; and "State Ownership and Regulatory Costs: A Law and Economic Analysis of State-Owned Enterprise in China," *31 Columbia Journal of Asian Law 1* (2017). These materials have been extensively revised and integrated to support the broader themes and arguments presented here.

LIST OF ACRONYMS

BOT	build-operate-transfer
BRICS	Brazil, Russia, India, China, South Africa, Iran, Egypt, Ethiopia, and the United Arab Emirates
CBRC	China Banking Regulatory Commission
CIC	China Investment Corporation
CIRC	Chinese Insurance Regulatory Commission
CPC	Communist Party of China
CSRC	China Securities Regulatory Commission (CSRC)
ESG	Environmental, Social, and Governance
GDP	gross domestic product
ICBC	Industrial and Commercial Bank of China
LGFV	local government financial vehicle
LGOE	local-government-owned enterprise
LTF	legal theory of finance
LTS	legal theory of SOEs
OECD	Organisation for Economic Co-operation and Development
OLA	Orderly Liquidation Authority
PICC	People's Insurance Company of China
PLICC	People's Life Insurance Company of China
PPP	public-private partnership
RMB	renminbi
SASAC	State Asset Supervisory and Administrative Commission
SIFI	systemically important financial institutions
SOE	state-owned enterprise
SPC	Supreme People's Court of China
SPE	sole proprietorship enterprise
TOT	toll-operate-transfer
TVE	township and village enterprise
UCB	urban commercial bank
UCC	urban credit cooperative
USD	United States dollar

Introduction

Since the 1960s, numerous nations have embraced the concept of privatization of state-owned enterprises (SOEs), transferring their equity stakes to private investors, and encouraging private investment in sectors traditionally under state control (Megginson and Netter, 2001, pp. 325–326). This wave of privatization aligns with the prevailing view that SOEs are inefficient, mainly due to the lack of incentives for government officials to reduce costs and promote innovation. The World Bank, in a highly influential report published in the 1990s, presented this argument and sought ways to reform "inefficient, loss-making state-owned enterprises that impose a significant burden on government budgets and scarce resources in many countries" (World Bank, 1995, p. 50). This view finds substantial support in empirical studies, consistently demonstrating the comparatively weaker financial performance of SOEs in relation to private firms (Megginson and Netter, 2001, p. 333).

Despite the widespread belief that SOEs are inefficient, SOEs remain a common phenomenon across the globe (Kowalski et al., 2013; Pargendler, 2019, p. 5). According to a report issued by the Organisation for Economic Co-operation and Development (OECD) on SOEs (Kowalski et al., 2013), 204 out of the 2,000 largest listed corporations in the world in 2010–11 were state-owned (Kowalski et al., 2013). Developing countries, especially the "Brazil, Russia, India, China, and South Africa (BRICS)," have a significantly larger number of SOEs than developed countries. Another report by the OECD in 2017 shows that the central governments of about 40 countries (excluding China) hold more than 2,000 SOEs, collectively valued at USD 2.4 trillion (Organisation for Economic Co-operation and Development, 2017). Of the BRICS, China has the largest number of SOEs – the Chinese central government holds over 50,000 enterprises collectively valued at USD 29.2 trillion (OECD, 2017).

Since 1978, China has endeavored to shift from a centrally planned economy to a market-oriented one by encouraging the development of private enterprises and transferring SOE ownership to private investors.

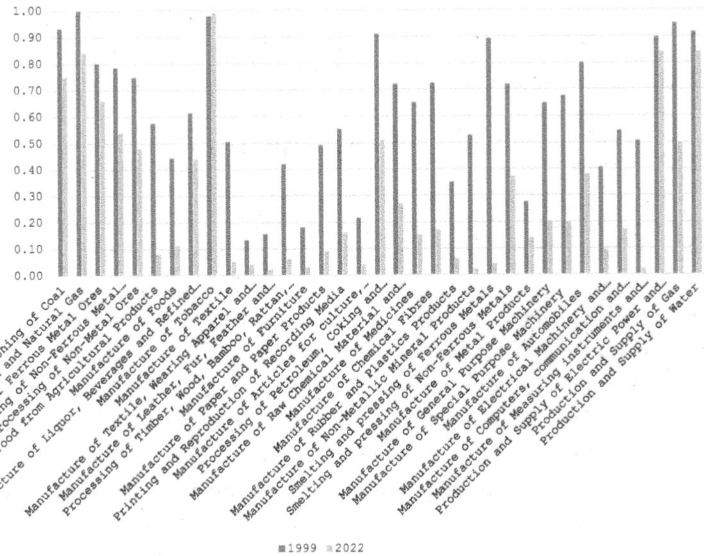

Figure 1 Proportion of assets held by SOEs across sectors.

Figure 1 illustrates the proportion of assets held by SOEs in different industrial sectors in 1999 and 2022, based on data from China's National Bureau of Statistics. In most sectors, the proportion of SOE-held assets has significantly decreased over the years. The manufacturing sectors, including food, textile, leather, furniture, timber, paper and paper products, rubber, and plastics, experienced the most substantial decline, with the proportion of SOE-held assets dropping below 10 percent. Similarly, the proportion of SOE-held assets fell below 10 percent in the processing of food from agricultural products, and printing and reproduction of recording media. In China, divergent viewpoints regarding the efficiency of SOEs coexist, although a majority of studies confirm their underperformance compared to private enterprises (Zhang, 1994; Bai et al., 2006b; Hu et al., 2006).

While the privatization of SOEs in many sectors has been successful, SOEs continue to maintain a dominant presence in specific sectors in China, including coal mining, petroleum and natural gas extraction, tobacco, and production and supply of electric power and water, as illustrated in Figure 1. This uneven distribution of SOEs across sectors is not exclusive to China and can be observed in other countries as well. According to a report by the OECD, SOEs globally tend to concentrate primarily in network industries such as electricity, gas, transportation, telecommunications, utility sectors, and the financial sector (OECD, 2017).

Given the general belief that SOEs are inefficient, why has China failed to further privatize the remaining SOEs in these particular sectors while it has succeeded in other sectors? This book seeks to offer an explanation for the historical development of SOEs and their uneven presence across various sectors in China, which are important both theoretically and practically. Over the past few decades, China has experienced a dramatic economic rise, becoming the world's second-largest economy. In 1994, China's GDP per capita was approximately $400. By 2022, this figure had surged to around $12,000. This remarkable growth has been the subject of extensive academic debate, largely because China's economic model – characterized by a significant presence of SOEs, substantial state intervention, and centralized planning – differs markedly from that of more liberal economies. China's economic development has sparked two competing views. One perspective argues that China's model, referred to as the "Beijing Consensus," has significant advantages (Ramo, 2004). Proponents of this view suggest that there are rationales behind the substantial involvement of the state in the economy. The opposing view contends that China's economic rise was driven by neoliberal economic reforms, particularly the privatization of SOEs and the loosening of state control over the economy (Zhou, 2014). This perspective holds that the economic liberalization initiated in the late 1970s, which encouraged private enterprise and market mechanisms, has been the true engine of China's growth. In recent years, as China's economic growth has decelerated, some have suggested that China may have reached "the end of its economic miracle" due to the lack of further reforms and the privatization of SOEs (Goldberg, 2023; Posen, 2023). Understanding the challenges facing the privatization of SOEs in China is crucial for comprehending the trajectory of China's development, a subject of significant interest given the country's substantial economic size and global influence.

Additionally, understanding the dynamics of SOEs is vital because they offer lessons that might be applicable globally. SOEs remain prevalent in many other developing countries, such as India and Brazil (OECD, 2017; Zhang, 2023). Even in liberal states such as the United States, government-owned entities are prevalent in the hospital, school, utilities, banking, and transportation sectors (Hanna, 2018, p. 18). Statistics show that 87 percent of the population in the United States receive piped water from public-owned utilities (Kapczynski and Michaels, 2024). The role of government ownership has increasingly been recognized as important in the implementation of the state's policy even in liberal states (Kapczynski and Michaels, 2024). As SOEs remain, and will likely continue to be, a significant organizational form in many states, this book contributes not only to discussions on Chinese economic and legal reforms but also provides important perspectives for other countries.

I. Main Arguments

This book aims to formulate a Legal Theory of SOEs (LTS) to explain the dynamics of SOEs and private enterprises in China. LTS posits that the development of SOEs and private enterprises is determined by two competing costs: ownership costs and regulatory costs. SOEs typically incur higher ownership costs relative to private enterprises due to the phenomenon of "soft budget constraints" – government officials overseeing SOEs do not face significant pressures to enhance performance because SOEs generally do not face the threat of bankruptcy. Additionally, ownership costs are high because government officials often lack incentives to pursue profits. However, private enterprises may incur higher regulatory costs compared with SOEs because of the social costs associated with using law rather than ownership to regulate enterprises, which include enactment costs, enforcement costs, and the costs resulting from the opportunistic behavior of the government or the enterprise. These costs arise because of uncertainty, bounded rationality, and asset specificity. In a rapidly developing country where the economy and society are evolving swiftly, the law tends to be incomplete, making it costly for the legislature or other lawmakers to establish sophisticated rules in advance (Pistor and Xu, 2002). Moreover, once rules are promulgated, both the government and private entities may engage in opportunistic behavior, resulting in social losses. For example, the government may alter rules after investors have made fixed investments, while private investors might exploit these regulatory loopholes or engage in regulatory arbitrage once the regulatory framework has been established and not yet updated.

LTS suggests that the extent of state ownership in the market is influenced by regulatory costs through both supply-side and demand-side mechanisms. From a supply-side perspective, the state may prefer to retain SOEs if it perceives that privatization could lead to instability. Post-privatization, the government loses direct control over these enterprises and must rely on regulatory frameworks to manage their conduct. Given the inherent limitations of legal systems, regulatory efforts may sometimes fall short of providing effective control compared to direct ownership. If regulatory costs are borne by the government, it reinforces the incentive to maintain SOEs. This is exemplified in the case of commercial banks' privatization. While the state can implement various financial regulations to mitigate risk-taking behavior by private banks, these measures may have their own deficiencies. Private banks might find ways to circumvent regulations, potentially leading to significant financial crises that require state intervention, ultimately burdening taxpayers. This risk of regulatory failure thus motivates the state to maintain control over critical sectors like commercial banking.

On the demand side, when private investors are tasked with bearing regulatory costs, it often results in a lack of private investment. In such situations, SOEs may step in as substitutes to fill this investment void and meet market demand, particularly when the government holds the ultimate responsibility for providing essential goods or services. Although strict adherence to rigid regulations might lead to adverse outcomes, governments may prefer to maintain some discretion and flexibility in law enforcement to avert such issues (Vermeule, 2009). However, this discretionary power can sometimes be abused, which can deter private investment, leading to the underinvestment problem. For instance, consider a scenario in which the government privatizes a water utilities enterprise. After its sale, the government faces the challenge of regulating water tariffs effectively. If, due to public pressure, it refrains from adjusting tariffs as needed, the water utilities enterprise may incur losses. As a result, the new private owners may face financial difficulties and choose to exit the market, or potential investors may foresee these regulatory challenges and hesitate to invest unless the conditions are exceptionally favorable. In such cases, where private investment is insufficient, the government may find it necessary to rely on SOEs to ensure the continued provision of these vital public services. This situation highlights the critical role of law and regulation in attracting private investment and in the successful reform of SOEs.

It should be recognized that underinvestment and the subsequent demand for SOEs cannot be resolved by simply enhancing the protection of private enterprises against expropriating regulations. The effects of regulation on private property are *reciprocal* in nature – government regulations impose costs on the private sector, and conversely, strengthening the protection for the private sector impacts the state's regulatory flexibility. Therefore, the solution extends beyond merely strengthening protections for private enterprises; it involves developing regulatory institutions capable of reducing the social costs associated with using legal and regulatory institutions.

The magnitude of regulatory costs likely varies across different sectors. This theory can explain the historical development and cross-sectional distribution of SOEs and private enterprises in China. LTS posits that in economic sectors where regulatory costs are high, SOEs play a larger role. Legal changes are more frequent in some sectors than others and the government possesses wide discretion in exercising its power. In these sectors, property protection and contract enforcement are likely to be weaker.

It should also be noted that LTS does not posit that the current level of SOEs in China is socially optimal. Determining the optimal level of state ownership is a complex question that this book cannot fully address. Importantly, LTS serves as an explanatory theory rather than a justificatory one (Coleman, 2001). The primary goal of this book is to deepen the understanding of the forces shaping the development of SOEs and to explore the reasons why privatization efforts sometimes succeed and sometimes fail, underscoring the influence of regulatory costs. Understanding the impact of regulatory costs is a necessary step for considering how best to reduce these costs by developing various institutions and innovative regulatory measures.

II. Contribution to the Literature

Given the significance of SOEs and the process of privatization, there exists a substantial body of literature and a long-standing history of discourse surrounding SOEs and privatization. LTS contributes to this literature and fills an important gap by highlighting the trade-off between state ownership and regulation and closely evaluates the social costs associated with SOEs as opposed to regulated private enterprises.

A. *Economic Theories of State Ownership and Privatization*

The prevailing scholarship mostly treats privatization and the prevalence of SOEs as intentional choices made by governmental authorities. In large part, these studies assume that privatization is a unilateral decision by the government, leading them to concentrate on analyzing privatization as a facet of public policy. The inquiries they undertake revolve around whether the state should pursue privatization, the rationales behind retaining SOEs, and whether privatization enhances managerial performance and overall efficiency. Their endeavors involve evaluating the effectiveness of privatization and gathering empirical data to assess the advantages it brings.

There exists a widespread belief that privatization enhances efficiency. Numerous factors can contribute to the potential underperformance of SOEs compared to private enterprises. Firstly, the objectives of SOEs may not align with profit maximization and market performance. Prioritizing social and political objectives over profitability can result in inefficiencies and suboptimal resource allocation within SOEs. As Andrei Shleifer notes, "private ownership should generally be preferred to public ownership when the incentives to innovate and to contain costs must be strong" (Shleifer, 1998, p. 136). Secondly, government control and intervention can impede the flexibility and decision-making autonomy of SOEs. Political considerations and bureaucratic processes may hinder effective management and resource allocation within these enterprises. Additionally, SOEs encounter the challenge of the soft budget constraint problem, whereby they often enjoy preferential access to financial resources and favorable policies. This grants their managers weaker market constraints and fewer incentives to pursue cost-cutting measures (Megginson and Netter, 2001, p. 331). In contrast, private firms typically face more stringent financial constraints, compelling them to enhance performance in order to secure low-cost funding. These factors collectively contribute to the potential performance disparities between SOEs and private enterprises, underscoring the rationale behind the drive for privatization.

Currently, the primary justification for state ownership in the literature lies in its potential to rectify market failures (Megginson and Netter, 2001, p. 329). State ownership has long been recognized as one of the means to address market failures, including natural monopolies, externalities, and transaction costs (Viscusi et al., 2005). However, scholars have provided various alternatives to address market failures other than state ownership (Viscusi et al., 2005, p. 503). A natural monopoly, for example, can be subject to rate regulation or competitive bidding that could also address the market failure, rendering state ownership unnecessary. States can intervene in private property rights by regulation regardless of whether they possess ownership. It thus remains questionable whether it is necessary for the state to own an enterprise at all. Additionally, privatization often leads to more regulation, which also addresses market failures (Vogel, 1996; Milhaupt, 1998, p. 1146; Keleman and Sibbett, 2004, p. 103). The need to address market failures alone does not explain the dominance of SOEs (Shapiro and Willig, 1990). A comprehensive explanation for SOEs thus requires the analysis of the precise market failure that state ownership aims to tackle and the mechanisms through which it does so. Likewise, some scholars contend that SOEs can address social issues such as income inequality (Megginson and Netter, 2001, p. 39). Yet, this argument raises the question of why alternative measures like taxation cannot achieve distributional goals at lower costs.

A similar perspective is that SOEs can offer public goods. Public goods are characterized by two key attributes: non-rivalry and non-excludability. Non-rivalry indicates that one person's consumption does not reduce the availability of the good for others, and non-excludability means it is not feasible to prevent anyone from using the good. Although private markets may not supply public goods at a socially optimal level, states can subsidize these goods to encourage their provision, thus making SOEs unnecessary.

Hart, Shleifer, and Vishny analyzed the efficiency of privatization and the appropriate role of government using the incomplete contract theory. They investigated the choices made by governments in terms of "contracting out" traditional state services to private parties or providing them "in-house" (i.e., inside the government or SOEs) (Laffont and Tirole, 1993, p. 638; Hart et al., 1997, p. 1127; Hart, 2003). Contracting out services to private firms can enhance efficiency by incentivizing cost-cutting measures to maximize profits. However, there is a risk that private firms may compromise on the quality of goods or services to reduce costs. Due to the inherent limitations of contracts, governments may struggle to exert full control over the behavior of privatized firms. Consequently, the theory of incomplete contracts presents a case for the provision of goods or services by the public sector (Hart et al., 1997, p. 1128; Williamson, 1999, p. 331).

Sappington and Stiglitz also point out that the choice between the public and private provision of goods depends on the transaction costs of governmental intervention (Sappington and Stiglitz, 1987, p. 567). Transaction costs stem from several sources. First, the private parties may have limited liability and hence do not bear the full costs of their actions. When the government and private party entered into a contract, the private party may default on the contract terms. While it can be held liable for the damages, the damages may be too high and its assets may be insufficient to bear the liability. This is especially true when the contract involves public interests, which are usually vast. Second, both the private parties and the government must find a way to make credible commitments. Each side may renege on their promises. If either the government or the private party anticipates that the risks of such breaches of contract are high, they would not easily enter into the contract in the first place or would do so only when the terms are highly favorable. Third, there could also be contracting costs and enforcement costs. Sappington and Stiglitz argue that government intervention in private firms is more costly than intervention in public firms, which justifies SOEs to the extent that government intervention is necessary.

The theory proposed in this book shares similarities with the analysis of Hart et al. (1997) and Sappington and Stiglitz (1987), but it offers several distinct contributions. Firstly, these studies primarily focus on the supply side and the public choice aspect of privatization, by considering the expected benefits and costs when choosing between public and private provision (Sappington and Stiglitz, 1987, p. 580). The discussion to be presented in this book will not be limited to government choices, but will also examine the choices made by private parties. In other words, it not only looks at how the government should decide between producing goods and services internally or outsourcing them to others (known as the supply side) but also considers situations where private parties don't show enough interest in investing (known as the demand side), leading to a demand for the goods and services provided by SOEs. The analysis of the demand side scrutinizes the incentives of private investors, examining their willingness to acquire ownership stakes from the government, invest in new enterprises, or increase their investments and expand their market presence. Throughout the book, special emphasis is placed on the crucial role played by robust legal institutions capable of upholding property protection and ensuring the enforcement of contracts.

Additionally, some of the analyses conducted by Hart et al. and Sappington and Stiglitz cannot directly apply in the context of China. This book refines their theoretical analysis by considering different assumptions based on experiences from China where the institutional arrangements differ significantly compared to the United States (Sappington and Stiglitz, 1987, p. 568).

Lastly, this book also makes the analysis of the supply side more complete. While Hart et al. and Sappington and Stiglitz focus on government-enterprise contracting and transaction costs, this book develops a theory that applies not only to situations where the government and the enterprise have a contractual relationship but also to cases where they have a regulatory relationship. This book thus addresses not just transaction costs but also regulatory costs – the social cost comparison between regulated private enterprises and SOEs that produce goods for consumers, which has yet to be sufficiently analyzed. This broader perspective is crucial because most of the enterprises in the economy do not directly engage in contracts with the government, thus expanding the scope of analysis.

Furthermore, current studies have not fully considered the relationship between law and state ownership. Current studies have discussed the advantages of SOEs versus contracting out. However, there is insufficient analysis of the relative advantages and disadvantages of using regulation rather than SOEs to achieve state-desired goals. If state ownership is meant to implement the state's policy, why not use the law to achieve the same goal? This book intends to show that law plays an essential role in this analysis because it is one of the major substitutes for state ownership. It will engage in an analysis of the different social costs associated with the trade-off between law and state ownership.

The argument that aligns closely with my thesis is put forth by Laffont and Tirole, who acknowledge that private firms must consider the interests of both shareholders and regulators. This dual responsibility can lead to inefficiencies because the two principals may "exert externalities on each other unless the agent [enterprise] carries full responsibility for social welfare" (Laffont and Tirole, 1993, p. 639; Tirole, 1994, p. 19; Pargendler et al., 2013, p. 575). This book aims to contribute to the existing literature by further developing this idea. It is important to highlight that Laffont and Tirole do not differentiate between regulation and contract, leading them to conclude that one disadvantage of public enterprises is under-investment. However, as demonstrated in this book, private enterprises may also under-invest due to the potential for regulatory policy changes initiated by the state. Moreover, this book seeks to emphasize the distinct characteristics of regulation and its associated social costs, which are separate from contract considerations. This aspect has not been fully recognized, as noted by Hart et al., who acknowledge that they do not explicitly address regulation but suggest that "any regulatory policy can be interpreted as an (incomplete) contract and vice versa" (Hart et al., 1997, p. 1131). This book also aims to improve the theoretical framework for analyzing the comparative costs of regulation and state ownership by clearly illustrating the sources of regulatory costs and examining the specific legal institutions and laws that support regulation. This includes an examination of administrative law, property protection, financial regulation, and corporate law.

LTS is broadly connected to the study on "new comparative economics" proposed by Djankov et al. (2003, p. 598). They argue that all societies face the danger of disorder and dictatorship (Djankov et al., 2003, p. 598). Private orderings, private litigation, regulation, and state ownership are four common strategies to contain disorder and dictatorship, each involving different levels of public control. States can choose among different institutions based on the cost of disorder and dictatorship. State ownership is sometimes necessary when the cost of disorder from private control is too high (Djankov et al., 2003, p. 604). This book further discusses the social costs associated with state ownership and regulation, how institutions affect the privatization process, and the factors that may contribute to or thwart this change.

B. Political and Political Economy Theories of China's State-Owned Enterprises

Another line of literature employs political and political economy theories to explain SOEs in China. From a political theory perspective, one may believe that SOEs are solely determined by the policies made by the Chinese central government. China has adopted a strategy of withdrawing capital from many industries, allowing private enterprises to develop, and maintaining a controlling position in "strategic industries" (Hsueh, 2017, p. 3), including the military, electricity, oil and gas, telecommunication, coal, aerospace and shipping industries, and relatively strong control in "pillar industries" such as automobiles. The policy decisions made by the Chinese government to control "strategic industries," however, do not fully explain the distribution of SOEs either. For example, the machinery and equipment sectors are regarded as pillar sectors, yet SOEs' share of gross output in this sector was only about 20 percent in 2009 (Szamosszegi and Kyle, 2011, p. 41).

More importantly, it is worth noting that in sectors not deemed strategic or pivotal, such as water utilities, SOEs continue to dominate. Despite the issuance of the Opinions of the State Council on the Development of Mixed-Ownership Economy in State-Owned Enterprises in 2015, which aimed to encourage private investment in sectors providing public goods and services like water, electricity, gas, heat, public transportation, and public facilities, the prevalence of SOEs has persisted.

Another explanation for the distribution of SOEs is the political logic (Wang, 2014, p. 666; Choi et al., 2016, p. 9). China's Constitution states that SOEs are to be the "leading force" in the economy. The Chinese governments may be affected by the socialist ideology, deciding to maintain SOEs in important sectors. In addition, SOEs may help the state achieve various goals, including maintaining social stability, making citizens dependent on the state, providing disaster relief and enhancing the government's legitimacy (Wang, 2014; Wen, 2022).

While political theories may explain SOEs in some areas, it does not account for their prevalence in many other sectors. For example, the socialist ideology has not prevented China from encouraging private investments in several strategic and pillar industries such as electricity, telecommunications, and petroleum. In addition, the political theory cannot easily explain the success of SOEs in competitive markets where SOEs and private firms coexist, as exemplified by the infrastructure sector. Additionally, the current political account of SOEs fails to distinguish between central and local governments in China. While the central government intends to maintain control in many sectors, local governments have different incentives, focusing primarily on economic development. Given that SOEs are usually regarded as inefficient, local governments may possess stronger incentives to privatize them. The political logic thus cannot fully explain the landscape of SOEs owned by local governments. LTS offers a better explanation for these phenomena than the political theory.

Another influential theory about SOEs in China is that they exist because they have captured the government to prevent privatization (Zheng and Huang, 2018). Zheng and Huang examine the political economy of SOE reform in China, arguing that certain governmental authorities, especially the State Asset Supervisory and Administrative Commission (SASAC), have become obstacles to the reform. They claim that SOEs have become too politically influential and have captured the state to some extent (Zheng and Huang, 2018). Sarah Eaton notes that the distribution of SOEs across industries is not even and discusses the history of the decisions made by the Chinese government (Eaton, 2015, p. 5). She then discussed various theories, including the theory of capture (Eaton, 2015, p. 20), calculation of national interests, and the influence of ideas regarding the significance of SOEs (Eaton, 2015, p. 21). State capture is generally regarded as a type of *government failure*. Unlike the economic theory that emphasizes the function of state ownership in addressing market failure, this theory implies that certain interest groups manage to capture the government, leading to inefficient policymaking.

Some point out that the problem of state capture is particularly acute in China because Chinese governments often wield extralegal control over private firms or may suddenly change the policies that affect their interests (Chen, 2012, p. 105; Acemoglu and Robinson, 2013, p. 438; Milhaupt and Zheng, 2014). In the late 2000s, commentators noted a trend of "advance of the state, retreat of the private sector" in China where private enterprises were nationalized with relatively low compensation. This raised the concerns that private enterprises are not well protected and that the market will be increasingly dominated by SOEs (Chen, 2012, p. 105; Eaton, 2015). SOEs may have captured regulators who then devised rules that limited market competition, prevented private firms from entering the market, and allowed them to extract economic rents (Yu and Pan, 2008; Luo and Liu, 2009; Wu et al., 2009; Tian and Zhang, 2013; Dong and Liu, 2022).

While all SOEs may obtain subsidies from the government and influence regulatory policies that limit market competition, many have failed to stop the tides of privatization in some sectors of China, such as manufacturing. Supporters of this theory may argue that SOEs with strong political bargaining power and close ties with political elites are more capable of capturing the government. However, a large number of small-sized SOEs that are less capable of capturing the government have not been privatized yet. Meanwhile, private enterprises may also capture the government to gain market access and subsidies. The ability of SOEs to capture government thus does not fully explain the uneven distribution of SOEs across industries.

Another line of literature, related to the theory of state capture, suggests that private enterprises can gain a competitive advantage by seeking state investment or employing executives with political backgrounds. This strategy offers benefits such as easier access to financing (Yu and Pan, 2008), tax incentives (Wu et al., 2009), regulatory permits (Luo and Liu, 2009), and protection of property rights (Tian and Zhang, 2013). Hou Yue examined how private entrepreneurs serve as officials of the People's Congress to protect their property rights (Hou, 2019). According to this perspective, even private enterprises may embrace state investment to exert influence over the government, leading to an increase in the prevalence of SOEs in the market (Dong and Liu, 2022). While these studies share similarities with LTS, they have not fully explained why state ownership is more prominent in certain sectors compared to others. Theoretically, enterprises across all sectors face the need for financing and interactions with tax authorities. LTS addresses this gap by suggesting that the degree of incompleteness of the law varies across sectors. In sectors where laws frequently change to accommodate the state's diverse objectives, the government possesses more authority to adjust policies. As a result, the property interests of some enterprises become more susceptible to state expropriation, leading to more state ownership. Furthermore, LTS proposes that the incompleteness of the law is inevitable in certain areas, providing a better explanation for the development of SOEs in China.

It is important to clarify that this book does not dismiss political and political economy theories as invalid. Indeed, certain empirical evidence presented in Chapter 4 lends partial support to the political economy theory. However, the book contends that these theories are incomplete and necessitate supplementation from LTS. To fully comprehend the diverse behaviors of SOEs across different sectors, it is essential to employ a combination of political, economic, and legal theories. Currently, legal theory has not been adequately emphasized. Grasping the interconnections between law and state ownership is crucial for developing effective policies in China and other regions.

C. The Role of Law in Privatization and the Promotion of Private Enterprises

The existing literature has not adequately explored the impact of law on the extent of privatization of SOEs. While some scholars have acknowledged the significance of efficient legal governance institutions for successful privatization (Stiglitz, 1999, Ramamurti, 2000; Dyck, 2001; Nellis, 2003), these studies do not examine the impacts of law on the level of privatization. Instead, they assess the performance of post-privatized firms and the size of privatization proceeds within jurisdictions characterized by varying degrees of robust legal institutions. For instance, Nellis (2003) concludes that privatization without well-established legal institutions may lead to unfavorable outcomes such as poverty and income inequality. Eagle and Christensen (1995) contend that the performance of privatized firms hinges on the legal framework that safeguards investors. Banerjee and Munger (2004) propose that the rule of law positively correlates with elevated revenues from privatization sales. This book does not focus on economic outcomes such as sales proceeds, firm performance, poverty, and income inequality. Instead, it considers how law affects the extent of privatization.

This book also provides a clearer illustration of the specific aspects of law and legal institutions that may influence the process of privatization. While existing research sometimes underscores the significance of legal institutions in successful privatization, there remains a lack of clarity regarding the specific dimensions of these institutions that drive such outcomes (Bortolotti et al., 2004; Smaoui and Boubakri, 2004). As an example, Bortolotti et al. (2004) resort to legal origin indicators as a proxy for the strength of legal institutions. Since legal origins encompass multifaceted dimensions, it remains unclear why certain legal origins affect the extent of privatization. Smaoui and Boubakri (2004) observe that governance institutions impact privatization proceeds relative to GDP. Nevertheless, their analysis relies on a composite of proxies for governance institutions, encompassing governmental stability, corruption levels, law and order, and bureaucratic quality. Delineating the precise influence of individual legal factors on privatization outcomes becomes difficult. This book further distinguishes different types of social costs associated with regulation, which deepens our understanding of how legal institutions may alleviate these costs.

Additionally, most of the existing studies that emphasize the importance of legal institutions view a strong and competent judicial system as crucial for preventing corporate insiders from expropriating the assets of the post-privatized corporations and alleviate agency costs (Black et al., 2000; Johnson and Shleifer, 2003). Lessons from Russia illustrate that privatizations conducted in the absence of strong legal frameworks often result in suboptimal outcomes for privatized firms. In theory, private investors in firms face threats of expropriation from private parties, such as corporate insiders, as well as from governmental actions. Current studies predominantly focus on the former, while this book concentrates more on the latter. The impact of government opportunism on the extent of privatization is direct: Without strong legal frameworks, private investors may hesitate to invest, which in turn limits the extent of privatization as measured by the proportion of private investment in the market.

Some existing studies also consider the function of state ownership in addressing defects of legal or regulatory institutions, similar to the arguments presented in this book. Yingyi Qian points out that state ownership is a second-best choice during the transitional period, given that many institutions, such as the tax collecting system, are not yet fully developed. He also argues that in regulated industries, such as the banking industry, SOEs should continue to exist (Qian, 2002, p. 1).

However, it remains unclear what makes tax collection and regulation in these industries particularly difficult and whether they are socially costly, raising questions about the necessity of maintaining SOEs in these sectors.

The argument proposed by Jiahua Che and Yingyi Qian also shares similarities with the analysis in this book, particularly in their exploration of the dynamics between local government-owned enterprises and private enterprises in China. Che and Qian (1998) argue that enterprises owned by local governments have advantages over private enterprises, notably due to their reduced propensity to conceal revenue for tax evasion purposes and their enhanced access to state protection for their property (Che and Qian, 1998, p. 468). However, their discussion does not fully address why private enterprises have managed to thrive in certain sectors despite these advantages of state ownership. This leads to an incomplete explanation that warrants further exploration. This book emphasizes the varying strength of private property protection across different sectors and its consequential impact on the success of private enterprises. The degree of regulatory oversight and intervention by the state plays a significant role in this dynamic. In industries subjected to stringent regulation, the state reserves the right to adjust policies and regulations over time, introducing a layer of uncertainty that can deter private investment. Such regulatory adjustments often entail higher costs for compliance and operation, disproportionately affecting sectors where state intervention is a recurring or predominant feature.

LTS is closely connected to the transaction cost theory developed by Ronald Coase and Oliver Williamson and the theory of the ownership of enterprises developed by Henry Hansmann (Coase, 1937; Williamson, 1985; Hansmann, 1988). Current studies have recognized that economic organizations serve to reduce transaction costs. Some studies have found that government expropriation limits the extent of private investment and contributes to the prevalence of SOEs (Troesken and Geddes, 2003; Masten, 2011). This book further extends the theory of transaction costs to the context of regulation, conceptualizing the law and regulatory rules as commitments made by the state to the people and develops a more comprehensive framework for understanding the various kinds of opportunistic governmental behavior, including the strategic use of tariff regulation, legal changes, or extralegal control. It also emphasizes that the opportunistic behavior of both the government and private parties are two sides of the same coin. SOEs can be viewed as a way to address the regulatory costs resulting from the incompleteness of the law, which can explain the continued presence of SOEs across sectors in China.

LTS is also related to the legal theory of finance (LTF) proposed by Katharina Pistor (Pistor, 2013). According to LTF, the financial market is constructed by law, which enforces legal claims hierarchically. At its core, the law is bent because strict enforcement may lead to the disability of the financial system. In liberal states, government intervention in the market is relatively rare, and the financial market is among the few examples where the government intervenes to prevent disastrous outcomes. In China, the government is more concerned with stability and decides not to enforce the law strictly. It thus intervenes in a more flexible way to maintain control, considering a broader range of sectors essential for maintaining control and enforces legal claims and private property hierarchically. In China, the entire economic system, not just the financial system, is hierarchical rather than "flat." SOEs are more likely to be prevalent in some areas where there are perceived needs for intervention.

LTS also contributes to the literature on law and development. Traditional views in this field emphasize that robust legal protection of private property encourages investment and fosters the growth of private enterprises (Trubek, 1972a; North, 1990; Clarke, 2003; Acemoglu and Robinson, 2013). It is often presumed that enhanced protection of private enterprises could stimulate investment, thereby diminishing the prevalence of SOEs in China's economy. However, LTS posits that strong property rights may restrict regulation. It underscores that the effects of regulation on private property are reciprocal: While regulations levy costs on private property, stringent property protections might also limit governmental regulatory agility. Therefore, the emphasis should shift from merely strengthening property rights to reducing overall regulatory costs.

III. Structure of the Book

The book will proceed in the following order. Chapter 1 will develop LTS, analyzing how law affects the development of private enterprises and the various costs associated with the incompleteness of the law. Meanwhile, private enterprises have an advantage in reducing the ownership costs, which include the agency costs between the owner and the manager of enterprises, the decision-making costs, as well as the costs of risk-bearing. While current studies have considered the ownership costs of SOEs, they have not systematically analyzed regulatory costs. This chapter will identify the factors that affect these costs and describe the potential mechanisms through which these costs affect the state ownership of the firm.

Chapter 2 will apply LTS to China's context and explain the evolution of SOEs owned by local governments and private enterprises in several sectors, including water utilities, coal, steel, iron, and commercial banking. It will present empirical evidence to support LTS, and provide a detailed account of how regulatory costs affect state ownership through the demand-side and supply-side mechanisms. It will also emphasize the strength of LTS in explaining the development of SOEs and private enterprises compared to the alternative political theories.

Chapter 3 delves into the demand-side mechanism and scrutinizes the extent of legal protection afforded to private enterprises in China. A widely held view attributes the dominance of SOEs and the underdevelopment of private enterprises in China's economy to the inadequate protection of private enterprises. However, this perspective does not adequately explain why SOEs are more prevalent in certain sectors than others. This chapter posits that the legal protection for private enterprises is hierarchical – the strength of protection varies across sectors. It investigates the legal protection provided to private enterprises during periods of legal transition. By analyzing disclosed judicial judgments, this chapter identifies the factors influencing the level of protection afforded to enterprises and illustrates the varying degrees of protection across different sectors. This analysis suggests that the theory of regulatory costs more accurately explains the relatively weak legal protection for private enterprises in China.

Chapter 4 will further examine private and state ownership of the public-private partnership (PPP) project companies in the infrastructure sectors. In China, the infrastructure landscape is characterized by significant participation from SOEs, though private enterprises are also permitted to compete in this sector. Presently, numerous local administrations across China deploy PPPs as a mechanism to promote investment in infrastructure projects, with competing firms engaging in a bidding process for these initiatives. This Chapter explores the impact of strengthening judicial power on privatization levels by analyzing a reform initiated in 2014. This reform curtailed the local authorities' control over the budgetary and staffing decisions of local judiciaries, which bolstered judicial independence. Empirical evidence shows that a judiciary with greater power is linked to an increased rate of privatization within China's PPP market. The findings imply that the dominance of SOEs in China can, to some extent, be attributed to the absence of a judiciary capable of safeguarding private investment against governmental appropriation. The promotion of judicial power boosts investor confidence, thereby enhancing privatization through a market-driven mechanism.

Chapter 5 will examine the development of the corporate form of SOEs in China. It will show that turning SOEs into state-owned corporations affects ownership costs and regulatory costs simultaneously. On the one hand, as SOEs become legal persons and more independent, ownership costs generally decline because the "soft-budget constraint" problem is alleviated. On the other hand, state-owned corporations have stronger incentives to pursue profits. They may then use the law to resist control from regulators, giving rise to higher regulatory costs. Today, some state-owned corporations remain different from private corporations. Many do not share the essential characteristics of corporations – limited liability, legal personality, transferrable shares, and delegated management. The theory proposed in this book can explain the changes in the organizational forms of SOEs in China.

Based on the above chapters, the final chapter will draw conclusions and consider several theoretical and policy implications. It will discuss the policies on privatization as well as on further development of the legal and regulatory institutions. While most scholars agree that SOEs reduce economic efficiency and call for privatization (Wu, 1994; Zhang, 1994), this book contends that the challenges associated with SOEs reflect deeper issues in China's legal and institutional architecture. Advancing the private sector therefore requires building more sophisticated legal and regulatory frameworks. Strengthening the legal institutions and allowing courts to curb opportunistic behavior of governments would promote private investment. However, it is also important to recognize that the incompleteness of the law is inevitable, especially in the short term. How well China could reform the SOEs thus depends significantly on its capability of developing effective regulatory and governance regime of the private sector.

1

Introducing the Legal Theory of State-Owned Enterprises

Given their influence, state-owned enterprises (SOEs) have been widely studied in the literature. However, current research has not fully explored how the law affects the historical development and sectoral distribution of SOEs. This chapter introduces LTS, a positive theory that provides a new lens for understanding the factors influencing the evolution of SOEs in China (Friedman, 1966, pp. 4, 9). This chapter lays the groundwork for applying this theory to explain the distribution and persistence of SOEs in China, which will be further explored in subsequent chapters.

I. The Concept of Regulatory Costs

A. *From Transaction Costs to Regulatory Costs*

LTS (Legal theory of SOEs) builds upon the influential work of Ronald Coase, particularly his seminal paper, "The Nature of the Firm," where he sought to provide an economic account of why firms exist (Coase, 1937). Coase's analysis compares firms to their closest alternatives, which are contracts. Market participants have the choice to either establish a firm or use contracts to conduct business. Coase posits that firms exist because negotiating and concluding contracts entail social costs (Coase, 1937, p. 4). This perspective revolutionized the understanding of firm theories.

Henry Hansmann further developed the theory of transaction costs into a theory of the ownership of firms (Hansmann, 1988). According to Hansmann, ownership confers the rights of control and residual financial interests. Hansmann argues that the allocation of the ownership of enterprise depends on economic forces – the sum of two types of social costs: transaction costs and ownership costs (Hansmann, 1988). Corporations and their patrons would enter into transactions that shift the ownership if it is not most efficiently allocated. This is because doing so could create a social surplus and the participants in the transfer of ownership could make a gain.

For example, investor ownership is usually efficient and hence the dominant form of ownership in modern societies because of two major reasons. First, it alleviates the transaction costs between a firm and the providers of long-term capital. Imagine that a financier invests funds in a firm that become specified assets. The financier expects to recover the investment over a long period. Suppose that the ownership is not allocated to the financier and instead is retained by the entrepreneur who controls the firm. The entrepreneur may act opportunistically when new circumstances arise and demand that the original term of investment be amended. The entrepreneur may also increase the risks of the firm to benefit herself/himself, even though doing so may negatively affect the interests of the financier. Knowing the risks in advance, the financier would refrain from investing unless promised a certain level of residual financial rights and control rights. In order to attract investment, the entrepreneur would also likely accept such terms. A second reason why investor ownership is prevalent is that it usually incurs lower ownership costs. Modern corporations are usually owned by a large group of profit-seeking shareholders who purchase shares with equal rights and participate in corporate decisions on a one-share-one-vote basis. Since shareholders largely have homogeneous interests, their decisions usually benefit shareholders as a whole.

While investor ownership is the most common type of ownership in today's society, other types of ownership, such as employee ownership and consumer ownership, can also be found in certain markets. For instance, legal professionals usually choose partnerships owned by employees. Such an arrangement has the important benefit of reducing the transaction costs between employees and law firms without significantly raising decision-making costs (Hansmann, 1988, p. 291). Compared to other firms owned by employees, the interests of the owners (partners) of a law firm are relatively homogeneous (Hansmann, 1988, p. 295). It is also relatively easier to devise compensation formulas to measure the production of different partners, reducing the decision-making costs in these firms (Hansmann, 1988, p. 295).

This book further expands the theory of the ownership of firm to the relationship between states and enterprises. In modern societies, governments frequently intervene in the business activities of private enterprises, which sometimes takes the form of a contract between the government and private enterprises. For example, a local government may enter into a public-private partnership (PPP) contract with a private firm, in which the firm agrees to construct infrastructure and operate the project for the government. Such a contract has the characteristic of a long-term relational transaction, which may give rise to transaction costs, similar to a long-term contract between two private firms. One mechanism to address the transaction costs is vertical integration: A private firm may acquire a part of the entire ownership of another firm if the concern for transaction costs looms large. By the same logic, state ownership of private firms may also alleviate the concern for opportunism that may arise under a government-firm contract.

If transaction costs were the only concern, state ownership would be relatively rare. In the literature, many consider whether governments should provide goods or services themselves directly or "contract out" to private parties (Hart et al., 1997). One concern is that the quality of the goods or services may be difficult to specify, which can incur transaction costs when contracting out. However, Andrei Shleifer argues that even if this is the case, government ownership is inefficient in most cases because the government lacks the incentives to cut costs (Hart et al., 1997). This may explain why SOEs are relatively uncommon in liberal states.

The analysis presented in current studies, however, is incomplete. The relationship between the state and the enterprise is not limited to contract. The state also wields regulatory power over enterprises. As Trubek notes, regulation can be viewed as "a hybrid of the universal rules of pure market and the specific directives of pure command" (Trubek, 1972b, p. 30). One common form of regulation is economic regulation. Market failures, including information asymmetries, natural monopolies, and externalities, may lead to social welfare losses. Regulators have formulated various methods to address these problems, including market entry control, standard setting, and information disclosure. The state can also intervene in the market by providing subsidies, tax incentives, and penalties to influence the decisions of private corporations. It can even impose an outright ban on more severe undesirable activities.

The state can impose regulations on the conduct of enterprises without ownership, because it possesses the police power to define property rights and interfere when the public interest is at stake. The precise extent of police power often remains unclear, enabling the state to impose certain limitations on private property or activities without providing compensation. For instance, the state may establish requirements regarding the capital adequacy of commercial banks to ensure they possess sufficient assets to honor their obligations to public depositors. Such measures are generally considered justified, and banks are not entitled to compensation for any resulting losses, as all banks are subject to similar rules upon entering the market. Banks cannot assert that they have incurred any loss due to the capital adequacy requirement since the law defines their operations in consideration of their significant impact on the public. Essentially, there is no inherent "right to operate" beyond the framework of the law. However, in cases where the state's actions exceed the scope of police power and constitute a "regulatory taking," compensation may be required. Nevertheless, the legal principles surrounding regulatory takings are usually carefully formulated to avoid unduly restricting the government's authority, recognizing the importance of flexibility in pursuing the public interest.

Using law rather than ownership to control firms also incurs certain social costs, which can be termed "regulatory costs." The theoretical explanation for the prevalence of SOEs thus resembles the theory of the firm. To understand the function of state ownership, one needs to consider its closest alternative. In this context, just as contracts are viewed as the alternative to forming a firm, the law is posited as a close alternative to state ownership of firms. Law can serve to accomplish almost every objective of state ownership. For instance, while state ownership is conventionally regarded as a solution to market failures, various regulatory measures can be employed to address these concerns. Consider the regulation of water utilities, often deemed natural monopolies. A private water utility might set tariffs at monopoly levels, prioritizing profit over public welfare. Conversely, a state-owned water utility might set tariffs with a view to social welfare. However, tariff regulation can also mitigate such market failures. In essence, the state can exercise control over enterprises through its legal authority rather than direct ownership. It can also achieve revenue collection and redistributive goals through taxation rather than relying on returns on investment as an enterprise owner. Thus, to fully understand the nature of state ownership, it is crucial to examine the limitations and drawbacks of depending exclusively on legal mechanisms to achieve governmental objectives.

Just like contracts incur transaction costs, regulations also incur significant social costs. Currently in the literature, many have recognized state ownership as a solution to market failures (Viscusi et al., 2005, p. 503); previous studies of the efficiency of SOEs largely focus on their financial performance. As Andrei Shleifer argues, "many of the concerns that private firms fail to address 'social goals' can be addressed through government contracting and regulation, without resort to government ownership" (Shleifer, 1998, p. 136). However, one should not presume that regulation can always effectively control market failures, and that state ownership is unnecessary. This section provides a new theoretical framework that considers not only the financial performance of SOEs but also their functions in achieving regulatory goals, which may explain the prevalence of SOEs in China.

B. The Components of Regulatory Costs

Regulatory costs include enactment costs, enforcement costs, and the costs of opportunistic actions by both the state and regulated firms. Regulators derive their power through public law created by political mechanisms. Law may be regarded as a commitment extended by the government to the public (Pistor and Xu, 2002, p. 958). It sets the boundaries of the government's power. Like contract, law is inherently incomplete due to policymakers' bounded rationality and the inability to foresee all potential circumstances. This incompleteness incurs certain regulatory costs. This book adopts a broad interpretation of regulatory costs, incorporating the social costs arising from diverse forms of governmental intervention such as regulations, taxation, and subsidies, along with other lawful government actions. Despite the diversity of these interventions, they share common characteristics and arise because of similar reasons. For clarity and simplicity, the term "regulatory costs" will be employed throughout this book to encompass all such costs associated with government intervention.

Enactment costs are the social costs associated with the enactment of the law and regulatory rules. The enactment process often involves significant procedural costs, similar to those created by the contracting process. Rule-makers need to obtain sufficient knowledge to write sophisticated rules that seek to cover as many foreseeable circumstances as possible, which is usually difficult (Laffont and Tirole, 1993, p. 643; Pistor and Xu, 2002; Pargendler et al., 2013, p. 575). The ability to enact complex rules needs to be developed over time. Thus, developing countries often lack the capacity to write sophisticated regulatory rules. The Internal Revenue Code of the United States, for example, contains thousands of sections, while the Individual Income Tax Law of China, as amended in 2011, contains no more than fifteen rules.

Even if rule-makers possess the ability to anticipate a sufficient range of future circumstances, the specific content of regulatory rules is determined through political negotiations. The costs associated with these regulatory bargains are often higher compared to those involved in contractual agreements, given that regulations frequently impact the interests of multiple interest groups. Regulatory rules establish the boundaries between public power and private property, which can lead to conflicts and disagreements. Effective regulation necessitates the inclusion of public input, typically through notice-and-comment procedures (where governments publish proposed rules and allow the public to provide feedback before finalizing regulations), and relies on specialized expertise in the relevant field. The state must establish fair procedures to justify its decisions and persuade both public stakeholders and private parties to accept them, which can prove challenging in certain countries. Moreover, when consensus is difficult to achieve, the costs associated with bargaining during regulatory rulemaking are likely to be high. For instance, individuals with varying perspectives may advocate for distinct environmental regulatory rules. Certain stakeholders may prioritize economic development over environmental protection, while others maintain an opposing stance. Harmonizing these divergent viewpoints and formulating a regulatory framework that garners wide acceptance pose a formidable and costly endeavor.

Enforcing regulatory rules can also pose challenges for the state, particularly in monitoring and ensuring compliance by private firms (Pargendler et al., 2013, p. 575). Private firms may intentionally conceal information from the government, making it difficult and costly to detect any wrongdoing (Shapiro and Willig, 2019, pp. 55–87). An illustrative case is Volkswagen, where they implemented software in their vehicles that triggered emission-reducing equipment during testing but deactivated it during regular driving (Gates et al., 2017). Advanced technology possessed by private corporations allows them to hide information effectively, making it difficult for regulators to detect such behavior consistently. Furthermore, private enterprises may declare bankruptcy before regulatory action can be taken, enjoying the protection of limited liability (Sappington and Stiglitz, 1987, p. 573). Consequently, the law often fails to provide sufficient deterrence to shareholders who may benefit from violating regulations.

Consider, for example, the government regulation of commercial banks. The 2008 financial crisis in the United States suggests that it is very costly to regulate large financial institutions. The United States, with its developed financial market, still suffers from a lack of regulatory capacity in devising effective regulatory regimes and enforcing them. These costs are presumably higher in developing countries that have less sophisticated institutions.

Sometimes, the enforcement of regulatory rules also involves reconciling different views about regulatory choices. As an illustration, let us examine tariff regulation within the context of water supply. The pricing of water supply impacts a considerable number of public consumers, each with varying preferences. Some individuals may prioritize high-quality water, demonstrating a willingness to pay a premium for superior equipment and enhanced water quality provided by the water utilities company. In contrast, others may favor cost-effective water supply solutions. Consequently, during a price hearing, reaching a consensus on the appropriate pricing may prove challenging. Regulatory decisions that fail to gain the support of the general public may damage the legitimacy of the government, which can also be considered as a social cost incurred by governments in the regulatory process.

Apart from enactment costs and enforcement costs, the regulation also incurs costs of opportunism (Ogus, 2007). Scholars have long recognized opportunism as a source of transaction costs that arises under the contractual context. Nobel Laureate Oliver Williamson defines opportunism as "self-interest seeking with guile" (Williamson, 1985, p. 47). In the contractual context, some define opportunism as "any contractual conduct by one party contrary to the other party's reasonable expectations based on the parties' agreement, contractual norms, or conventional morality" (Cohen, 1992, p. 957), or the "residual behavior that would be contracted away if ex-ante transaction costs were lower" (Smith, 2020, p. 1078). Others argue that opportunistic actions occur "when a performing party behaves contrary to the other party's understanding of their contract, but not necessarily contrary to the agreement's explicit terms, leading to a transfer of wealth from the other party to the performer" (Muris, 1981, p. 521).

Opportunism also emerges in regulatory contexts. The government may act opportunistically when it promulgates or modifies laws or policies, or exercises discretion in ways that cannot be foreseen and are contrary to the reasonable expectations of private investors based on existing laws, political agendas, and social norms. Such regulatory changes may not necessarily serve the public interest and may instead result in a transfer of wealth from the regulated party to the government, its officials, or another entity. After corporations have made significant investments in an industry, the state may suddenly change its policies or enact new laws that impose excessive costs on these corporations, impeding their ability to operate profitably (Vickers and Yarrow, 1991, p. 114). Consequently, in sectors with ambiguous rules, enterprises may seek to invite government investment, making the government more cautious about engaging in opportunistic behavior. When these measures prove insufficient, private investors may refrain from investing, thereby failing to meet market demand.

One crucial question remains: Do the state or the regulators have incentives to act opportunistically? While not all states would take advantage of the loopholes in the enabling statutes and regulations to hurt private parties, there exist strong reasons to believe that state opportunism is highly possible in China's context. The analysis of the state's opportunism depends on the behavioral model one adopts to understand regulators. Even if the regulatory officials intend to pursue specific regulatory goals, they may still fail to fully recognize the costs their regulations place on the private businesses or further internalize them, a problem commonly known as "fiscal illusion" in the literature (Fischel and Shapiro, 1988). For example, the environmental regulators may be driven by concern for curbing carbon emission and fail to fully consider the financial interests of private firms. Additionally, one may believe in the private interest theory of regulation and view the regulators' actions with suspicion. Regulators may exercise their power in a way that creates obstacles to the operation of private businesses in order to extract private benefits. The regulators' decisions may be influenced by interest groups inside and outside an industry, which may be heterogeneous. For example, in the nuclear power industry, firms with better safety measures may suffer a reputation loss if other firms without these measures create a problem, giving the public the impression that nuclear power is unsafe. Therefore, these firms may urge the regulators to devise stricter rules. Additionally, the change of rules may lead to the damage of some parties outside the industry, for example, consumers, who cannot efficiently influence the decisions of the regulator. In these cases, regulators may act opportunistically in a way that affects the interests of some parties while benefiting others, even though it appears that they are pursuing regulatory goals. Since regulators do not bear the full costs of the rule-changing, they may revise the rule to fulfill their goal or further the interests of certain officials without due consideration of the costs borne by private parties.

The failure of the government to make credible promises is sometimes referred to as the "credible commitment" problem (Schuck, 1999). This problem worsens when "asset specificity" arises. Private corporations may not easily withdraw their investment from their projects unless they suffer a great loss, because the assets cannot be used for other purposes.

Facing the uncertainty that the state may increase the regulatory burden on them at any time, private parties may lack sufficient incentive to invest. As Laffont and Tirole note, while the lack of commitment "leads to underinvestment by fear of expropriation," a justification for not committing is "the difficulty of signing complete state contingent contracts in an uncertain environment" (Laffont and Tirole, 1992). Since interest groups often cannot agree on the optimal level of regulation, regulatory rules may remain ambiguous and unpredictable, which may give rise to opportunistic actions (Schuck, 1999).

Private parties may also act opportunistically when the law has certain loopholes that can be exploited. The widespread belief in the corporate law literature that corporations should maximize shareholder welfare also contributes to the cost of opportunistic actions. It encourages corporations to pursue the welfare of shareholders, while imposing externalities on outside stakeholders (Bratton, 2001–2002). This understanding of the corporation presumes that the state can effectively control private corporations through regulation, just as it presumes creditors and other stakeholders can control corporations with contracts. Yet when regulatory costs are too high, the emphasis on shareholder wealth maximization encourages opportunistic actions, prioritizing profits over societal welfare and leading to undesirable consequences for external stakeholders.

The use of taxation can illustrate regulatory costs associated with governmental intervention. Scholars have long recognized the utility of Pigovian taxes in addressing externalities. For instance, in the case of a corporation emitting pollution into the air, a Pigovian tax would enable the corporation to internalize the social costs associated with such externalities. Indeed, many economists and legal scholars consider the Pigovian tax as the optimal policy for mitigating externalities (Mankiw, 2009, p. 15; Shavell, 2011). However, utilizing taxation as a regulatory tool also presents certain challenges. The state must establish tax laws in advance, specifying the regulated actions and their corresponding tax consequences. It is widely acknowledged that private corporations can engage in tax avoidance strategies by exploiting loopholes in tax laws. Consequently, the state may need to implement anti-avoidance measures. However, such measures often encounter difficulties, as courts frequently become involved in costly legal disputes to determine the distinction between tax avoidance and legitimate tax planning. The utilization of taxation to regulate corporate behavior undoubtedly incurs regulatory costs, including the expenses associated with drafting tax regulations, enforcing them, and addressing the residual effects stemming from opportunistic corporate behavior when tax laws are incomplete.

The above analysis so far presumes that regulation mainly leads to losses of wealth by private corporations. It is also possible that a certain regulatory measure would increase their wealth. For example, during a financial crisis, the state may decide to bail out some private financial institutions to prevent the risks they generate from affecting the entire financial system. Similarly, when a large corporation becomes bankrupt during an economic crisis, the state may also want to rescue it to protect the interests of the employees and the economy. Such measures would not constitute an expropriation of the property interests of the corporation. However, they also incur certain social costs. First, because of the expectation that the state would rescue firms that are "too big to fail," firms would tend to expand too much to increase their sizes in order to be rescued. As a result, these firms would have an overinvestment problem, which may not be socially optimal. Second, while the transfer of wealth from the state to private corporations does not itself change the total amount of wealth in society, it does raise distributive concerns. The decision to bail out the corporation thus may cause political upheavals, which is also costly. In addition, the state would need to engage in greater efforts to redistribute wealth. Such efforts would no doubt be very costly, since the state would need to spend resources on collecting information, enforcing the tax laws, and dealing with tax avoidance activities.

To address concerns regarding opportunistic behavior by private enterprises, the law often provides a certain degree of flexibility for government intervention. In countries where governments have a significant presence in economic activities, the checks and balances on political institutions tend to be weaker, as procedural constraints on the government may impede its ability to exert influence on the markets (Reitz, 2005). However, this can further exacerbate the issue of credible commitment, deterring private investment and resulting in efficiency losses.

It must be pointed out that these regulatory costs are social costs in the sense that they are not a transfer of wealth from one party to another, but a decrease in social welfare. The credible commitment problem in regulation may lead to under-investment in the market. The inability of the state to regulate private enterprises also leads to market failures that negatively affect market efficiency. The harm caused by public regulation on private enterprises is *reciprocal*, as avoiding the harm inflicted by regulation would impose harm on the government and the public interest it represents. Regulatory costs are socially undesirable regardless of who bears the costs. The opportunistic actions undertaken by both the government and private enterprises are two interconnected aspects of the same issue and cannot be easily resolved by simply enhancing the rigidity or flexibility of the legal rules.

A significant limitation of the law lies in its inherent incompleteness (Pistor and Xu, 2003). Similar to a contract, the law is inevitably incomplete because the legislature could not foresee all the circumstances that might arise after the law is made. Thus, new circumstances may render strict enforcement of the law problematic. The law thus contains "black holes" and "grey holes," which refer to areas where statutes, judicial decisions, and institutional practices either explicitly or implicitly exempt the executive branch from legal constraints (Vermeule, 2009). These arrangements are inevitable because of the difficulty of foreseeing future circumstances. The scope of emergencies is arguably broader in China, where the economy and society change more drastically than in liberal states such as the United States. Hence, the law is likely to be more incomplete in China, giving rise to higher regulatory costs.

The inherent limitations of the law become most apparent during times of emergencies. In such circumstances, such as during times of war, the state may intrude upon private properties to a much greater extent. This intrusion can manifest in various ways, with the most direct being the state's uncompromising expropriation of private property without any legal basis. Alternatively, the state could enact new legislation to achieve similar objectives, which would align more closely with the principles of the rule of law. However, this approach may introduce delays, as the legislative process requires time, and ultimately still results in encroachment upon private property.

In a liberal state, the law typically grants preemptive powers to the government to address emergencies, which fundamentally contradicts the principles of the rule of law. Regardless of the specific form it takes, governmental authority during times of emergency carries the risk of abuse. If a state lacks sufficient self-restraint, private investment will be deterred. Conversely, excessive constraints during emergencies may impede the state's ability to respond with flexibility and agility. Even in a state where the rule of law is highly developed, the government is still granted the power to handle emergencies (Vermeule, 2008).

LTS exhibits certain parallels with the LTF put forth by Katharina Pistor (Pistor, 2013). LTF posits the modern financial market relies on a delicate structure that necessitates a degree of flexibility at its apex, where the law is malleable. If legal obligations were consistently and rigidly enforced, the financial market would collapse. Pistor refers to this as the "law-finance" paradox. In the context of a too-big-to-fail financial institution facing a liquidity crisis, strict enforcement of all legal obligations would trigger a broader financial crisis. Thus, the law operates hierarchically, with stringent enforcement at the periphery but flexibility at the apex. LTS introduces a similar concept, highlighting the incompleteness of the law. Strict adherence to the law inadvertently hampers effective regulation of misconduct. Consequently, when unforeseen emergency situations arise, rigid enforcement of the law can lead to adverse consequences. On the other hand, bending the law may undermine its legitimacy. State ownership offers a potential solution to this predicament. By conferring residual control, ownership empowers the government to regulate the behavior of a firm and make specific decisions that are not predefined, all without requiring legal contortions.

C. *Regulatory Costs of State-Owned versus Private Enterprises*

As previously discussed, regulatory efforts often entail substantial social costs akin to transaction costs, including enactment costs, enforcement costs, and the costs incurred by opportunistic behavior. SOEs can help alleviate these regulatory costs through various means.

Before we delvie into the function of SOEs, it is necessary to clarify the scope of SOEs considered in this book. A broad definition of SOEs is used, encompassing all enterprises that are either wholly or partially owned by the government. Two key elements – the government and the type of enterprise – warrant further clarification. The term "government" here refers to both central and local governments. Therefore, municipal corporations, which are commonly found in some developed countries, are also regarded as SOEs in this book. Admittedly, the boundaries of this definition are not entirely clear. Sometimes, the government owning the firm is a self-governing local organization, such as a village collective. The critical point is that the government can use its ownership to control the firm in pursuit of certain regulatory objectives and align its financial interests with those of the firm.

The term "enterprise" can also be a source of contention. Generally, enterprises are understood to be business organizations that pursue profits. However, some enterprises aim to achieve both profits and other public-interest goals. Indeed, in many liberal states, government-owned entities operate in sectors such as hospitals, schools, and prisons. These entities often take the form of nonprofit organizations and are considered public institutions rather than traditional enterprises, as they do not primarily seek profits. The significant difference between nonprofit organizations and business organizations, such as corporations, is not that the former do not pursue profits, but rather that they do not distribute profits to investors (Hansmann, 1980, p. 838). In fact, many nonprofit organizations also generate profits and charge fees from users. Meanwhile, profit-seeking firms may also pursue certain nonprofit goals, such as Environmental, Social, and Governance (ESG) objectives. Consequently, this book does not differentiate between enterprises based on whether they are "profit-seeking" or nonprofit, but rather considers them together instead. Additionally, some enterprises serve the government as their primary clients rather than the general public, such as in sectors like prisons and toll-free roads. When the government directly purchases products and services from these enterprises, transaction costs are usually incurred. However, even if the government does not engage in direct purchases, regulation may still apply, resulting in regulatory costs. This book argues that the ownership of these enterprises can be analyzed similarly within the same framework.

State ownership of enterprises aligns the interests of enterprises and the government and enables the government to internalize the costs associated with opportunistic actions, akin to vertical integration (Williamson, 1975, p. 104; Troesken and Geddes, 2003, p. 379; Zeng, 2017a; Lin, 2020; Lin and Milhaupt, 2021). For instance, consider the regulation of prices for natural monopolies. If the state sets the price too low, which could adversely impact the enterprise's interests, it can provide subsidies to compensate private businesses. Conversely, if the price is set too high, the additional profits function as a form of government-collected tax that can be utilized for the public good.

The precise manner in which state ownership alleviates the opportunistic actions of governments is a complex matter that depends on the specific institutional design. Typically, the government establishes dedicated departments or entities to exercise control and financial rights over SOEs. These specialized bodies often possess a certain degree of influence, enabling them to shape the decision-making processes of the governmental entities responsible for regulating the SOEs. For instance, in China, SOEs owned by higher-level governmental authorities frequently participate in infrastructure projects initiated by lower-level governments. The political power wielded by the owners of these SOEs empowers them to influence the behavior of the lower-level governments and alleviates concerns about opportunistic actions.

Another way state ownership reduces regulatory costs is by granting the state more instruments to control and influence the decisions made by the enterprise (Sappington and Stiglitz, 1987, p. 568; Laffont and Tirole, 1993, p. 638). The state can use external regulatory measures with legal authorities as well as internal incentive measures based on ownership to achieve its goals. State ownership may take many forms. Some SOEs exist as independent corporations; some operate as branches of the government rather than separate entities. No matter which form it takes, ownership confers the residual rights to control and earnings. The control based on state ownership, what Laffont and Tirole call "internal control," affects firm decisions mainly through the state's control over managers (Laffont and Tirole, 1993, p. 637). With ownership, the state can use reward and penalty instruments, including "employment, promotion, remuneration and internal resource allocation" (Williamson, 1971, p. 114). Managers and employees are placed under the state's control and are selected by the state. It can thus control their incentive more effectively, examine their backgrounds, and place them in a long-term relationship with the state.

Control rights of the state can be structured in different ways. The state may remove managers at will, in which case the managers lack autonomy completely and must follow the state's orders. The state may also grant certain autonomy to the managers. For example, a public listing SOE may be operated by a board of directors, while the state can only exercise its rights as a shareholder pursuant to the corporate charter. If the state completely owns an enterprise or holds more than 51 percent of the shares, it can use its control rights to command the managers to fulfill regulatory goals. There may be different arrangements for allowing minority shareholders to have a say in the selection of managers. At this point, it is convenient to assume that state ownership confers full control over the enterprises. Of course, as the equity interests of the state in the enterprise decline, the control of the state generally weakens. It is also assumed that the managers have no means to resist the control of the owners. In the short term, managers of a firm may be able to resist the majority shareholders' influence. However, in the long run, the owner can likely replace the managers. For example, a corporation may adopt a staggered board regime, which allows the shareholders to replace only a part of the board members each year. However, the shareholders would eventually be able to replace all members of the board and gain control of the corporation.

Although the state can also regulate managers in private enterprises, such regulatory efforts may encounter difficulties because regulators may not easily control private investors, who may incentivize their managers to evade regulatory scrutiny. Regulation generally involves fewer control rights than state ownership (Trubek, 1972b, p. 30). For example, banking regulators use a capital adequacy requirement to regulate the financial risks taken by commercial banks, instead of controlling each transaction. Thus, privatization can reduce governmental interventions in the economy, which may be desirable to some extent. However, it may also lead to difficulties in controlling and regulating the enterprises.

China's insurance sector can serve as a pertinent example. China's insurance industry encompasses a variety of ownership structures, including companies owned by the central government, local governments, SOEs, and private investors. State-owned insurance companies are corporations that are directly or indirectly controlled by the central government. Notable examples of such companies include People's Insurance Company of China (PICC), People's Life Insurance Company of China (PLICC), Chinese Reinsurance Company, and China Taiping Life Insurance Company Limited, along with their respective subsidiaries. Over the past decades, the insurance regulator has granted approvals for the entry of many new insurance companies into the market, including those owned by both foreign and domestic private investors. Furthermore, the regulator has facilitated the participation of more domestic private investors in the market.

In the insurance industry, SOEs are generally subject to stronger control by the state compared to other insurance companies, although both types are subject to regulation. While the regulation of insurance companies continues to develop, state ownership serves as a mechanism to mitigate opportunistic behavior exhibited by these companies. For instance, one way to compare the difficulties of insurance regulating different types of insurance companies is to examine the number of complaints filed against state-owned and other insurance companies. Starting from the second quarter of 2020, the Chinese Banking and Insurance Regulatory Commission began publicly disclosing the number of complaints per hundred million RMB insurance premiums in each quarter. The number of complaints launched against state-owned life insurance companies is generally lower than that for private life insurance companies, as can be seen in Table 1.1. These figures suggest that SOEs might engage in less opportunistic actions, thereby making regulation less difficult.

A counterargument posits that even private corporations in China are effectively under the state's control, owing to the country's institutional framework. The examination of Party-building amendments mandated

Table 1.1 *Average number of complaints per hundred million RMB in insurance premiums*

	State-owned insurance companies	Private insurance companies
Q2, 2020	2.77	4.06
Q3, 2020	2.72	5.52
Q4, 2020	2.4	2.94
Q1, 2021	1.15	2.49
Q2, 2021	3.57	3.71
Q3, 2021	3.29	3.26
Q4, 2021	3.16	3.52
Q1, 2022	0.77	1.86
Q2, 2022	1.98	4.61
Q3, 2022	2.2	4.16
Q4, 2022	2.43	4.39

Source: Chinese Banking and Insurance Regulatory Commission

by the government conducted by Lin and Milhaupt (2021) supports this perspective. Their findings reveal that fewer than 90 percent of the listed SOEs adhered to the state's directive, while approximately 6 percent of private corporations also incorporated Party-building amendments into their corporate charters. While Milhaupt and Lin emphasize that the line between SOEs and private corporations is blurred in China, their findings also suggest the Chinese government retains significant control over the majority of SOEs, with only a small fraction of private corporations affected. Furthermore, among these private corporations, the incorporation of Party-building amendments is predominantly symbolic in nature. Consequently, the state's control mechanism is notably stronger when it maintains ownership of the corporation (Lin and Milhaupt, 2021, p. 205).

State ownership of enterprises provides the state with an avenue to acquire more information about these entities. As shareholders, the state can appoint directors or exercise shareholders' rights to access information. While the state can also obtain information from private enterprises through legal means, there is a risk that private entities may conceal relevant information about the corporation. For example, the state might designate accountants to assist in gathering information. However, regulating accounting practices poses significant challenges. The Enron scandal, for instance, exposed the difficulties in overseeing accountants who may have incentives to comply with the directives of the corporations they audit and possess informational advantages over regulators. These challenges highlight the potential benefits of state ownership in improving transparency and information flow, while also illustrating the limitations of relying solely on legal mechanisms to obtain accurate and comprehensive corporate information.

Certainly, while state ownership may allow the state to command the enterprises to comply with regulations or to further governmental goals, the state may not actively exercise this power because of the sheer number of SOEs it controls (Milhaupt and Zheng, 2014). SOEs are also more likely to obey regulatory rules because they can be structured to consider the public interest rather than to focus exclusively on financial performance, and hence have a weaker incentive to evade regulation. Reducing the profit-seeking motive itself may effectively limit opportunistic behaviors and prevent hazardous activities. SOEs can thus internalize the costs of their actions. In many industries – such as public transportation, municipal utilities, and hospitals – profit-seeking corporations pose a severe threat to public safety and welfare. By contrast, SOEs can be similar to nonprofit organizations, which incur lower risks of fraud and infringement on relevant stakeholders (Hansmann, 1987, pp. 27–42). In addition, SOEs also face media scrutiny. Studies have found that wrongdoings of SOEs in China are more likely to be corrected after the media exposes them (Li and Shen, 2010; Pargendler et al., 2013, p. 589). While the state sometimes wants SOEs to pursue profits and improve performance, state ownership allows the state to structure internal incentives as it wishes. It may incentivize them to fulfill regulatory goals, which can promote cooperation and resolve many conflicts between the enterprises and other stakeholders.

Moreover, the senior managers of SOEs are usually placed in a long-term relationship with the government. By contrast, private enterprises may be liquidated or may go bankrupt at any moment. In developing countries where the credit system is less developed, private investors may even get away with the violation of regulatory rules by escaping to foreign countries or using fake identities. SOEs, by contrast, can be expected to consider the long-term relationship with the government and hence would not act opportunistically for short-term gain.

II. Ownership Costs of Private and State-Owned Enterprises

While state ownership may reduce regulatory costs, it also incurs higher ownership costs. In the academic literature, two major explanations for the low efficiency of state ownership co-exist: the "political view" and the "agency view." According to the "political view," politicians may interfere in the business of SOEs to pursue political goals (Shleifer and Vishny, 1994), which may reduce the profits of SOEs. However, if the political goals are socially desired, political intervention in SOEs' business decisions may not be inefficient. Whether the political goals are themselves worth pursuing is another question that depends on the specific circumstances.

The agency view provides more convincing grounds for questioning SOEs efficiency. Agency costs arise because owners need to monitor and control the conduct of managers of enterprises. Shleifer, in his important article "State versus Private Ownership," points out that state ownership is usually inefficient because government officials do not actually own the enterprise and thus lack any incentive to promote the management and financial performance of the enterprise (Shleifer, 1998).

In China and elsewhere, several reasons suggest that SOEs incur higher ownership costs than private enterprises. The first reason for the high ownership costs is that managers of SOEs simply are self-interested and only consider their own benefits (Titternbrun, 1997, pp. 56–64). They may lack incentive to improve performance, because they do not actually own the enterprise, and hence would not put resources to the most efficient use (Demsetz, 1974, p. 348). Second, SOEs have two goals – to promote shareholder welfare and to fulfill various social purposes, which may harm efficiency because managers can engage in self-benefiting management activities under the disguise of the pursuit of social purposes (Macey, 1999). The third problem with state ownership is the so-called "soft budget constraint" problem. SOEs can usually obtain more capital from the state when they face financial distress, which weakens the market disciplinary effects on managers (Kornai, 1986; Vickers and Yarrow, 1991). Managers of the enterprise thus face limited pressure to improve the financial performance of the enterprise to regain capital through issuing new stock or borrowing more money. Whether these problems associated with SOEs are real remains an empirical question. So far, the evidence in China is that SOEs are generally weaker in performance compared with private corporations, while the reform of SOEs, including corporatization and privatization, promotes their financial performance (Liu, 2013).

III. Developing the Legal Theory of State-Owned Enterprises

With the above theoretical concepts, it is now possible to develop LTS that can be employed to explain SOEs in China. This theory posits that

Table 1.2 *The social costs of SOEs v. regulated private enterprises*

	Ordinary sectors	Some regulated sectors
Private enterprises	Low regulatory costs + Low ownership costs	**High** regulatory costs + low ownership costs
SOEs	Low regulatory costs + **High** ownership costs	Low regulatory costs + **High** ownership costs

the development and distribution of SOEs are significantly affected by law. Framed in theoretical terms, the distribution of SOEs is determined by the social costs associated with SOEs and private enterprises, including both ownership and regulatory costs. As Table 1.2 shows, in ordinary sectors, the social costs of private enterprises are generally lower because of the lower ownership costs. Private enterprises are thus likely to be the most common form of enterprises in the market. By contrast, in some regulated sectors, the advantages of private enterprises become smaller because while they incur lower ownership costs, they may incur higher regulatory costs. Meanwhile, SOEs may prevail because of their advantages in alleviating regulatory costs. Exactly why regulatory costs are high in these sectors is a more complicated question, which will be left to subsequent chapters.

The different levels of social costs associated with SOEs and private enterprises may affect both the supply and demand of SOEs. The specific mechanisms can take two forms: public choice or market dynamics, contingent upon whether the regulatory costs are borne by the government or the enterprises themselves. In a regulatory relationship, the burden of regulatory costs may fall on either the government or the enterprise and its private investors.

Firstly, regulatory costs affect the supply of SOEs. When regulatory costs are borne by the government, they influence the public choice regarding the provision of SOEs. If the government perceives it to be challenging to regulate SOEs effectively, it may opt against privatizing them. Once private enterprises enter the market, if the government deems the risks of losing control to be too high, it might impose stricter regulatory rules that diminish investment returns. Additionally, the government may introduce new laws or policies that result in the nationalization of private enterprises with inadequate compensation. It is important to note that while this book acknowledges the significance of the government's public choice, this analysis differs from current political or political economy theories, as the government's decision is influenced by concerns about regulatory costs rather than political ideology or state capture. LTS emphasizes the choice between law and state ownership, which is typically not a primary consideration in political theories.

Secondly, regulatory costs also impact the demand for SOEs through a market mechanism. Private investors face the costs associated with opportunistic actions by the government, which discourages their entry into certain regulated markets. Those who have already entered the market may encounter state expropriation and subsequently decide to exit, resulting in an underinvestment problem. This scenario fosters a heightened demand for goods or services that private entities fail to supply adequately. Faced with the necessity to ensure the availability of public goods or services, the government is compelled to step in, often resulting in an increased presence of SOEs in the marketplace. SOEs can help alleviate the underinvestment problem because once they make their investments, the government's interests become more aligned with the interests of the SOEs, reducing the likelihood of opportunistic behavior. Hence, SOEs tend to be more prevalent in regulated industries where the regulatory costs are relatively high.

Under China's particular context, the regulatory costs are most likely borne by private investors rather than the government. Unlike in a liberal state, where the government would be strictly limited by the law, the Chinese government is likely to retain significant power or choose not to be bound by the law when it decides to achieve a certain goal or handle an emergency. It also often engages in extralegal measures in practice (Milhaupt and Zheng, 2014, p. 685). Thus, when a new circumstance arises that is not previously foreseen by the legislature, the powerful government may impose the new regulations, leaving the private enterprises to bear the negative consequences.

An illustrative example, explored in greater depth in Chapter 4, revolves around the employment of exclusivity clauses within the context of PPP agreements. Here, the government engages with private entities in contractual agreements to undertake infrastructure projects, such as bridges or toll roads, with an assurance of exclusivity. This exclusivity is pivotal, as the introduction of competing government projects at a later stage could significantly dilute the interest in the initially agreed project. Yet, this commitment to exclusivity could potentially restrict the government's ability to adapt to new developments. Chinese law chooses to permit the government to either terminate or amend these contracts for the public interest, thereby predisposing private entities to bear a greater share of regulatory costs in comparison to their counterparts in more liberal jurisdictions.

This book suggests that China's rise has followed a combination of two models. On the one hand, it has developed, at least to some extent, legal institutions that enforce contracts, protect private property, and safeguard the interests of minority investors (Clarke, 2003; La Porta et al., 2008). These institutions are crucial for promoting a large number of investments made by private investors and corporations that are financed by dispersed equity investors. On the other hand, the rule of law has its limits in China. China has maintained its control over legal institutions and the government has wide extralegal power. Where the law is elastic and bent, private investors face more severe challenges. This is where state ownership plays a dominant role.

The hierarchical enforcement of the law is not unique to China and has been acknowledged by other scholars. Katharina Pistor argues that in liberal states, the financial system is constructed hierarchically rather than flatly (Pistor, 2013, p. 315). Strict enforcement of the law may lead to systemic risks and the suspension of the law is sometimes necessary to protect the financial system. Hence, Pistor argues that "[f]inancial systems are not state or market, private or public, but always and necessarily both" (Pistor, 2013, p. 322).

This book highlights that China's economic landscape also exhibits a hierarchical structure that extends beyond the financial sector. In China, the legal system provides hierarchical protection to private enterprises across a broader spectrum of economic sectors. As Benjamin Liebman observes, Chinese governments often derive their legitimacy from the outcomes they deliver and frequently display a tendency to be "over-responsive to individual or group protests" (Liebman, 2011, p. 104). This over-responsiveness reflects their deep-seated concern for maintaining stability in a diverse array of situations, at times making them hesitant to fully commit to the rigidity of the law, fearing that it might restrict their capacity to respond effectively to instances of instability. Such a "law-stability" paradox sometimes leads the governments to wield extralegal control or swiftly amend the law unexpectedly. This paradox contributes to the escalation of regulatory costs across a wide spectrum of sectors within China, as private enterprises may find themselves operating in an environment devoid of stable and predictable legal guidelines. In sectors where regulatory costs are particularly high, SOEs tend to assert their dominance due to their capacity to navigate the complex regulatory landscape more effectively.

IV. Major Factors That Affect the Magnitude of Regulatory Costs

The theory offered in this book posits that high regulatory costs are associated with a larger proportion of SOEs. It is thus important to discuss the determining factors of regulatory costs. This part will consider some of most influential factors.

A. *The Needs for Intense Regulation*

The extent of regulatory costs is shaped by the necessity for either regulatory intervention or direct government control, driven primarily by two considerations. The first is to rectify market failures, where the market alone fails to efficiently allocate resources or ensure fair competition and consumer protection. The second reason pertains to the state's imperative to maintain oversight and control over critical sectors or activities, ensuring that broader socioeconomic objectives are met.

1. Market Failures

The state may need to regulate when there are certain market failures. This can occur for a variety of reasons, including natural monopolies, information asymmetry, or externalities. The regulation of these market failures often entails regulatory costs, which can be mitigated through state ownership. As a result, the extent of regulatory costs within a particular sector is closely tied to the existence of market failures and the nature of the required regulations.

Virtually all enterprises today are regulated to some extent concerning their business scope, bookkeeping and accounting, land use, or emission of environmentally harmful substances. The more aspects of the business the state needs to regulate and the more difficult it is to define the state's control, the higher the regulatory costs become. Consequently, state ownership is more likely to arise when regulatory institutions are underdeveloped. In some industries, the state engages in the regulation of a specific aspect, which also incurs certain social costs. However, regulators can easily define their control rights by using certain standards and need not engage in other aspects of private businesses. For example, almost all private enterprises need to comply with state laws related to taxation, occupational health, safe production practices, fire safety, environmental standards, and consumer protection laws. In other words, the regulator imposes restrictions on some of the aspects of the firm's operation. Thus, the boundaries between public power and private property can be drawn relatively easily. Nonetheless, in certain industries, delineating a distinct boundary between government authority and private ownership can prove to be more challenging. Consider, for instance, the water utility sector, where private enterprises may be subject to tariff regulation. To determine the appropriate water tariffs, regulatory agencies must assess whether the expenses incurred by these enterprises are reasonable, necessitating a comprehensive examination of various facets of the enterprise's operations. When regulation requires the state to intervene in many aspects of an enterprise's business, regulatory costs become higher.

In many states, SOEs operate within sectors characterized by market failures, largely due to the challenges associated with regulating private entities effectively. For instance, a significant number of water utilities in the United States are municipally owned, a choice attributed to the complexities of enforcing an efficient tariff regulation system (Troesken and Geddes, 2003; Masten, 2011). This phenomenon extends to utilities sectors in other countries such as India, Italy, South Korea, and France, highlighting a global reliance on SOEs in these areas (Zhang, 2023). Moreover, in the commercial banking sector, where financial regulation is stringent, SOEs hold substantial market shares in several developing countries. Notably, state-owned banks account for 67 percent of the assets in India, 46 percent in Brazil, and 47 percent in Vietnam, underscoring their prevalence in environments where private sector regulation poses significant challenges (International Monetary Fund (IMF), Fiscal Affairs Department, 2020, p. 48; Zhang, 2023).

2. Control Goals

The government in China may consider it necessary to maintain control in the economy, while privatization would loosen its control. This concern can arise because of several reasons. First, China often deems it essential to maintain social stability. As a commentator notes, "social stability is a major concern at every level" in China (Qiao, 2023a). Jinglian Wu, a leading economist who actively participated in the reform of Chinese SOEs, also commented that "[t]he state regarded SOEs as instruments to achieve its political and economic objectives" (Wu, 2005). President Xi Jinping also stated that "SOEs are an important part of the foundation for the administration of our Party" (Wu, 2009). In addition, China's government sometimes adopts changes in policies that negatively affect the interests of private enterprises when their activities threaten economic or social stability.

China also retains oversight of specific sectors vital for emergency disaster relief efforts (Wang, 2014, p. 666). In the event of significant natural catastrophes, like earthquakes or hurricanes, the government often steps in to offer disaster relief, bolstering its public image and legitimacy. To this end, it may direct businesses to contribute to disaster relief efforts by providing essential services such as electricity, water, and transportation (Ren and Liu, 2006). For example, the state owns the two main electricity grid companies in China: the State Grid Corporation and the Southern Power Grid Company. These grid companies frequently participate in executing government directives, including disaster relief initiatives and providing subsidies to rural communities. For the ruling party, its abilities to ensure a stable electricity supply for certain national events, to undertake rescue missions during disasters, and to extend subsidies to rural areas are deemed vital components of legitimacy. In the event of a hurricane, the state-owned grid corporations will be ordered to maintain the electricity supply and to prevent power outages, even during holidays and usually without any compensation. As a commentator notes, "[W]ithout such political control, no enterprise that operates on a commercial basis would be willing to pursue those objectives" (Wang, 2014, p. 666). To enhance its legitimacy, the state needs to control the electricity provider to ensure that electricity is available even during the worst circumstances. The state may also control certain sectors to facilitate the implementation of macroeconomic policies in response to a financial crisis or an economic recession even when doing so adversely affects their financial interests. Thus, most private enterprises are precluded from these key industries.

China also seeks to maintain significant financial resources. The government may control SOEs in some lucrative sectors such as tobacco and commercial banking, so that it has the necessary resources to pursue various state goals. Private enterprises may thus be barred from entering these state-monopolized sectors to ensure the government can collect revenues from them. Indeed, the state may also extract revenues from private enterprises in the form of taxes. However, driven by profit-seeking motives, private enterprises may take various measures to evade taxation, while SOEs may have the opposite incentives – they may tend to submit a large amount of tax since officials may get rewarded for doing so.

However, China does not necessarily need to maintain control in all sectors. It only needs to control certain sectors that are necessary for the state to maintain stability, provide disaster relief, or extract revenues. The development of private enterprises in certain sectors sometimes contributes to the state's ability to maintain stability, given that private enterprises submit taxes, increase the employment rate, and hence stabilize society. The goal of profit-seeking activities pursued by private enterprises and the interests of a non-liberal state are often aligned. Thus, this book posits that regulatory costs are higher in some but not all sectors where the state needs to maintain control.

B. *The Degree of Uncertainty and Asset Specificity*

Law is inevitably incomplete because of bounded rationality, uncertainty, and opportunistic actions. However, the degree of uncertainty varies across sectors (Pistor and Xu, 2003, p. 932). Some sectors undergo more changes in the law than others. The degree of uncertainty depends on several factors, including changes in the market and the macroeconomic environment. Regulatory costs are higher when regulators need to cope with issues that change rapidly over time, and lower when the environment is relatively static. This factor directly influences enactment costs. When environments change rapidly, states and enterprises need to renegotiate their regulatory contracts. In a developing country such as China, or a newly developed industry, traditional laws are ineffective in dealing with new circumstances. There are also more loopholes in the regulation under these circumstances. The problem of bounded rationality thus becomes more severe, leading to higher regulatory costs. It also discourages the government from making credible commitments, because they may be more concerned about foreclosing options and losing control of the situation.

In some industries, fixed investments are needed upfront whereas profits come in the long run. Investors face the asset-specificity problem: their investments become specified and cannot be used for other purposes, which renders them more susceptible to government predation. Private investors may not enter the market when they find it too difficult to calculate the risks ex ante, leading to underinvestment and hence a decrease in efficiency.

C. *Institutions That Support Regulation*

1. Judicial Capacity and power

The government may lack the ability to provide strong legal protection, a problem commonly referred to as the "credible commitment problem" (Levy and Spiller, 1994). This problem arises when governments fail to guarantee and enforce contracts and commitments, leading to concerns of government opportunism. A powerful judiciary acts as an impartial arbitrator, safeguarding the rights of individuals and businesses. When the court is entirely beholden to the government, its ability to act as a check on government actions is compromised. Therefore, the establishment of a powerful judiciary that can adjudicate the disputes involving the government impartially is crucial to ensuring fair and just outcomes.

A related concept is judicial capacity. Judges not only need to be powerful but also capable of adjudicating disputes between the government and enterprises. Several factors can indicate a robust judicial system. One such factor is the quality of judicial decisions. A strong court should exhibit sound reasoning, consistency, and fairness in its judgments. Additionally, the extent of investment made by the state in the judicial system reflects its commitment to ensuring a reliable and efficient legal framework. Adequate financial resources, infrastructure, and staffing are essential to enhance the capacity of the judiciary.

One example arises when the government modifies the laws or regulations that govern private entities. In order to ensure robust legal protection for private enterprises, it is imperative for the court to impose substantial constraints on the government, thereby facilitating the establishment of credible commitments. Nonetheless, excessive constraints within the law can undermine its flexibility. Over time, government policies and regulations may undergo revisions due to changing societal needs and economic circumstances. Judges must be capable of assessing the nature and intent of these changes and distinguishing between opportunistic actions taken by the government and legitimate changes in the law or regulations.

2. The Cost of Lawmaking

Regulatory costs include the costs of enacting and adjusting regulatory rules. Their magnitude thus depends on the costs of lawmaking. The costs vary across different states, depending on the relevant institutional arrangements and the size of the state. China has a unitary system instead of a federal system, although local governments also enjoy some discretion in policymaking. It has adopted a hierarchical control of legal authorities, leaving legislative power to deprive the property interests of private parties to the national legislature. According to Article 8 of the *Legislative Law (li fa fa)*, local governments are barred from enacting laws that expropriate the property interests of private enterprises, adopt new taxes, or adopt measures that limit individual liberty. Such an arrangement significantly limits the power of the local governments. One possible justification for China's approach is that it might have been adopted due to the concern of local protectionism – different provinces may enact rules or policies that discriminate firms from other regions, which would be inefficient. Since the government officials' performance in different regions is measured by the local GDP growth, government officials in a region have incentives to adopt policies that limit the development of firms from another region in order to win the "performance tournament" (Zhou, 2007). However, it does significantly raise the enactment costs. In addition, given the size of the country, China may face significant needs for policy flexibility – different provinces are likely to have different policy preferences and a uniform approach may lead to negative consequences.

3. Alternative Mechanisms

Another factor influencing the magnitude of regulatory costs is the availability of alternative solutions to the state's need for regulation or intervention. When the market is capable of rectifying its own failures without state intervention, fewer regulations are necessary, reducing regulatory costs. In some countries, nonprofit organizations play a pivotal role in mitigating market failures (Hansmann, 1980, p. 838). Unlike for-profit entities, nonprofit organizations do not distribute profits to their members, shareholders, or individuals in control. This characteristic makes them less likely to prioritize profit over other stakeholders, potentially requiring less regulation (Hansmann, 1980, p. 838). However, nonprofits face several operational challenges, such as difficulties in accessing capital and adapting to changing investment and expansion needs (Hansmann, 1980, p. 897).

The reputation of business enterprises can play a crucial role in mitigating market failures. Even without regulation, enterprises in the market may consider their reputation among the public and would not act opportunistically because the long-term benefits of maintaining a good reputation may be higher than the short-term gains of opportunistic actions. The reputation mechanism makes regulation unnecessary and thus reduces regulatory costs. However, in many developing countries, significant information asymmetry still exists, and reputations take a long time to build.

Societies may also encourage enterprises to achieve social objectives using economic or legal incentives. Communities, environmental organizations, or other social advocacy groups can initiate boycotts against companies that harm public interests (Gunningham et al., 2004, p. 334). Such protests often put pressure on regulators, prompting them to adopt a stricter approach toward these corporations (Gunningham et al., 2004, p. 328). However, these strategies are effective only when social groups are well-organized (Gunningham et al., 2004, p. 332). Furthermore, the effectiveness of reputation-based mechanisms requires the corporation to be a consistent, long-term participant in the market. The extent of regulatory costs within a jurisdiction is influenced by whether these alternative mechanisms are present and capable of effectively advancing social objectives.

V. Responses to Potential Challenges and Counterarguments

One major challenge to LTS is that the prevalence of SOEs is largely influenced by government decisions, making it difficult to infer their efficiency solely based on their prevalence. As LTS is developed based on the framework of Hansmann's theory of the ownership of enterprise and Ronald Coase's theory of transaction cost, it is helpful to compare how empirical evidence has been offered to support these previous theories. The Coase theorem suggests that people would willingly trade their entitlements when transaction costs are low. This principle does not necessarily require extensive empirical support since individuals who do not follow this theorem would likely bear negative consequences (Stigler, 1989, p. 631). Similarly, Hansmann's theory of the ownership of enterprise also assumes that market competition would affect the ownership pattern. It is more difficult to provide robust support for LTS than the Coase theorem and the theory of the ownership of enterprise because it involves the government's decision, which may deviate from the decisions made by profit-seeking, rational market participants.

However, this book posits that the pattern of state ownership in different markets depends not only on the government's choice but also on private choices made by investors and consumers. Chapters 2–4 will show that where the law frequently changes and the government may act opportunistically, private investors may be more cautious and choose not to invest. Hence, even if the government has decided to promote private investment, regulatory costs may constitute a barrier. The prevalence of SOEs in some markets can be explained, at least in important part, by the regulatory costs faced by private market participants.

It is important to acknowledge that the optimal levels and methods of market regulations are subject to ongoing debate, which lies beyond the scope of this book's analysis. If the regulations themselves are inappropriate, one potential approach for China to enhance efficiency would be to reduce the extent of state control over the market. The theory presented in this book focuses on exploring whether the social costs associated with regulation can help explain the prevalence of SOEs in China, without evaluating the necessity of the regulations themselves.

2

Explaining Local-Government-Owned Enterprises in Different Sectors in China through the Legal Theory

This chapter begins to apply the Legal Theory of State-Owned Enterprises (LTS) to explain the development of state-owned enterprises (SOEs) in China. It focuses mainly on local-government-owned enterprises (LGOEs) and private firms across various sectors in China for several reasons. First, unlike the SOEs controlled by the central government, LGOEs are less intensely affected by political concerns. They are widely present in sectors that are not considered strategically important, such as the water utilities sector. Studies have shown that local governments in China have very different incentives than the central government, often focusing more on economic goals such as promotion of GDP growth, raising fiscal revenue, and improving the employment rate (Bai et al., 2006a, p. 355; Zhou, 2007). Their decisions are thus more likely to be affected by the social costs associated with regulation and state ownership. Second, LGOEs in different parts of China behave differently, and there are significant disparities among the LGOEs. While some local governments privatize LGOEs to promote GDP growth or employment rates, others maintain LGOEs for stability and other concerns. This variation provides a wealth of empirical evidence regarding the development of LGOEs, which can be leveraged to test various theories related to state ownership.

This chapter will first provide an overview of the ownership costs and regulatory costs facing these enterprises in China, outlining the basic legal framework and reviewing the literature on the level of protection received by private and state-owned enterprises. It will then delve into several case studies. As analyzed in Chapter 1, one of the mechanisms through which regulatory costs affect state ownership is the demand side mechanism; in sectors with significant regulation and high regulatory costs that are mostly borne by private enterprises, there might be an underinvestment problem, leading to a higher demand for the goods or services provided by the SOEs. This chapter will first focus on this demand side mechanism by analyzing the extent of regulatory costs in several heavily regulated sectors, including water utilities, iron, steel, and coal. After these discussions, this chapter will proceed to consider financial regulation and the development of state-owned banks in China. It will shift the focus to the supply side and analyze the governments' incentives to maintain or relinquish control in the financial sector. These case studies combined illustrate the varying degrees of protection for private enterprises across different sectors and offer an explanation for the heterogeneous landscape of state ownership observed in these sectors.

I. Ownership Costs and Regulatory Costs in China: An Overview

Since the late 1990s reform, China has successfully privatized a large number of SOEs, while maintaining SOEs in a few designated sectors. The State Asset Supervisory and Administrative Committee (SASAC) has stated that China needs to retain control over seven strategically important industries, including the military, electricity grid, oil and petroleum, telecommunications, coal, airline, and shipping industries (Ren and Liu, 2006). Private investments are encouraged, and the proportion of SOE assets is below 30 percent in almost all manufacturing fields: food, textile, timber, furniture, paper, medicines, raw chemical materials, chemical products, rubber and plastics, nonmetallic mineral products, metal products, machinery, computers, and measuring instruments. The manufacturing of automobiles is an exception, as it is regarded as a pillar industry where SOEs hold over 40 percent of the assets. According to a report by the *China Daily*, in 2023, private enterprises contribute over 50 percent of tax revenue, over 60 percent of the GDP, over 70 percent of technological innovation achievements, over 80 percent of urban employment, and over 90 percent of the total number of enterprises (Wang, 2023).

China's decision to privatize SOEs and promote private enterprises has been primarily motivated by an emphasis of economic development. (Gilson and Milhaupt, 2011) The central government has recognized the efficiency of privatization and actively advocated for its implementation. Numerous studies have indicated that privatizing SOEs has resulted in enhanced performance (Wei and Varela, 2003, pp. 65–82; Bai et. al., 2006b, pp. 4–13; Chen and Tang, 2014, pp. 13–23; Zhang et al., 2016, pp. 32–41; Hao and Gong, 2017, pp. 122–135; Qian and Liu, 2019, pp. 185–188; Zhang et al., 2023, pp. 5–25). Bai et al. (2006b) examined the effects of privatization during the period of 1998–2003 and observed a substantial improvement in the economic efficiency of privatized enterprises. This improvement was primarily attributable to the reduction in agency costs, which was specifically reflected in decreased management expenses. Chen and Tang (2014) investigated the reform of SOEs from 1999 to 2007 and identified a reduction in the policy burdens imposed on SOEs, including excessive staffing and welfare responsibilities, which reduces ownership costs. Qian and Liu (2019), utilizing data from 2011 to 2016, discovered that SOEs that underwent mixed-ownership reforms exhibited superior performance. Nonetheless, it is worth noting that some studies, such as those by Li and Zhang (2008), have not consistently demonstrated improved performance following privatization of SOEs.

It is important to recognize that government officials spearheading privatization efforts may not be solely motivated by efficiency considerations. They have their own incentives and constraints as well, which may prevent them from fully capturing all the advantages of privatization. Guo and Yao (2004) investigated five different hypotheses explaining the privatization of SOEs by Chinese governments. They concluded that, apart from efficiency concerns, local governments are likely motivated by the imperative to enhance fiscal revenues, with officials incentivized through compensation for facilitating privatization (Guo and Yao, 2004). Zhang and Li (1998) posit that privatization was made feasible through decentralization, as local governments, driven by competition in the provision of goods and services, sought ways to gain a competitive edge.

Many of these benefits of privatization align with the theory of ownership costs. Privatization enhances revenue generation by reducing ownership-related expenses. As private firms benefit from lower ownership costs, privatization facilitates the acquisition of SOEs' ownership interests by private investors, thereby increasing the income of local governments (Guo and Yao, 2004, p. 6). Additionally, privatization improves managerial performance, resulting in higher tax revenues for the government.

Although China has made significant efforts to privatize its SOEs and invite private investment since its economic reform, regulatory costs remain a major barrier to the development of the private sector. Due to the incompleteness of law, the government often wields significant regulatory power over enterprises or may issue new laws or regulatory rules. These powers can be exercised in an unpredictable way, which sometimes infringe upon the property interests of enterprises.

To understand the magnitude of regulatory costs faced by private enterprises in China, one must first examine the legal institutions that offer protection. China has promulgated many laws, policies, regulations, and plans that sought to offer stable protection to private enterprises. China has developed a set of administrative laws to protect investors' interests. For example, Article 8 of the *Chinese Legislation Law* stipulates that the expropriation of the assets or property of a non-state-owned enterprise must have a basis in a national statute. Both state and Party policies confirm the decision to respect private property. For instance, in 2005, the State Council issued "*Opinions On Supporting, Guiding And Encouraging The Economic Development of The Private Enterprises*" (关于鼓励支持和引导个体私营等非公有制经济发展的若干意见), which proposed rules for promoting investments by private enterprises and emphasized protecting their legal interests. In recent years, China has issued rules that aim to improve the business environment (营商环境), which also strengthen the protection of private property. The Chinese State Council has also made significant efforts to encourage private investment.

Although numerous studies have indicated that Chinese courts often provide inadequate protection for private enterprises, it is important to recognize that the Chinese government has certain incentives to offer at least some level of protection, driven by the desire to promote economic development (Clarke, 2003; Gilson and Milhaupt, 2011). Since the Chinese government generally considers economic development as a major source of legitimacy, both the central and local governments of China have incentives to offer strong property protection to business enterprises.

Moreover, China has developed institutions that incentivize local governments to make credible commitments in promoting growth and fostering strong investor confidence. In China, local government officials compete with each other in promoting economic growth to advance their careers. This model institutionalizes development as a key metric in explaining government decisions, referred to as a "promotion tournament" (Zhou, 2007). Thus, local governments have incentives to offer strong protection to private enterprises that can drive up the employment rate, increase tax revenues, and promote GDP growth (Zhang and Zhou, 2008). When private enterprises in a local area perform well, the local government officials also benefit from their performance. Consequently, local governments often form strategic partnerships with local enterprises and compete with those in other areas (Zhou, 2018). The competition between different development partnerships also promotes the protection of private property.

Some private corporations are not only encouraged to develop but also regarded as "national champions" critical to the country's economic growth and national interests, allowing them to receive favorable treatments such as government subsidies or low-interest bank loans. Milhaupt and Zheng note that private corporations can capture the state by promising growth (Milhaupt and Zheng, 2014). They thus can receive protection of properties and obtain state-generated rents or other favorable treatments. One major type of preferential treatment is low-cost land. It has been noted that Chinese local governments frequently provide low-cost lands to attract investment from manufacturing corporations because the development of these corporations can significantly promote GDP growth and increase the tax revenue of the local government (Lan, 2021). Although some local government officials still expropriate private enterprises for their personal benefit, such activities are strictly monitored by upper-level bureaucrats (Hou, 2019).

Scholars have presented empirical evidence indicating that the level of protection for Chinese private enterprises is often inadequate. Anecdotal evidence supports this claim, suggesting that private enterprises in China encounter greater regulatory costs compared to their counterparts in liberal states. Weak property protection for business enterprises could take several forms.

First, the government sometimes engages in extralegal direct expropriation of financial interests by soliciting informal payments from private enterprises. These payments can take many forms, such as prepaid taxes and donations to public projects (Hou, 2021). Chinese government officials have a strong incentive to collect informal payments from private enterprises for their personal gains due to the relatively low salaries of civil servants in China (Ang, 2009). Private enterprises may be willing to hand over the payments either because they believe that they may gain something in the long term from dealing with the government – such as obtaining loans from state-owned banks, low-cost lands, or seeking approval on their projects – or because they fear that the government may impose sanction on them using its regulatory power if they resist the expropriation (Hou, 2021). According to one study, government officials could impose informal taxes, fees, and fines on private enterprises. However, the payments collected are usually not unlimited; otherwise, the private enterprise would not survive, and the government officials would lose their income sources. Empirical evidence on some enterprises shows that the level of expropriation is about 5 percent of their profits (Hou, 2021).

Second, some studies show that Chinese governments engage in extralegal control of private enterprises. By definition, extralegal control is exercised by the government without a formal legal basis, thereby violating the fundamental principles of the rule of law. Such control imposes regulatory costs on private entities by transgressing legal boundaries, significantly undermining investors' expectations and potentially deterring investment. A typical way for the Chinese government to wield extralegal control is through the use of "informal interviews" to "persuade" private enterprises to follow the state's orders even when such orders negatively affect their property interests (Milhaupt and Zheng, 2014). For example, the state may intervene in price-setting decisions, even though the law does not authorize price regulation. The state may also order financial firms to purchase shares or commercial banks to extend loans in a financial crisis, even when doing so may lead to financial losses for these firms. The magnitude of regulatory costs depends on the financial interests adversely affected by such informal order.

Third, the law in China frequently changes, which imposes significant regulatory costs on private enterprises. Undoubtedly, legal transitions that adversely affect the property interests of private enterprises are not uncommon in liberal states (Kaplow, 1986). For example, the deregulatory policies adopted by the United States in the late 1990s led electric utilities to lose more than $34 billion without triggering the compensation required under the Taking Clause in the US Constitution (Rose-Ackerman and Rossi, 2000). Scholars generally argue that investors themselves should be left to bear the losses caused by legal transition as long as the new rules are formulated under the formal legislative procedures (Kaplow, 1986). However, in non-liberal states, changes in the law may be even less predictable. In addition, given the drastic speed at which China's economy and society have developed in the past few decades, changes in the law are generally more frequent and unexpected in advance, rendering private enterprises more susceptible to losses caused by legal transitions. This can explain why SOEs are relatively more prevalent in China than in many other developed states.

It should be noted that the governments' intervention in private businesses occurs more frequently in some sectors than others. In other words, the level of regulatory costs varies across sectors because of the state's goals of promoting development and imposing regulations in some sectors but not others. This discrepancy can explain the evolution of private and SOEs within these different sectors. As illustrated above, the government may intervene to address market failures or maintain control. In a large number of manufacturing sectors, market failures are mild. Additionally, China does not deem it important to maintain control in many of these sectors. Their success in these areas may even reinforce the state's power when they submit a large amount of tax, increase the employment rate, and promote GDP growth (Milhaupt and Zheng, 2014). In fact, the protection of private manufacturing may contribute to economic development. As discussed earlier, local governments in China are under a "performance tournament" – they compete in promoting the economic development of the local region to gain a higher chance of promotion (Zhou, 2018). They thus may develop ties with private corporations that protect their property interests to encourage further investment (Zhou, 2018). Therefore, in these sectors, private enterprises predominantly operate within the framework of the law. They are obligated to adhere to various regulations such as taxation, environmental standards, and workplace safety. However, the regulatory rules in these sectors are relatively well-defined, resulting in lower regulatory costs. As a result, private enterprises in these sectors, with lower regulatory costs and well-defined rules, often excel due to their superior management capabilities compared to SOEs.

However, in sectors characterized by market failures or where state control is deemed necessary, private enterprises face a higher risk of government intervention. Many case studies highlighting China's weak property protection focus on sectors with these characteristics. For instance, Acemoglu and Robinson, in their influential work "Why Nations Fail," argue that China's protection of private property remains inadequate. They cite the example of Tieben, a private steel corporation, whose property interests were infringed upon by the Chinese government (Acemoglu and Robinson, 2013, pp. 437–438). As the following sections will demonstrate, the steel industry is subject to extensive state regulation and control. The Tieben case thus may not be a representative example of the landscape of property protection under Chinese law.

The above theory that legal protection offered to private enterprises varies across sectors is further supported by a recent study based on the Chinese Private Enterprise Survey, conducted by several Chinese governmental authorities, including the State Administration for Market Regulation in 2016 (Zeng, 2025). The survey questionnaire was randomly distributed in March 2016. In total, over 7,000 enterprises replied to the survey. Among them, over 2,000 are in the manufacturing sector. The survey includes three questions that gauge the respondents' perception of property protection. The first question is whether changes in government policy pose risks to their business, with response options of "No" or "Yes." Twenty-two percent of the respondents believe it poses a risk to their business. In the survey conducted in 2008 by the same authorities, there was a question of whether the respondent agreed that their enterprises faced confiscatory measures from the government.

Regarding the risk posed by changes in government policies to businesses, empirical evidence shows that manufacturing firms experience fewer policy changes than most other sectors, such as agriculture, with the difference being marginally statistically significant (Zeng, 2025). Additionally, enterprises in the manufacturing sector were less likely to face confiscatory measures (Zeng, 2025). Enterprises with government investment also show a reduced likelihood of facing confiscatory measures (Zeng, 2025).

It is important to acknowledge a selection bias in this type of studies. The survey was conducted among existing private enterprises, which may not fully represent the perspectives of those who have already exited the market due to significant government expropriation. Additionally, investors who have chosen to invest in a specific sector have likely taken into account their relationship with the government beforehand. For instance, if a private investor decides to invest in the mining sector, which is known to face higher risks of government expropriation, it is likely that the investor is more capable of navigating government interactions. Therefore, the perception of strong property protection within a particular sector does not necessarily indicate overall strong protection across the market. However, it should be noted that the survey asks respondents whether changes in government policy pose risks to their business, rather than asking them whether they are satisfied with the level of risks. Thus, even enterprises capable of managing their relationship with the government may still report facing risks from policy changes, which mitigates the concern of self-selection to some extent.

Overall, the survey results support the hypothesis that private enterprises in different sectors largely receive different levels of protection. These findings align with the LTS, suggesting that the weak protection of private enterprises in certain sectors in China is not merely due to the state's unwillingness to offer strong protection. If that were the case, we would expect all private enterprises to be weakly protected. Instead, it appears that the weak protection of some enterprises arises because delineating the boundaries between public power and private property is more complex in their sectors. This complexity can be attributed to the higher regulatory costs associated with the frequent need to adjust regulatory policies.

II. Water Tariffs Regulation and the Privatization of Water Utilities

To further illustrate how the magnitude of regulatory costs varies across sectors, this section will discuss several specific industries. The water utilities industry is an appropriate case where the state's rate regulation often remains unstable, which may negatively affect investors' confidence and lead to underinvestment by private investors, resulting in the rise of SOEs' market share through a demand-side mechanism. Water utilities are usually natural monopolies and therefore need to be regulated. Moreover, there is a relatively long history of privatization in this industry. Significant discretion has been granted to local governments to carry out privatization and price regulation. It thus creates an opportunity to examine the relationship between state ownership and regulation over time in various cities.

Before 1998, an overwhelming majority of capital investments in the water utilities sector in China, amounting to 95 percent, was contributed by multilevel governments. This significant figure underscores the dominant role of the government in this vital industry. To illustrate the evolution of state involvement in the water utilities sector, Figures 2.1 and 2.2 present the shifts in the state's equity share within the industry over time. Over the years, there has been a noticeable decline in the state's contribution as a percentage of the total capital investment. However, this trajectory has not been linear or uniform. Notably, during the periods of 2011–12 and 2016–17, there was a reversal in this trend. The state's proportion of capital investment experienced an uptick, indicating a temporary halt or slowdown in the privatization process. These deviations highlight the complexities and challenges in consistently implementing privatization policies within the sector.

A. *Problems of Tariff Regulation and the Role of State Ownership*

Water utilities are usually subject to tariff regulation because they are natural monopolies. Although local governments have the incentive to privatize, tariff regulation is underdeveloped, creating a major barrier for privatization. In China, water tariffs are usually determined by cost-of-service regulations. According to the Municipal Water Supply Price Management Measures, a national regulation, water utilities can submit a request to the price department, a branch of the prefecture-level government, to adjust water tariffs. Before approving the adjustment,

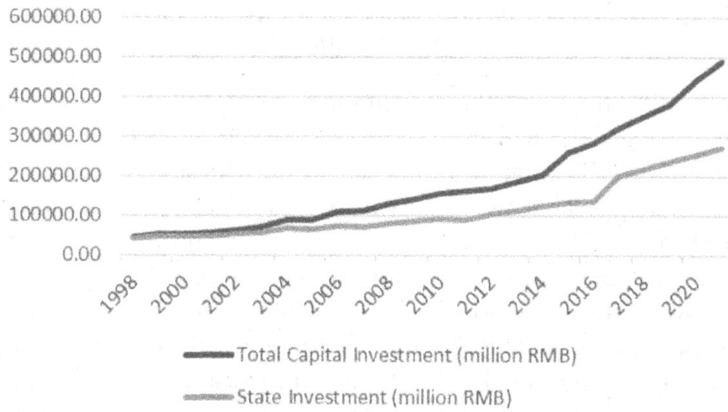

Figure 2.1 Total capital investment and state investment in the water utilities industry.
Source: China Economic Information Center (CEIC) China Premium Database

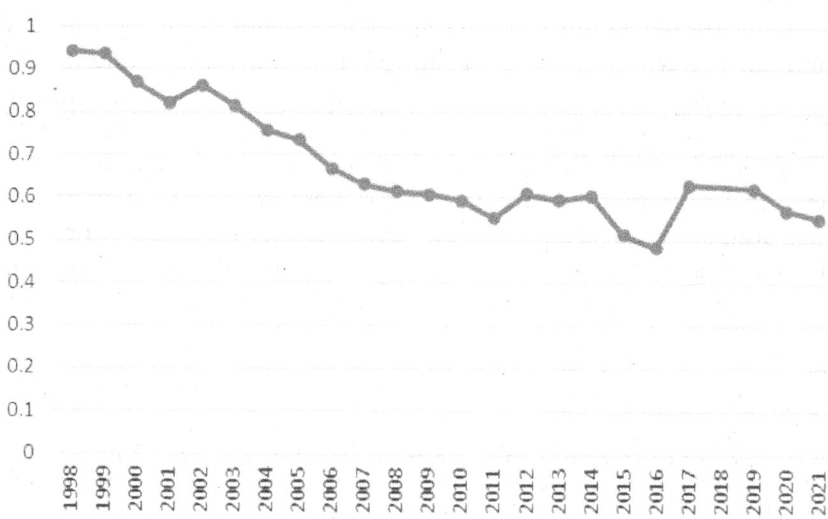

Figure 2.2 Percentage of capital investment contributed by the governments in the water utilities industry.
Source: China Economic Information Center (CEIC) China Premium Database

the price regulator conducts a hearing process, inviting experts and the public to participate. Based on the opinions gathered in the hearing, the price regulator and the prefecture government will determine whether to approve the adjustment. If approved, the adjustment will be reported to the higher level of government.

This process incurs significant procedural costs, requiring considerable time and resources. Moreover, it draws significant criticism from public consumers as well as scholars (Wang, 2006). As some scholars have pointed out, it is a one-sided decision-making process (Wang, 2006). Without sufficient knowledge and capacity, public representatives often cannot fully understand the accounting reports on the costs of water utilities when attending the hearing (Fu, 2011, p. 17). Under the expectation that the public should have a say in the adjustment of water tariffs, the hearing process is criticized as having no substantive impact on the final decision (Fu, 2011, p. 17). The tariff regulation also involves distributional concerns – a lower water tariff for residential use would benefit low-income individuals since they spend a larger portion of their income on water usage. Thus, it is sometimes difficult for the public to reach a consensus on the appropriate level of water tariffs.

Additionally, determining the cost of supplying water as a basis for calculating water tariffs is inherently challenging. Consequently, price regulators must oversee numerous business decisions made by water utility companies, necessitating substantial resources. For instance, many water utilities offer high salaries to their employees. When regulators assess whether to approve tariff adjustments, they must also scrutinize these salary structures. Public dissatisfaction often arises from the regulatory constraints imposed on water utilities aimed at reducing supply costs. Furthermore, the ambiguity of many accounting terms used in cost determination allows for easy manipulation, complicating tariff regulation efforts. These regulatory challenges are not unique to China and can be observed in other countries. In the United States, where governmental ownership of water utilities is rare, scholars have identified similar issues. Cost-of-service regulation can lead private owners to overinvest, whereas government ownership may mitigate these problems and reduce "relational friction" between consumers and utility enterprises (Masten, 2011, pp. 618–621). This comparison underscores the complexities involved in regulating water tariffs and highlights the potential benefits of state ownership in addressing regulatory inefficiencies.

The law on the regulation of water tariffs grants discretionary approval power to local governments. The regulatory rules allow local governments to consider the development of water utilities, the growing needs for water supply, and the burden on the public. These objectives are often in conflict with each other, which essentially allow local governments to make decisions with unbounded discretion because they can always find a justification for their decisions. The public's distrust and scholars' criticism have put enormous pressure on local governments, making them reluctant to adjust water tariffs frequently (Fu, 2011, p. 21; Wu, 2013). Some local governments chose not to adjust water tariffs for a long period of time, even though the costs of supplying water had risen significantly (Fu, 2011; Wu, 2013). When the costs of water supply increase, they are borne by the water utilities and shared by all investors. Local governments can thus externalize some of the costs to private investors (Troesken and Geddes, 2003). Due to these costs, private investors may be deterred from investing, leading to an underinvestment problem and a shortage of water supply (Troesken and Geddes, 2003, p. 379). When local governments use SOEs to supply water, they cannot act opportunistically: If water tariffs do not adequately cover supply costs, local governments must subsidize the enterprise. Thus, SOEs are not subject to the social costs of opportunistic actions as would private enterprises.

B. *Empirical Evidence in Different Cities*

In order to illustrate the impacts of tariff regulation on private investment, this chapter conducts a statistical study using data in different cities. The data used in this study come from the Chinese National Sizable Industrial Enterprise dataset. The dataset includes all industrial enterprises that have revenue of over 5 million RMB and all SOEs regardless of their size from 2005 to 2006, all industrial enterprises with revenue of over 5 million RMB (including SOEs and private enterprises) from 2007 to 2010, and all industrial enterprises with revenue of over 20 million RMB after 2011. The difference in selection criteria may cause problems for the study because after 2011, the percentage of SOEs may become larger in some cities relative to others, depending on the size of the private enterprises and SOEs. To resolve this problem, I thus excluded all enterprises in the dataset with revenue below 20 million RMB. The time frame for this analysis spans from 2005 to 2014, given that data after 2014 remains currently unavailable.

Within each city, water tariffs for residential, industrial, and business uses typically differ, but they are often adjusted simultaneously. For this study, I focused on industrial-use water tariffs across thirty-six cities, utilizing data accessible through the CEIC China Premium Database. The thirty-six cities include four municipalities, twenty-seven provincial capitals, and five major cities with provincial-level (*sheng ji*) status: Shenzhen, Qingdao, Xiamen, Dalian, and Ningbo.

The dependent variable is the ratio of the aggregate capital investment contributed by the government to the aggregate capital investment from all sources in such city in water utilities in a given city. The dataset contains information of the capital contribution from various sources to each enterprise, including capital investment from the state, individuals, legal persons (usually corporations), collectives, and foreign investors. I calculated the percentage of capital investment by the government through two steps. First, I took the variable of the governments' capital investment provided in the dataset and divided it by the total capital investment. Second, since the capital investment of some enterprises comes from corporations whose owners are unknown and can be government owned, I treated the investment from legal persons as state investment if the water utility company reports being controlled by the state, but the state's capital investment does not exceed half of its paid-in capital.

The independent variable in my study is the number of times a city had adjusted its water tariffs since January 2005. Given the fact that the costs of supplying water had risen drastically from 2005 to 2014, water tariffs needed to be adjusted frequently to reflect the increase in costs. Water utility firms risk incurring significant losses if their production costs rise without a corresponding adjustment in tariffs. A smaller number of adjustments of water tariffs indicate a tendency of the local government to avoid using regulation, which may harm the financial interests of the enterprises and discourage private investment in this sector. Later in the study, I also examined the relationship between the proportion of state investment and the size of the water tariff. A summary of the major variables used in the study is listed in Table 2.3.

To examine the relationship between state ownership and regulation, I conducted a regression analysis with fixed effects and random effects models using panel data. The model is specified as follows:

$$\boldsymbol{State\ Ownership}_{y,i} = \beta \boldsymbol{Adj}_{y,i} + \boldsymbol{\theta}_y + \boldsymbol{\lambda}_i + \boldsymbol{X}_{y,i} + \epsilon_{y,i}$$

$\boldsymbol{State\ Ownership}_{y,i}$ denotes the percentage of the state's investment in city i in year y calculated in the ways stated above. $\boldsymbol{Adj}_{y,i}$ denotes the number of times that city i has adjusted its water tariff from January

2005 to the end of the year *y*. I included three control variables in the vector $\boldsymbol{X}_{y,i}$, GDP per capita, fiscal revenue per capita, and the Consumer Price Index (CPI). Areas with higher GDP, fiscal revenue, and CPI might have a different level of state and private enterprises. $\boldsymbol{\theta}_y$ represents year indicators and $\boldsymbol{\lambda}_i$ represents city indicators. Table 2.3 of the Appendix provides a summary of the major variables by year and by number of water tariff adjustments.

The results of the regressions are presented in Table 2.4 of the Appendix. The coefficients of "Adjustment" are statistically significant at the 0.01 level in all models. In all models, clustered standard errors were used to calculate the level of statistical significance. These results strongly indicate that the more times a city adjusts its water tariffs, the lower the proportion of state investment becomes.

To enhance the clarity of the results, the dataset was narrowed to include only the years 2005 and 2014. Figure 2.3 presents a scatterplot that correlates the frequency of water tariff adjustments with the shifts in state investment proportion from 2005 to 2014. The figure visually represents that, with an increase in the number of tariff adjustments,

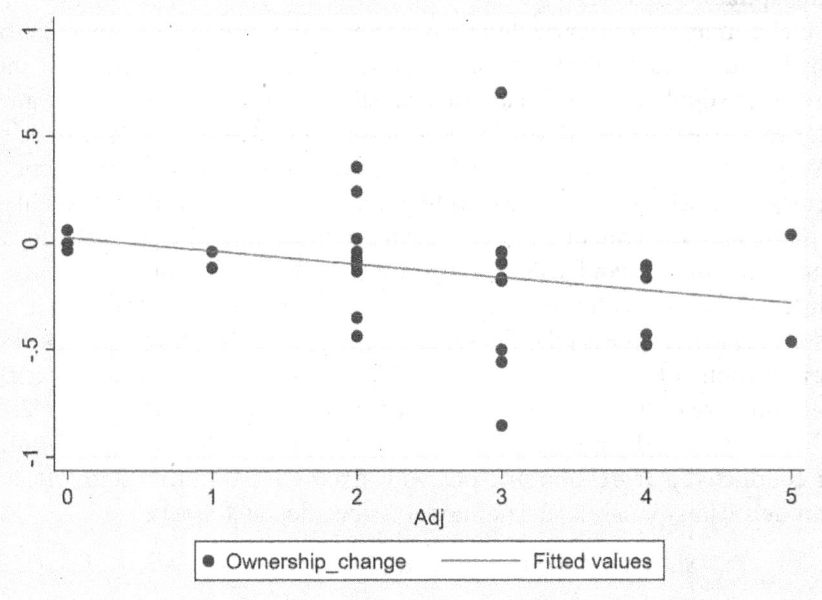

Figure 2.3 Number of adjustments of the water tariff for industrial use and changes in state ownership from 2005 to 2014.

the observed changes in state ownership – quantified by the proportion of state investment – tend to be negative.

It should be noted that the above analysis faces an endogeneity problem. One alternative interpretation for the findings is that private enterprises possess a stronger motivation to influence regulators into modifying water tariffs compared to SOEs. Consequently, a negative correlation emerges between the proportion of state investment and the frequency of tariff adjustments. Another possibility is that both the tariff regulation and the decision to privatize are influenced by an unaccounted variable, muddling the observed effects. For instance, certain governments might opt to privatize SOEs and simultaneously heighten regulatory measures, driven by the desire to enhance revenue or the efficiency of water services.

Nonetheless, these alternative interpretations do not diverge from the core argument but suggest that private investors place considerable importance on the tariff's regulation regime. For the privatization of state-owned water utilities to proceed successfully, it is important for governments to demonstrate a commitment to consistent and predictable regulatory practices concerning price adjustments. A failure to adjust water tariffs could jeopardize the investors' property interests, deter investments, and consequently, raise the demand for services managed by SOEs.

Alternative theories cannot easily explain these findings. Specifically, conventional economic and political theories fall short in accounting for the evolving ownership patterns observed in water utilities across different cities. Despite being natural monopolies, the ownership of these utilities' changes over time. Moreover, the classification of water utilities as nonstrategic industries, meaning they are not always under strict government control. As a result, the local authorities have significant discretion to privatize them.

Additionally, the political economy's explanation of SOEs, including the regulatory capture theory, also does not explain all the findings above. Regulatory capture refers to the circumstances in which regulated enterprises successfully turn the regulator into their "servant" (Posner, 2013, p. 49), usually because they are relatively better organized (Stigler, 1971). Scholars have expressed the worry that SOEs may capture regulators and affect regulatory policies. Regulatory capture is closely related to the concern of protecting existing interest groups during the reform of SOEs. Current research indicates that a significant obstacle to privatization in China is the concern of social instability resulting from unemployment (Han and Dai, 2008). In the context of the privatization of water utilities, if the employees of the SOEs are not fully compensated, they may object to privatization.

While the capture theory argues that SOEs can resist privatization by swaying government policies to their advantage, it falls short in explaining the inverse relationship between tariff adjustment frequency and the proportion of state investment observed. Contrary to what capture theory might suggest – that SOEs would benefit from more favorable regulatory treatment – the data shows that in cities where state ownership in water utilities is prevalent, changes to tariffs are notably infrequent. Although it is plausible for SOEs to receive government subsidies, the capture theory does not fully explain why SOEs would choose subsidies over influencing regulators to raise tariffs. LTS offers a more nuanced understanding, highlighting the inherent complexities and costs associated with regulating water tariffs.

There are two slight variations of the capture theory that may explain the above findings. Firstly, after private investors enter the market, they may influence regulators to more frequently adjust water tariffs. This phenomenon suggests that frequent adjustments follow rather than stimulate private investment. However, this explanation fails to explain why SOEs are unable to exert similar influence on tariff regulators to increase the frequency of adjustments. Moreover, if private investors indeed had sway over the regulators, one might logically expect them to push for significant increases in tariffs. Empirical evidence presented below will demonstrate that such scenarios are not substantiated by the data.

A second explanation aligned with capture theory posits that local governments may aim to reacquire equity stakes in water utilities from private entities, particularly when they believe they could collect higher profits from these enterprises. This could be accomplished by reducing the frequency of tariff adjustments, thereby lowering the utilities' valuation and enabling the government to repurchase equity at a diminished cost. Following such a repurchase, local authorities could increase water tariffs to boost profits. This implies that tariff rates tend to be lower under private ownership and higher when in state hands. However, as the forthcoming empirical analysis will demonstrate, this hypothesis does not find support in the data.

To critically examine these alternate hypotheses, I conducted a placebo test focusing on the size of water tariffs across cities. The analysis employs the following model to probe the relationship between water tariff levels and the SOE ownership share:

$$State\ Ownership_{y,i} = \beta Water\_Tariffs_{y,i} + \theta_y + \lambda_i + X_{y,i} + \epsilon_{y,i}$$

$Water\_Tariffs_{y,i}$ is the size of the water tariff in city i in year y. The results are shown in Table 2.5, which shows that the coefficient of ***Water_Tariffs*** is not statistically significant under the random effects model. The coefficient is only marginally statistically significant under the fixed effects model. These results suggest that the major concern of private investors is the infrequent adjustment of the water tariffs rather than the absolute level.

In conclusion, the difficulties of privatizing the water utilities sector can largely be attributed to the regulatory complexities surrounding water tariffs. By contrast, SOEs remain shielded from the opportunistic government actions, primarily because local governments bear the responsibility to financially support them, ensuring the continuity of water services to the public. Moreover, this situation underscores the government's challenge in making credible commitments to private investors in tariff regulations. Water tariff regulation is generally believed to be necessary to prevent monopolistic pricing. Consequently, local governments may exploit their regulatory authority to satisfy public consumers, shifting the political and financial burdens onto private water utilities after specified investments are made. Hence, this explains the predominant presence of SOEs in the water utilities sector, a phenomenon inadequately explained by the capture theory.

III. Environmental and Energy Regulation and the Advance of the State in Iron, Steel, and Coal Industries

This section further examines the trend of the "advance of the state, retreat of the private sector" (*guojin mintui*) in the iron, steel, and coal sectors, where the nationalization of private enterprises occurred with relatively low compensation, which was cited by many scholars as evidence of weak property protection in China (Qian, 2002; Chen, 2012; Acemoglu and Robinson, 2013, pp. 437–438). Many observers interpret the increasing influence of the state and the diminishing role of the private sector in China as indicative of a lingering adherence to socialist ideology (Eaton, 2015), raising concerns about the country's prospects for success. Following this logic, China has reason to be concerned about this trend. A deep understanding of the reasons behind this trend is thus crucial for any further policy proposals regarding SOEs.

A. *Iron and Steel*

A comprehensive analysis of the increasing involvement of the state in the iron and steel sectors reveals a nuanced picture. Figure 2.4 shows the proportion of SOEs as a fraction of the total number of enterprises in the smelting and processing of ferrous metals, including iron and steel, iron, manganese, and chromium, has dropped below 10 percent since the 1990s. The proportion of assets held by SOEs in this industry has dropped gradually from about 90 percent in 1999 to below 60 percent in 2006. However, the proportion of SOEs rose slightly during 2006–09 and 2013–18, suggesting that private enterprises faced certain policy risks, and there was a trend of nationalization of the industry to a small extent, consistent with the observation of the "advance of the state, retreat of the private sector."

Current studies cannot easily explain the evolution of SOEs and private firms in these sectors. Firstly, the existing political theory falls short of fully explaining the state's growing presence in these sectors. The

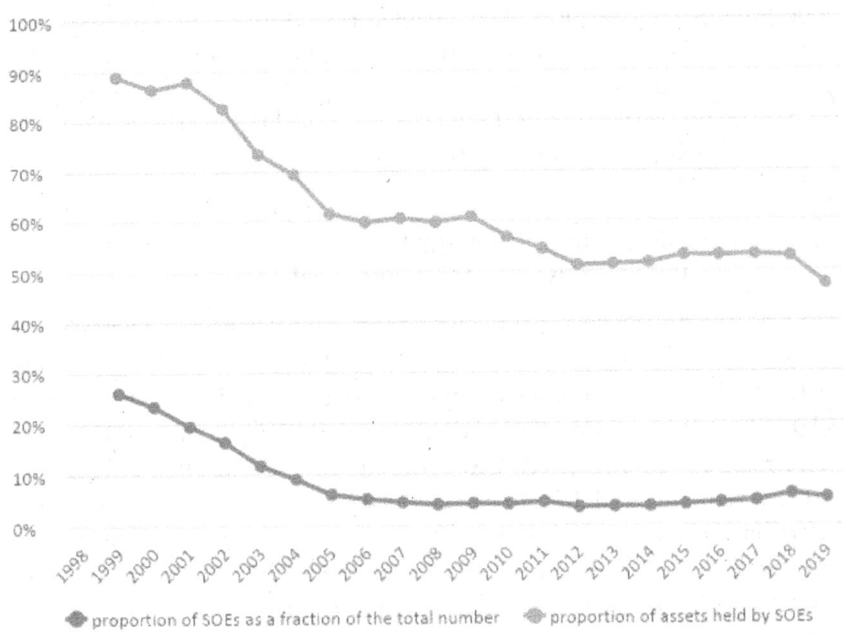

Figure 2.4 SOEs in the ferrous metal smelting and pressing industry.
Source: China Statistical Yearbook

SASAC has identified seven strategic industries where state control is deemed necessary, with the coal sector being one of them. However, the iron and steel sectors are considered important "pillar" industries in which the state should maintain a significant role but not exert absolute control (Ren and Liu, 2006). Other pillar industries include automobile manufacturing, machinery equipment, construction, and the electronic and information industry (Ren and Liu, 2006). These pillar industries differ from strategically important sectors in that private enterprises hold a substantial proportion of assets in many of them. For instance, in the manufacturing sectors of computers, communication, and other electronic equipment, private enterprises account for over 60 percent of all enterprises. Consequently, the existing political theory does not fully explain the reasons behind the state's increasing presence in the iron and steel industry.

Another possible explanation is that SOEs in these sectors managed to capture the government. As a result, the state has increased its proportion of investment in these sectors. However, this theory faces the challenge of explaining why the government has not been similarly captured by SOEs in other sectors. As discussed in the Introduction chapter, SOEs in most manufacturing sectors play a relatively small role, and there is no observed trend of the advance of the state and the retreat of private investors in these sectors. The theory of state capture needs to be supported with further empirical evidence.

LTS provides a more compelling explanation by suggesting that in sectors with frequent policy changes and where the government retains broad discretion, an environment of heightened legal uncertainty is created for private enterprises. Moreover, the court imposes less stringent restrictions on the government during these policy changes. Consequently, private enterprises face increased legal uncertainty and potential losses, leading them to withdraw from the market.

While the Chinese government does not seek to maintain control of the iron and steel industry, it still faces some level of regulatory costs because investments in these sectors conflict with the state's other goals. China has adopted industrial policies to eliminate the outdated technology and the excess production capacity in this sector, generating significant uncertainty for private investors and deterring private investment. This policy was criticized by economists as likely to undermine China's economy, since the relatively weak protection for private properties may lead to underinvestment (Chen, 2012). Additionally, some enterprises in this sector may generate high pollution, contradictory to the state's decision to promote green energy. With China committed to becoming carbon neutral by 2060, a decline in private investment in these sectors is consistent with the state's policy, since the state may find it easier to control pollution emitted by SOEs than private enterprises driven by financial incentives.

China adopted unfavorable industrial policies regarding the iron and steel industry in 2003 when the State Council promulgated the "Opinions on Curbing Blindly Investment in the Iron and Steel Industry." This document recognized that many local governments encourage investment in the iron and steel corporations, likely leading to excess production capacity, heavy pollution, and waste of resources. The State Council decided to set up market entry requirements, tighten environmental regulation, and enhance the supervision of bank loans offered to the iron and steel corporations. Since 2006, the central government's report stated China's decision to reduce the excessive production capacity in the iron and steel industries (Cai, 2016). In these areas, the central government directed relevant departments and local governments to exercise control over new projects, reduce production capacity, and encourage mergers and acquisitions. Although these efforts were interrupted in 2008 due to the fiscal stimulus package (Bai, 2016), the State Council subsequently released further regulations that prohibit any increase of iron and steel production capacity in environmentally protected areas. Frequent legal changes in this sector likely contributed to the lack of investors' confidence, leading to a slight reversal in the trend of privatization.

B. Coal Mining

Coal mining is another industry where the state implements significant environmental and energy regulations. First, it is recognized as an industry with substantial pollution, prompting the state to enact regulations aimed at shutting down small private coal mines that fail to comply with the state's environmental standards. Additionally, the state frequently promulgates new environmental regulations concerning coal mining activities, which introduce a certain level of uncertainty regarding the investment confidence of private investors. These ongoing regulatory changes can deter private investment by creating an unpredictable business environment.

Second, China also considers coal mining as a strategically important industry because it pertains to the state's energy safety and national security. Controlling coal production can help the state ensure a sufficient energy supply and avoid economic shocks from an energy shortage (Schizer, 2017). A state's dependence on foreign countries to provide energy may incur military costs. The United States, for example, has spent significant funds on maintaining the oil supply (Schizer, 2017). As China's energy consumption depends heavily on imports, it also incurs financial costs in maintaining good foreign relationships with countries that have abundant energy resources. Second, dependence on foreign countries may weaken a state's geopolitical power, as its rivals gain more financial resources (Schizer, 2017). China may be concerned about maintaining its energy supplies and hence tend to regulate the mining of coal, which is an important substitute for oil.

Third, coal mining often leads to significant workplace safety concerns. Accidents in coal mines since the 1990s have created social problems in China, threatening social stability and government legitimacy (Wang, 2004). Statistics show that in 2003 alone, 6,750 people died from coal mine accidents, constituting 39 percent of all deaths caused by production activities (Wang, 2004). The death of miners drew widespread criticisms of the governments, and many called for actions against smaller coal mines (Wang, 2004). By nationalizing private coal mines, the government can better control and regulate workplace safety.

Statistics show that the death rate in state-owned coal mines is generally lower than in private mines. There are three major types of coal mining companies in China: those controlled by the central government, those controlled by local governments, and Township and Village Enterprises (TVEs). Central and local SOEs have very different incentives. Local government officials are constantly under pressure to pursue higher GDP growth to get promoted. Consequently, they tend to grant less priority to noneconomic government objectives. The pursuit of GDP growth may even lead them to disregard regulatory goals (Zhou, 2004). Compared with companies owned by local governments, TVEs more closely resemble private enterprises and have an even stronger incentive to evade regulation (Byrd and Gelb, 1990; Huang, 2008). In the coal mining industry, the death rate per million tons is lower in state-owned mines than in mines controlled by the local government, which in turn is lower than the death rate in TVEs, as shown in Figure 2.5. The comparison between these three types of enterprises suggests that more extreme forms of state ownership incur lower regulatory costs. During the 2000s, however, the difference between the death rates for different types of enterprises has narrowed. A possible explanation for this trend is the increase in regulatory capacity and the development of sophisticated

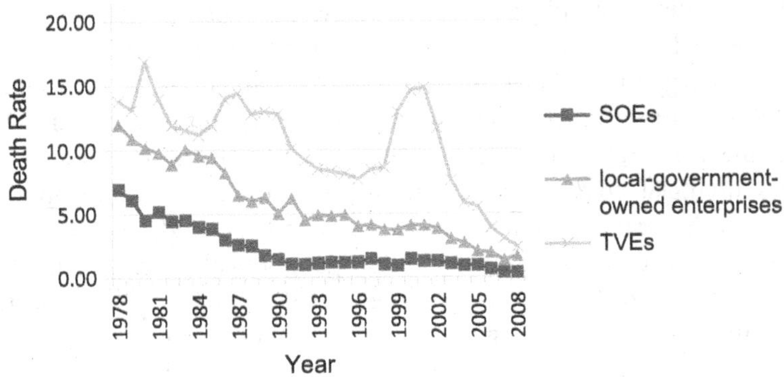

Figure 2.5 Death rate per million tons of coal production.
Source: China Coal Industry Yearbook 2008; Figure created by the author

regulatory rules on liabilities. Additionally, China has incentivized many private corporations to grow in size through mergers and acquisitions, while gradually closing down small-sized coal mines. As private corporations become larger, regulatory costs may decline, because large private corporations have a stronger incentive to comply with regulatory goals. They have more to lose when their licenses are revoked due to violations, rendering all fixed investments worthless, which increases the deterrence effect of regulation. These factors may explain why the gap between the three types of enterprises has become smaller over time.

Figure 2.6 illustrates the ratio of SOEs to the total number of coal enterprises and the asset share possessed by SOEs. It reveals that, even with the notable rise in the number of private enterprises since 1999, SOEs continue to dominate over 70 percent of the industry's assets. Throughout the 1990s, the revenue share attributed to SOEs within the sector remained relatively stable. From 2014 onward, there has been a marginal increase in the asset proportion controlled by SOEs. This suggests that the state has maintained a steadfast grip on the industry.

The Chinese central and local governments have promulgated a series of rules that fundamentally affect the financial interests of private enterprises in this sector. In Shanxi Province, the local government acquired private coal mines through various means. For example, the government demands that all mines with production capacity below a certain level be closed or sold to other enterprises (Wang, 2009). According to the 2018 Annual Development Report of the Coal

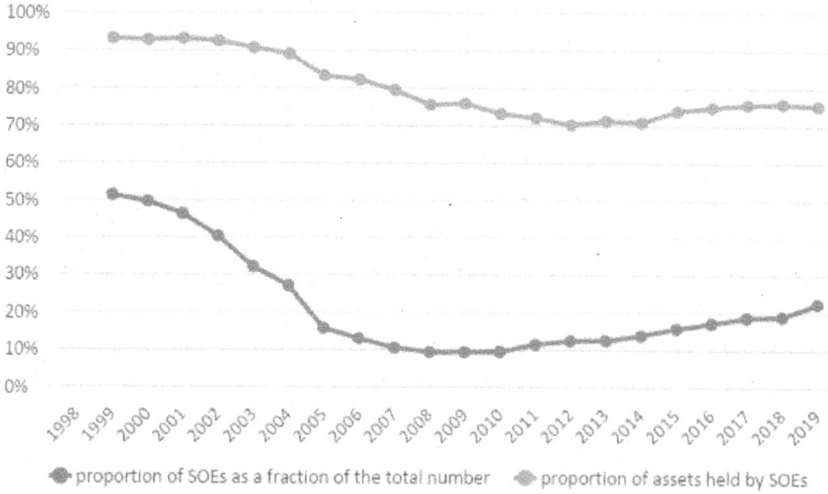

Figure 2.6 SOEs in the coal mining and processing industry.
Source: China Statistical Yearbook; Figure created by the author

Industry issued by the China National Coal Association, the number of coal mines was 6,794 in 2017. In 2018, the number dropped to around 5,800. As Figure 2.7 shows, the overall number of private enterprises in the coal mining and processing sector declined since 2008.

The political theories, however, cannot fully explain the changes in private investment in these sectors. Admittedly, the coal industry was designated as a strategic industry by SASAC in 2006. Many have noted the trend of "advance of the state, retreat of the private sector" in the coal mining and processing sectors. Although the number of private enterprises has generally declined, the value of assets held by private enterprises in this sector has not significantly changed. The value of assets held by private enterprises in the coal industry continued to grow from 2006 to 2014, as Figure 2.8 shows. The value of assets held by private enterprises declined only slightly from 2014 to 2020 and rose again in 2021.

LTS suggests that the increase in the proportion of coal enterprises owned by the state was likely mainly driven by the significant regulatory costs generated by the new environmental and safety standards. The state mainly closed down small mines and encouraged larger mines to acquire smaller mines in order to improve the efficiency of the use of energy and reduce pollution (Ma, 2012). This policy does not necessarily harm the

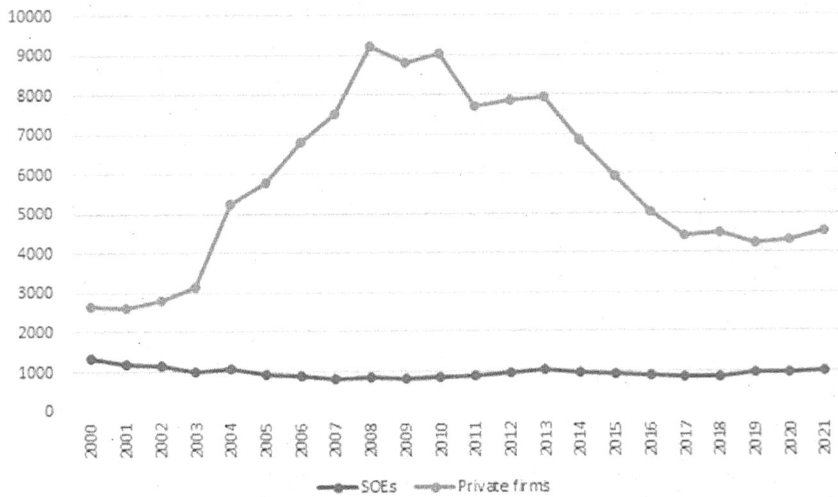

Figure 2.7 Number of firms in the coal mining and processing sectors.
Data source: CEIC China Premium Database; Figure created by the author

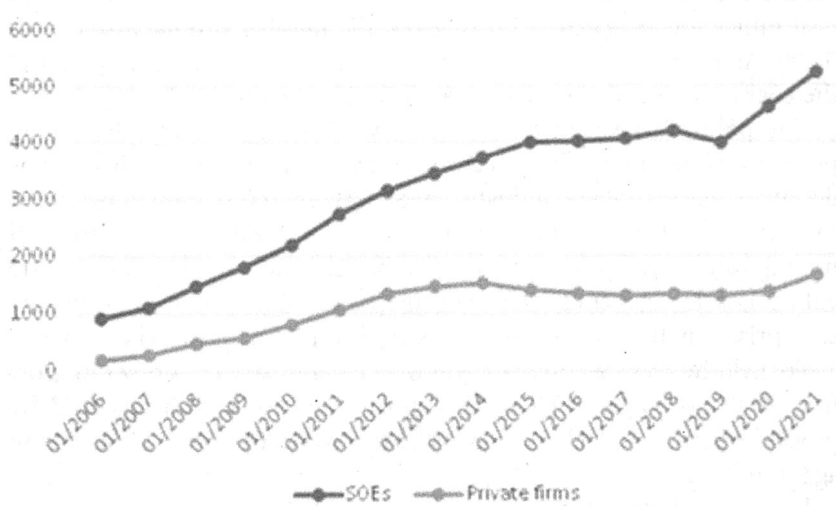

Figure 2.8 Value of assets held by firms in the coal mining and processing sectors.
Data source: CEIC China Premium Database

interests of large private coal corporations – larger private coal corporations might also receive strong protection for their property interests to the extent that they could help achieve the state's goals. As a manager of a mid-sized coal corporation stated:

> The merger and acquisition policy adopted by the Shanxi province is a good thing. Our company has been hoping to acquire other coal mines. If the government did not implement the policy, it would take many years ... Many small mines originally did not want to be acquired. However, they eventually understood the trend and made a balanced move. After all, the operational risk of small mines is too high. My company acquired six private coal mines. (Chen, 2010)

The government's policy of closing down small mines may lead some private mines to be sold to larger private coal corporations through market negotiation, also benefiting private investors. It thus explains why the total value of assets held by private coal enterprises did not drop significantly, although the total number of private enterprises had declined.

The political economy theory offers a different explanation for the changing landscape of SOEs and private enterprises in the coal industry, which suggests that the government's wide discretion in policymaking allows it to exploit their power and extract rents from private enterprises. As SOEs typically maintain closer ties with the government, they have an advantage that contributes to their increased market share. While the political economy theory has some merits in explaining the evolution of SOEs in the coal mining industry, it falls short of providing a complete explanation. To illustrate this point, one can compare the development of SOEs and private firms in the coal mining sector and the mining of nonmetal ores. The mining of nonmetal ores is not considered a strategically important industry or a pillar industry. In addition, there are not many SOEs in this sector. The state's proportion of capital investment in this sector has already dropped to around 10 percent in 2008. Thus, it is likely that SOEs in this sector, as an interest group, do not exert as much influence over regulatory rulemaking as those in the coal mining sector. However, the trend of the "advance of the state" has also been observed in this sector. Figure 2.9 illustrates the trend of the state's capital investment in the mining and processing of nonmetal ores sector. There was a notable increase in the state's proportion of capital investment relative to the total capital investment in this sector during two periods: 2008 to 2010 and 2017 to 2020.

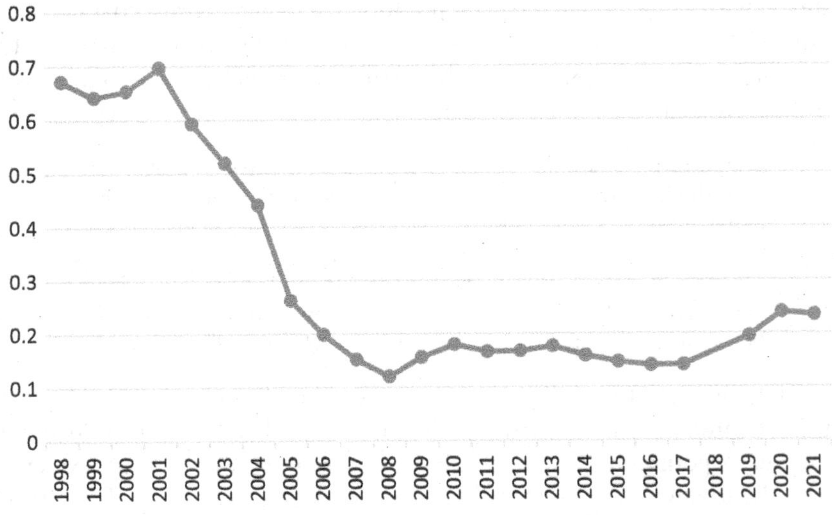

Figure 2.9 State's proportion of capital investment in the mining and processing of nonmetal ores.
Data source: CEIC China Premium Database

LTS provides a better explanation. The Chinese central government has introduced new policies related to the mining of nonmetal ores during the same period, often driven by environmental protection concerns. As Chapter 3 will further illustrate, the governments enjoyed significant discretion in implementing these policies while the courts offer little protection for the private enterprises in this sector, significantly increasing the regulatory costs. Restricting this discretion may have unintended consequences, as it limits the state's ability to adjust policies. Therefore, the political economy theory needs to be complemented by LTS to fully understand the evolution of SOEs in these sectors.

In summary, the analysis in this chapter emphasizes the role of the law rather than politics in the explanation of SOEs in China. The current political theory offered by scholars to explain SOEs in China largely posits that the prevalence of SOEs is determined by the unilateral decision of the state to develop and maintain SOEs in certain "strategic industries" (Eaton, 2015). This explanation, however, is incomplete for it cannot fully explain the changes in the development of SOEs and private firms in these industries.

IV. Financial Regulation and State Ownership in the Commercial Banking Sector

The financial industry provides further evidence of the relationship between state ownership and regulatory costs. Banks and financial institutions typically require regulatory oversight, which can be a costly endeavor. State ownership can help mitigate these challenges and reduce regulatory costs. State-owned banks, for instance, are generally less driven to pursue excessive profits by evading regulations. Additionally, the state possesses greater control mechanisms over state-owned banks, enabling the implementation of more effective regulatory measures. Unlike the sectors examined above, this section will focus more on the supply-side mechanisms, considering how government's regulatory goals have affected the historical development of state ownership in the commercial banking sector.

A. Regulatory Costs in the Banking Industry

1. The Need for Financial Regulation

Banks operate with a capital structure that relies heavily on leverage, making them vulnerable to potential bank failures (Kaufman, 1996). Their liabilities primarily consist of deposits and other short-term funds that can be easily withdrawn. Meanwhile, their assets primarily consist of long-term loans extended to individuals and enterprises, which cannot be quickly liquidated. This inherent imbalance exposes banks to the constant risk of a bank run. If a large number of depositors simultaneously lose confidence in a bank and withdraw their funds, the bank can easily become insolvent. Additionally, banks often operate with high levels of leverage and may invest in complex and opaque financial instruments, further intensifying financial risks (Kaufman, 1996, p. 20).

When commercial banks are owned by investors, they often face incentives to engage in excessive risk-taking. Investors benefit from the protection of limited liability and are typically not personally liable in the event of a bank's failure. Consequently, they may exert pressure on the bank's board of directors to pursue riskier activities. Directors are generally presumed to be risk-averse, as they have invested human capital in the banks they oversee and risk losing their positions or suffering reputational damage in the event of a bank failure. As a result, directors are likely to be more cautious and less inclined to undertake excessive risks compared to shareholders. However, the extent to which directors can mitigate these risks depends on the corporate governance structure in place. Two major arrangements may affect their incentives. First, many directors hold stock options that align their interests with the shareholders. They thus may also seek excessive risks to pursue strategies that could boost the stock price for personal gain. Second, directors are selected by the shareholders and are thus under pressure to be removed if they directly oppose shareholders' directives. Thus, banking regulation becomes necessary to prevent them from taking excessive risks.

Although bankruptcy is prevalent in today's market, governments are generally concerned with the failure of banks and other financial institutions. This concern arises because bank failures can have a contagious effect, spreading losses among interconnected banks and other industries (Bossone, 2000, p. 5). The collapse of one bank can significantly impact the solvency of another bank (Mitts, 2015, p. 11). Furthermore, banks play important public roles, such as facilitating money circulation. Their failure can lead to a spillover effect on the market and inflict severe damage on the economy (Kaufman, 1996, p. 20). In that case, borrowers may face immediate demands for repayment, leading to a wave of liquidations and bankruptcies. Public depositors may lose confidence in banks, resulting in higher interest rates. This can cause market irrationality, leading to widespread economic downturns. To prevent this disastrous outcome, governments often step in to support and bail out banks and creditors during emergencies. However, this intervention creates issues of moral hazard and adverse selection. Creditors may lack sufficient incentives to choose safer banks, relying instead on the expectation that the government will bail them out. Therefore, state intervention is necessary in regulating the business activities of this sector.

2. The Costs of Financial Regulation and the Role of State Ownership

Private banks and other financial institutions present significant challenges in risk management, and relying solely on regulation may not effectively mitigate their propensity for excessive risk-taking. One of the primary difficulties lies in the inherent complexity of formulating sophisticated and effective regulatory frameworks. The dynamic nature of financial markets and the innovative strategies employed by these institutions can outpace regulatory measures, rendering them less effective.

A common financial regulatory measure is the capital adequacy requirement. Regulators impose a minimum capital-to-asset ratio on commercial banks, aiming to enhance their stability. Risk-based capital requirements are often utilized, taking into account the varying risk levels associated with different types of assets. Assets are classified into different risk-weighted categories, and a risk-based capital ratio is calculated accordingly. However, asset categorization itself can be challenging. For instance, in the United States, home mortgage loans were considered relatively safe before the 2008 financial crisis, but the actual risks associated with some mortgage loans turned out to be higher than initially believed (Calem and LaCour-Little, 2004, pp. 647–648).

Using asset categorization and capital adequacy ratios provide a level of control over commercial banks that is less extensive than direct state ownership. This allows the state to concentrate on specific areas of the banks' operations. However, it is important to acknowledge that these regulatory measures may not always succeed in achieving their intended objectives (Calem and LaCour-Little, 2004, p. 651). The capital adequacy ratio may not accurately capture the true financial risks faced by banks. Furthermore, private banks can employ various strategies to circumvent the limitations imposed by the capital adequacy ratio.

Deposit insurance regulation also faces significant problems (Macey and Miller, 1988). The deposit insurance fund, usually operated by the government, promises to repay public depositors if a bank fails, and charges a premium from the bank in exchange. However, deposit insurance suffers from the moral hazard problem commonly found in private insurance. It diminishes depositors' incentives to carefully choose banks and demand higher interest rates from riskier institutions (Carnell et al., 2009, pp. 326–328). Moreover, deposit insurance lacks many of the mechanisms available to private insurance that can effectively mitigate the moral hazard problem. For instance, the deposit insurer is unable to exclude certain banks from its coverage. If a bank is deemed too risky to insure, the deposit insurer cannot simply cease providing coverage, as this would signal to the market that the bank is in trouble and could trigger a bank run. However, continuing to provide insurance coverage to such a bank creates moral hazard by allowing the bank to engage in excessive risk-taking.

Similarly, the deposit insurer's ability to establish risk-based premiums is constrained. Imposing higher premiums on high-risk banks would further deteriorate their financial position and undermine their capacity to manage risks effectively. Once a commercial bank secures a license from the state regulator and benefits from deposit insurance, the state's ability to discipline the bank is limited by concerns about adversely affecting public depositors. This limitation represents a cost associated with the opportunistic actions of the regulated enterprises.

Regulation is also subject to the challenges of regulatory arbitrage. Regulated entities are often incentivized to exploit discrepancies in regulatory frameworks or loopholes in the law to circumvent restrictions through various means. Prior to the 2008 financial crisis, many banks in the United States utilized asset securitization, a practice that involved bundling loans together and transferring the interests of these financial instruments to other financial institutions through financial engineering. By doing so, banks were able to remove these assets from their balance sheets and transfer them to "shadow banks" that were not subject to the same level of regulatory oversight. This allowed banks to engage in excessive lending, as long as there were willing buyers for these products within the financial system (Barr, 2012). Consequently, a substantial number of highly risky subprime mortgage loans were generated. When the housing market bubble burst, the market prices of securities backed by these subprime loans sharply declined (Barr, 2012). Faced with a liquidity shortage, major financial institutions were compelled to rapidly sell off their assets, triggering a downward spiral of declining prices and causing financial difficulties for other institutions (Barr, 2012).

In short, regulating commercial banks and other financial institutions is difficult. The Financial Crisis Inquiry Commission in the United States recognized that the 2008 financial crisis was a result of regulatory failures, particularly in relation to the shadow banking system. Certain financial derivatives such as credit default swaps that were largely unregulated turned out to have created significant risks. After the 2008 financial crisis, governments worldwide reviewed their regulation frameworks and attempted to redress the defects (Barr, 2012, p. 99). This suggests that regulation is inherently difficult and that regulatory failures can impose substantial costs.

In addition to the aforementioned challenges, banking regulators in China face the issue of self-dealing and embezzlement by bank controllers, at least in the early stage of its development. The controllers of banks could exploit related-party transactions and other methods to divert the bank's assets for personal gain or provide preferential loans to their relatives. Unfortunately, the corporate law in China had several shortcomings in addressing these problems. The 1995 Corporate Law failed to adequately tackle self-dealing issues, and although the 2005 amendment introduced some regulations, it still fell short of addressing the involvement of interested shareholders in decision-making processes (Shi and

Du, 2007). While self-dealing was a concern across all corporations, the activities of bank controllers posed a greater risk to public interests, necessitating increased state intervention. Moreover, as the leverage of a commercial bank increases, the controller's motivation for self-dealing also grows because the short-term gains may outweigh the long-term benefits from cooperative actions. This created significant challenges for consumers seeking legal recourse when bank shareholders embezzled their funds, often leaving behind corporate shells with no assets to satisfy outstanding debts. These factors collectively contributed to the difficulty of addressing self-dealing and embezzlement in the Chinese banking sector, calling for comprehensive reforms and stronger regulatory measures.

The difficulties of regulating private banks can explain China's decision to maintain state ownership in this sector. On the one hand, state ownership provides incentives for financial firms to avoid excessive risks to some extent. State-owned banks may not have such strong profit-seeking motives as private banks, and therefore may not engage in excessive risks-seeking activities. The function of state-owned banks in promoting the stability of the financial system has gained recognition after the financial crisis. On the other hand, the state has more control instruments to influence the activities of banks and can arrange internal mechanisms that incentivize managers to consider more regulatory goals. Last but not least, state ownership may alleviate self-dealing, as the state investor may have weaker incentives to engage in tunneling compared to private investors, given that government officials are generally placed under stricter supervision and have incentives to maintain a long-term relationship with the government.

Notably, bank runs have been relatively rare in China in recent decades. Even during the 1999 Asian financial crisis, when state-owned financial banks were burdened with over one trillion RMB in nonperforming loans, equivalent to more than 20 percent of their assets, there was no significant bank run (Davis, 2013). This was largely due to the state's intervention and implicit guarantee of deposit safety. The state established four asset management corporations to acquire these nonperforming loans from the banks, effectively removing them from their balance sheets. With the public's awareness of the state's commitment to safeguarding deposits, there was little incentive for depositors to withdraw their funds during the crisis, thereby mitigating financial risks.

Indeed, this model may lead to the "soft-budget constraint" problem, resulting in insufficient incentives among banks to select their lenders carefully and manage risks. Nonetheless, it is worth noting that similar incentives exist in many countries, where private banks also expect government bailouts during crises. State ownership, on the other hand, grants the state greater power to intervene proactively by exercising control over bank managers, aiming to avert bank failures before they arise.

State ownership of banks can help address the fairness problem associated with bailouts. When state-owned banks receive financial assistance during economic downturns, it may be perceived as less politically unjust compared to using taxpayer's money to support private banks. This is because state-owned banks are owned by the government, and the fiscal support provided to them can be offset by the profits they generated during economic booms. As a result, state-owned banks contribute to a more equitable distribution of benefits and burdens. Conversely, if the state elects to nationalize commercial banks after they have become insolvent, concerns of fairness may arise. In such situations, private investors and employees receive dividends and bonuses during periods of economic prosperity, while taxpayers are left to assume the burden of the banks' debts when economic conditions deteriorate (Selvarajah, 2010). This dynamic further underscores the advantages of state ownership in addressing inequities within the financial sector.

B. *Evidence of the Regulatory Function of State Ownership*

The historical evolution of state ownership in the banking industry and the corresponding regulatory developments can be explained by the concerns of regulatory costs. While China has made efforts to introduce private investment in this sector, mostly due to efficiency and ownership cost concerns, such efforts are met with regulatory challenges. This section reviews the historical development of local-government-owned banks and private banks in this industry to illustrate the various forces behind the use of state ownership.

1. An Overview of the Changes in State Ownership and Regulations in the Banking Industry

When China embarked on its marketization reforms in the late 1970s and early 1980s, state-owned commercial banks – including the Agricultural Bank of China, Bank of China, China Construction Bank, and Industrial and Commercial Bank of China – held a dominant position in the banking industry. Prior to 1985, these commercial banks operated within distinct sectors, experiencing minimal competition.

During the 1990s, China's state-owned banks faced significant challenges due to their loans to state-owned enterprises (SOEs), many of which became nonperforming loans that eroded the banks' asset quality (OECD Development Centre, 1997, p. 21). In response, the government initiated financial system reforms in 1993 aimed at reducing state intervention in the four largest state-owned banks. These reforms included the establishment of debt-to-asset ratio guidelines and the implementation of risk management systems. Additionally, in 1994, three policy banks – the China Development Bank, the Export-Import Bank of China, and the Agricultural Development Bank of China – were created to fulfill specific policy objectives, such as lending to export-oriented corporations and supporting agricultural development.

The reforms also introduced competition among state-owned commercial banks and implemented an evaluation system to reward or punish managers based on their banks' performance. In 1995, the Commercial Bank Law was enacted, preventing government interference in lending decisions. Article 4 of the *Commercial Bank Law* states that "[c]ommercial banks should work under the principles of efficiency, safety and fluid with full autonomy and full responsibility for their own risks, profits and losses and self-restraint." Article 85 provides that

> [d]isciplinary action shall be taken against those who are directly in charge or responsible for forcing commercial banks to issue loans or provide guarantee; those who cause damages for the actions should undertake the whole or part of the responsibilities of repayment. Disciplinary action shall be taken against employees of a commercial bank who do not refuse to provide forced loans or guarantees; those who cause damages for the action should undertake relevant responsibilities of repayment.

The People's Bank of China further reinforced lending regulations in 1996 with the issuance of the *General Rules on Lending*. These rules included penalties for lenders involved in transactions with related parties and for government or other entities that exerted undue pressure on lenders to grant them loans.

In 2003, the state decided to further enhance banking regulation by establishing the China Banking Regulatory Commission (CBRC), which oversees the risk management activities of state-owned banks, while the People's Bank of China continued to conduct macroeconomic policies. In the same year, the CBRC loosened the previous regulation on foreign investors, and allowed foreign investors to hold up to 25 percent of the stocks in Chinese commercial banks (Berger et al., 2009).

In 2005, the Chinese government initiated efforts to attract foreign private investors to hold shares in state-owned banks, with the aim of leveraging their advanced risk-management techniques and management skills. Notable examples include Bank of America's acquisition of a 9 percent stake in China Construction Bank and Bank of China's introduction of Royal Bank of Scotland and Temasek as minority shareholders. In 2006, Industrial and Commercial Bank of China (ICBC) also brought in several foreign financial institutions as strategic investors, including Goldman Sachs Group Inc.

The state also introduced private investments in these state-owned banks by allowing them to list on the Hong Kong and Shanghai Exchanges, enabling the securitization of their ownership and transforming them into listing corporations similar to joint-stock commercial banks. However, the state still maintained control over these banks after they have been listed. The Central Huijin Investment Ltd., established in 2003 as a holding company for the state's equity interests in major central financial institutions, is the nominal majority shareholder of the four largest state-owned banks (Szamosszegi and Kyle, 2011, p. 117). Initially a branch of the People's Bank of China, Central Huijin Investment Ltd. came under the ownership of China Investment Corporation (CIC) in 2007, which is directly controlled by the State Council (Szamosszegi and Kyle, 2011). Managers of these state-owned banks are appointed by the Organizational Department of the Communist Party of China (CPC) and are expected to consider both the banks' profitability and the safety of their financial risks.

Apart from the state-owned banks, there are various other types of commercial banks that are not controlled by the central governments. These include joint-stock banks, urban commercial banks, township and village banks, rural commercial banks, and various other financial institutions in rural areas. Figure 2.10 presents the amount of assets held by these different types of banks over time since 2001. In this part, I will focus on the changing landscape of commercial banks in the urban area, because the state-owned banks have a weaker influence in rural areas, making it hard to analyze the relationship between state ownership and regulations.

Since the 1980s, China has introduced the concept of "joint-stock banks," which allows for the establishment of banks with a dispersed ownership structure under Chinese corporate law. These banks are often initiated by SOEs, particularly state-controlled corporate groups, but also involve private companies holding equity interests. One notable example

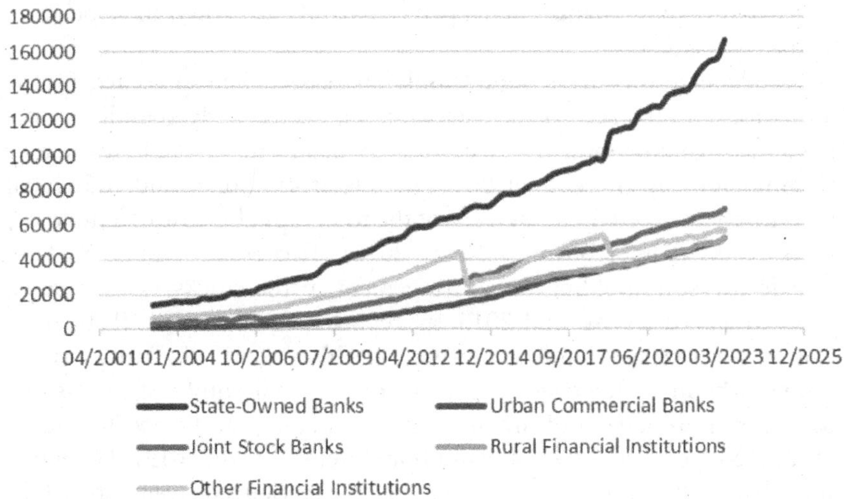

Figure 2.10 Total asset of different types of banks (billion RMB).
Source: CEIC China Premium Database

is the China Merchants Bank Co., Ltd, established in 1987, with the China Merchant Group, a state-owned corporation under the Transportation Department of the central government, holding 18 percent of the bank's stocks as the largest shareholder. Another joint-stock bank, the Bohai Bank, was formed in 2005, with Tianjin Teda, a state-owned company controlled by the Tianjin Government, and Standard Chartered as its two largest shareholders. Many of these joint-stock banks have chosen to list on the Shanghai and Hong Kong exchanges, providing an opportunity for private investors to purchase their stocks and share in their profits. This arrangement enables private participation and investment in these commercial banks, creating a platform for both state and private entities to benefit from their success.

The joint-stock banks in China were proactive in attracting foreign strategic investors even before the state-owned banks. A notable example is the China Everbright Bank, a joint-stock commercial bank controlled by a state-owned enterprise directly under the State Council. In 1996, the bank invited the Asian Development Bank to acquire 1.9 percent of its shares. This move demonstrated its receptiveness to foreign investment and collaboration. This early engagement with foreign strategic investors highlights the joint-stock banks' willingness to leverage external expertise and resources to enhance their operations and strengthen their position in the market.

Private investors have significantly increased their presence in the joint-stock commercial banks, signaling an increasingly significant role in China's banking industry. According to data from the Bank Regulatory Commission, by the end of 2011, private institutional and individual investors accounted for 42 percent of the total capital investment in joint-stock banks (China Business News, 2015). This trend continued, with private investors holding up to 51 percent of the stocks in joint-stock commercial banks by mid-2015, as reported by the Bank Regulatory Commission (State Council Information Office, 2015). In 2018, private capital accounted for over 40 percent of the total equity of joint-stock banks, over 50 percent of urban commercial banks, and over 80 percent of rural cooperative financial institutions (Reuters Staff, 2019). The joint-stock banks, fueled by private capital, have experienced steady growth in the past decades. In 2023, the assets of joint-stock commercial banks comprised about 17 percent of the total assets in the banking industry, while state-owned commercial banks accounted for 42 percent (China Banking Regulatory Commission, 2014). By comparison, in 2003, the figures were 10 percent and 58 percent, respectively (China Banking Regulatory Commission, 2006).

Despite the increasing presence of private investors in joint-stock banks, their ability to exercise control rights is often limited due to the dispersed nature of their ownership. A notable example is China Merchant Bank, which is listed on the Hong Kong Stock Exchange. The China Merchant Steam Navigation Co., an SOE, retains control of 12.54 percent of the bank's stocks, making it the largest shareholder of the corporation. The state's influence persists in the form of substantial ownership and decision-making power within these banks, even with the participation of private investors (Sina Finance, 2015).

2. The Development of Local-Government-Owned Banks

In addition to state-owned banks and joint-stock banks, the banking sector in China includes numerous Urban Commercial Banks (UCBs). These UCBs were previously known as Urban Credit Cooperatives (UCCs) before 1995. The development of UCBs serves as a striking illustration of the way regulatory capacity can impact the dynamics of state ownership within the banking industry.

Since 1978, China has gradually embraced the development of its non-state sector as a means to stimulate economic growth. While state-owned banks and major joint-stock commercial banks primarily served the interests of SOEs, UCCs were established to cater to the needs of private enterprises and individual businesses (OECD Development Centre, 1997). The growth of UCCs was closely tied to the expansion of the non-state economy, with a significant portion of UCC loans being directed towards private and collectively owned businesses. According to a report issued by the OECD, by the end of 1994, UCCs had extended outstanding loans of 48.72 billion RMB, with 13.13 billion going to industrial collectively owned enterprises, and 4.47 billion RMB to individual businessmen (OECD Development Centre, 1997). A survey conducted by the OECD on 56 sampled UCCs revealed that there was a total of 18,257 shareholders, with each UCC having an average of 50 to 270 entity shareholders and individual shareholders, respectively (OECD Development Centre, 1997). Among these shareholders, collectively owned enterprises accounted for 29.7 percent, while private enterprises, self-employed individuals, residents, staff, and communities held shares representing 10.6 percent, 5.9 percent, 21.8 percent, 10.2 percent, and 9.2 percent, respectively (OECD Development Centre, 1997).

Shareholders of UCCs exercised their voting rights based on their shareholdings to elect the cooperative's general council, which was responsible for important matters such as dividend distribution. Research indicates that the general councils often consisted of large shareholders who held a majority of the cooperative's shares and possessed expertise in financial institution management (OECD Development Centre, 1997). The council appointed the general manager, typically nominated by the largest shareholder, to oversee the operations of the UCCs (OECD Development Centre, 1997). The general manager was primarily responsible for approving lending activities, with the council and shareholders being well-informed about such decisions (OECD Development Centre, 1997).

Figure 2.11 presents the number of UCCs developed in China in the 1980s and 1990s. During the 1980s, UCCs experienced remarkable growth. The first UCC was established in 1978, and by the end of 1986, there were already 1,114 UCCs in China (OECD Development Centre, 1997). The number of UCCs doubled by 1988, reaching 3,265. However, the rapid expansion of UCCs brought forth numerous challenges. The People's Bank of China faced difficulties in enforcing regulations due to the overwhelming number of UCCs and limited resources and staff available (OECD Development Centre, 1997). Many investors who had pledged capital to UCCs failed to fulfill their commitments, or chose to

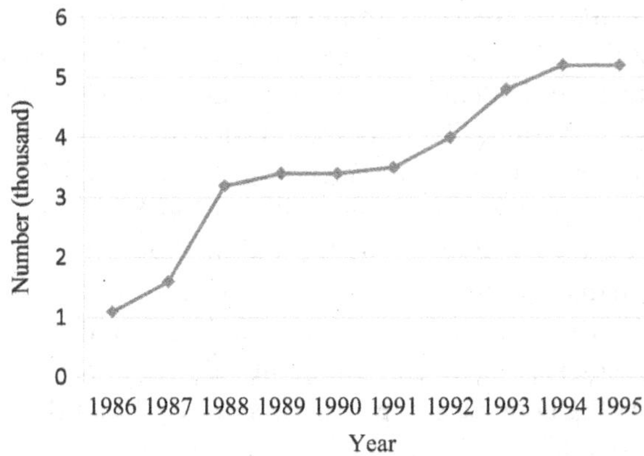

Figure 2.11 Number of UCCs.
Source: Almanac of China's Finance and Banking

withdraw their investments after the establishments, resulting in insolvency for the UCCs (OECD Development Centre, 1997). Some even established illegal subsidiaries, further complicating the situation.

During the 1990s, the financial crisis in Asia had severe repercussions on UCCs. In Guangdong province alone, approximately 2,000 local financial institutions were closed by the government. To mitigate the impact, the government allocated 38 billion RMB to bail out the creditors of these institutions (Xu, 2003). In Hainan Province, several UCCs were involved in problematic practices, including engaging in related-party transactions. This involved providing loans to investors or companies connected to the investors at preferential interest rates and lenient repayment terms (Xu, 2003). Furthermore, some managers even absconded with the deposits held by the banks, exacerbating the situation (Xu, 2003).

Although regulatory measures were introduced, they fell short of addressing the risks associated with UCCs. In 1988, the People's Bank of China implemented the *Regulation on Urban Credit Cooperatives*, which mandated the adoption of an asset-liability ratio management system. This included requirements such as maintaining a minimum capital-asset ratio of 5 percent. Additionally, the People's Bank of China issued a supplementary document in the same year, stipulating that no new UCC licenses would be granted until the financial system was stabilized. In 1994, the People's Bank of China imposed restrictions on the total amount of loans that these cooperatives could extend. However, the predominant issues persisted, particularly related-party transactions and the misappropriation of cooperative assets. The regulation of related-party transactions remained unclear, and the sheer number of financial institutions further complicated the overseeing tasks for regulators.

Recognizing the need for stronger control over UCCs, the state implemented regulatory reforms aimed at transforming these cooperatives and employed state ownership to stabilize the market. In line with the "*Decisions to Further Reform the Financial System*," the State Council initiated the conversion of UCCs into "Urban Cooperative Banks" in 1995. These banks operated as corporate entities governed by corporate law principles. The People's Bank of China subsequently issued the *Administration Measures on City Cooperative Banks* in 1997, stipulating that local governments would become the largest shareholders in city cooperative banks, holding less than 30 percent of the shares. Private investors were also allowed to invest, with a maximum limit established by the People's Bank of China for all private investors across financial institutions. In 1999, the Urban Cooperative Banks were renamed as UCBs to differentiate them from the cooperatives. Their operations were confined to the localities in which they were situated. Most UCCs were merged into UCBs, leading to a gradual decrease in their numbers from over five thousand to just eight hundred by 1999. The state recognized the risks associated with an excessive number of financial institutions and the challenges in regulatory oversight. Consequently, by the end of 1999, only ninety UCBs were permitted to be established, a significantly smaller number compared to the UCCs. Table 2.1 illustrates these changes in the late 1990s.

The ownership landscape of UCBs underwent significant changes over time. In 2005, the state introduced the "*Opinions of the State Council on Encouraging, Supporting and Guiding the Development of Individual and Private Economy and Other Non-Public Sectors of the Economy*," aimed at promoting private capital in the banking industry. Various local

Table 2.1 *Number of Urban Credit Cooperatives (UCCs) over time*

Year	1994	1995	1996	1997	1998	1999
Number of UCCs	5,229	5,104	4,630	3,716	3,190	836

governments, especially in Zhejiang Province, allowed private investors to acquire equity interests in UCBs. By 2010, private investors held 42.6 percent of UCB equity (China Banking Regulatory Commission, 2010), which further increased to 54 percent by the end of 2012 (China Banking Regulatory Commission, 2012). According to the Banking Regulatory Commission, by the end of 2014, private investors held over 50 percent of shares in approximately 70 percent of joint-stock and UCBs (Wang, 2015).

With the Banking Regulatory Commission's authorization for UCBs to engage in mergers and acquisitions and the removal ofgeographical restrictions on their business in 2006, these banks gained greater flexibility and attracted more private capital. Consequently, UCBs have played an increasingly influential role in China's banking sector. In 2023, the assets of UCBs accounted for 13 percent of the total assets held by all commercial banks in the country.

As private banks have experienced growth, the regulatory framework has also evolved to address the challenges they face, particularly concerning self-dealing and related-party transactions. In 2003, the Banking Regulatory Commission uncovered cases of self-dealing and embezzlement involving UCBs. In response, they issued the "*Opinions on Enhancing the Management of Equity Ownership of Commercial Banks.*" This policy mandated local branches of the Banking Regulatory Commission to scrutinize the backgrounds of private investors and their affiliated parties. Under this policy, the Banking Regulatory Commission obtained the authoritative power to undertake several actions. They could order shareholders involved in improper practices to sell their stocks, mandate the removal of directors from the bank, and impose fines on the commercial bank itself. Prior to the reform of urban commercial banks, such measures were not in place, despite the existence of state-owned banks and joint-stock banks that preceded the year 2004. The evolution of UCCs illustrates how regulatory challenges have necessitated state intervention in bank ownership control.

3. New Commercial Banks Promoted by Private Investors

The state's decision to allow private investors to participate in the establishment of commercial banks further highlights the interplay between regulation and state ownership. In November 2013, during the third plenary session of the 18th Central Committee of the CPC, it was determined that qualified private investors could establish small or midsized financial institutions, including banks, as long as they adhered to regulatory requirements. Various social groups submitted suggestions and proposals to the Banking Regulatory Committee, which influenced the implementation of this state policy.

The Banking Regulatory Committee set out several conditions for granting licenses to new private banks. Private banks were expected to demonstrate risk management capabilities and have sufficient capital input. They were also required to establish sound governance structures, define key areas of focus and business plans, and implement mechanisms to prevent self-dealing. Additionally, private banks were obligated to present promising business strategies, marketing targets, and establish resolution plans or "living wills" to handle potential insolvency (Ouyang, 2014). Despite the interest from numerous investors, the Banking Regulatory Committee only granted licenses to five private banks in the first round, emphasizing the stringent evaluation and selection process carried out to ensure compliance with regulatory standards.

The Banking Regulatory Commission has also developed regulatory measures similar to those provided in the Dodd-Frank Act of the United States. In response to the financial crisis, the United States introduced the Dodd-Frank Act to address regulatory issues and reduce the reliance on taxpayers' money to rescue large financial institutions in the future. The act implemented measures such as Title I resolution plans and Title II Orderly Liquidated Authority (OLA) to achieve this objective. Under the Dodd-Frank Act, Systemically Important Financial Institutions (SIFI) with assets exceeding $50 billion are required to develop a Title I resolution plan, commonly known as a "living will." This plan outlines a strategy for ensuring financial stability during crises. If regulators are dissatisfied with the resolution plan, they may impose stricter capital adequacy requirements or even restrict the company's operations. While these plans may differ slightly, many financial groups have indicated that the bank holding company would provide support to key bank subsidiaries and other major operating financial subsidiaries.

The living will requirements in China share similarities with those in the United States. In China, the promoters of each of the first five licensed private banks have made guarantees to individual depositors regarding the debts owed to them. For instance, Shanghai Hua Rui Bank Co., Ltd, one of the pioneering licensed private banks, has publicly stated that shareholders holding more than 5 percent of the bank's stocks would personally compensate depositors in the event of insolvency. The compensation amount is capped at the shareholders' investments, and each depositor would be reimbursed up to a maximum of 500,000 from the shareholders' own funds (Wall Street, 2021).

Increasing shareholders' liability of the banks may be effective in addressing bank failures, but its success relies on the ability of bank shareholders to absorb the losses. This is why China places emphasis on thoroughly examining the backgrounds and capital resources of shareholders before granting them the opportunity to establish new private banks. Additionally, by limiting the number of shareholders, regulators can mitigate the regulatory costs associated with tracking down numerous dispersed shareholders in the event of bank failures (Zeng, 2017b). Having a simplified ownership structure plays a crucial role in controlling regulatory costs and fostering the growth of private banks.

The characteristics exhibited by the first five licensed private banks indicate the regulator's concern regarding the potential risks incurred by private banks. Each of these banks is backed by at least two investors or promoters, a measure implemented by the regulatory committee to establish a check and balance mechanism and prevent self-dealing. Typically, one investor holds approximately 30 percent of the shares, while the second-largest investor holds around 20 percent. This setup allows the second shareholder to oversee the banks and act as a deterrent against any misconduct by the controlling shareholder (Wall Street, 2021). Furthermore, these promoters are often reputable private companies, including renowned entities like Alibaba and Tencent, which enhances confidence in their ability to contribute to effective bank oversight.

The banking regulator in China purposefully implements regulations on the ownership structure of private commercial banks by imposing limits on individual shareholder positions. This approach aims to establish a "moderately concentrated ownership" structure, which is relatively uncommon in China. Studies in the field of Law and Finance have demonstrated that concentrated ownership tends to emerge in countries with weaker corporate law frameworks (La Porta et al., 1998). This is because a dispersed ownership structure enables the board of directors to exert substantial control over the corporation, resulting in significant agency costs in settings with relatively weak corporate law (La Porta et al., 1998).

The moderately concentrated ownership structure employed by private commercial banks serves as a mechanism to maintain checks and balances among shareholders and prevent misappropriation within the banks. By avoiding a scenario where a single private investor holds a majority share and dominates the board of directors, the structure safeguards the interests of minority shareholders and public depositors. In an ideal situation, minority shareholders would have the ability to take legal action against the majority shareholder, providing additional protection for the public consumers. The imposition of limitations on shareholder positions reflects the regulator's recognition that corporate law alone may not be sufficient to deter self-dealing. However, it is important to acknowledge that this ownership model has its flaws. For instance, collusion between the largest and second-largest shareholders could lead to misappropriation of company resources instead of effective checks and balances. The ultimate superiority of this ownership structure over others is still subject to further evaluation.

Regulators' stringent measures to oversee private banks – including reputation screening, loss-bearing requirements during insolvency, and interventions in ownership structures – reflect their persistent concerns about self-dealing and financial risks. These adjustments in the ownership structures of commercial banks in China signify the state's cautious efforts to introduce private investors to enhance the efficiency of financial resource allocation while maintaining control over potential risks associated with private banks. This process underscores that the development of private banks ultimately depends on the state's confidence in its ability to regulate the risks these institutions generate.

C. The Macroeconomic Function of State-Owned Banks

Apart from financial regulation, state ownership plays a significant role in fulfilling the state's macroeconomic policies. In times of economic downturn, the state can direct commercial banks to support its macroeconomic objectives by encouraging increased lending to struggling businesses. Studies have highlighted that state-owned banks possess the advantage of being able to receive informal instructions from the government, enabling them to align with broader economic goals. This aspect underscores one of the advantages state-owned banks may have over their private counterparts (Hamdani and Kamar, 2012).

While the desirability of such economic stimulation is debatable, this section aims to examine whether state ownership provides a broader avenue for economic stimulus and enables the state to intervene in the market with fewer regulatory barriers. Monetary policy, particularly interest rate adjustments, is a common tool for macroeconomic management. By influencing money supply, the central bank can impact short-term aggregate demand and overall economic output. This is often done through purchasing government debt or treasury bonds to inject more money into the market. However, the effectiveness of monetary policies may be limited by the zero lower bound (Listokin, 2019). Once interest rates reach zero, further stimulation through rate cuts becomes challenging since holding cash becomes costless. In contrast, instructing commercial banks to increase lending can be a more impactful measure compared to altering monetary policies. This capacity of state ownership cannot be achieved solely through regulatory means, as the state lacks the authority to dictate private banks to provide additional loans during recessions.

Despite China's tendency to maintain limited control over its state-owned banks and the separation of regulators from SOEs, there are instances where the government directly intervenes and commands banks to achieve national objectives. The 2008 financial crisis serves as a compelling example.

Before the 1990s, China implemented an annual practice of issuing orders that specified the lending amount for state-owned commercial banks. The People's Bank of China directly regulated the loan volume of these banks (Huang, 2013). However, in 1998, the central bank decided to move away from direct control and adopt alternative policy tools, such as open market operations. While the central bank continued to provide guidance on annual loan amounts, the banks were granted more autonomy in their decision-making processes.

However, in 2007, when the total loan amount exceeded 20 percent of the guiding number, the Chinese central bank made the decision to reassert its power and strictly enforce this restriction for ten months as a measure to control inflation. This policy changed again in November 2008 when the financial crisis had a profound impact on the Chinese economy. China's central bank ceased enforcing this control until July 2009.

During the 2008 financial crisis, the sharp decline in demand from foreign markets caused significant losses for many enterprises. In response, the Chinese Banking Regulatory Committee instructed state-owned banks to increase lending, despite the high level of risk involved (Liao, 2010; China Securities Journal, 2009). Data reveals that the total amount of loans provided by commercial banks in 2009 reached a peak of 9.59 trillion RMB, surpassing the guiding number set by the central bank. This suggests that the state exerted informal influence on the banks to expand lending through unofficial channels (Liao, 2010; China Securities Journal, 2009).

Empirical evidence suggests that private commercial banks have provided a significantly lower amount of loans compared to state-owned commercial banks and banks with substantial state ownership (Chu

Table 2.2 *Amount of newly issued loan*

Year	2002	2003	2004	2005	2006	2007	2008	2009
Guiding amount of loan	1.30	1.80	2.60	2.50	2.50	3.00	3.87	5.00
Real amount of newly issued loan	1.90	2.80	2.20	2.40	3.18	3.60	4.91	9.59

Source: Huang (2013)

et al., 2012). This disparity can be attributed to the higher financial risks associated with extending loans during a crisis. Private banks are generally hesitant to assume such risks on behalf of the state. Given the stringent regulation in the banking industry, mandating private banks to increase lending during a crisis is neither feasible nor acceptable. Private banks may argue that such a command interferes with their property rights and would incur considerable costs. Since the regulatory approach alone cannot effectively address this issue with privately owned banks, it helps explain why the current state policy primarily focuses on introducing private capital into small and medium-sized commercial banks at the urban and rural levels, which have a limited impact on macroeconomic policy.

D. State-Owned Banks and Distributive Concerns

The significance of state ownership of banks can also be examined in terms of distributive justice concerns. As mentioned earlier, the vulnerability of commercial banks necessitates the state's role as the lender of last resort and the need to bail out banks during financial crises. However, such bailouts involve the state providing assistance and granting significant benefits to private financial institutions, while the taxpayers and the general public – who are not responsible for causing the crisis – must bear the cost of the bailouts, raising concerns of fairness.

The issue of distributive concerns can also be understood through the lens of LTF. According to Professor Pistor, the financial system is inherently unstable because banks engage in maturity transformation, where they offer long-term loans using short-term funds that can be withdrawn at any time. Given this instability, predetermined legal obligations cannot be rigidly enforced as they could lead to a financial collapse. As a result, the law tends to be more flexible in the financial market, particularly at the apex of the system, while remaining rigid at the periphery. Although such unequal treatment may be necessary for the system's survival, it raises a serious concern of distributive justice.

State ownership of commercial banks can partially address the fundamental problem in the financial system. If financial institutions, especially those at the system's apex where favorable laws apply, are owned by the state, it theoretically mitigates concerns about a specific group of investors benefiting from bailouts. Thus, although state-owned financial institutions may incur higher ownership costs compared to private ones, the extent of privatization depends significantly on how effectively legal and regulatory regimes can govern private financial institutions and thereby reduce regulatory costs.

Appendix

Table 2.3 *Summary statistics*

Variable	Observation	Mean	Std. Dev.	Min	Max
State Ownership	291	0.78	0.29	0.00	1.00
Adj	291	1.68	1.28	0.00	5.00
GDP per capita	250	0.08	0.08	0.01	0.48
CPI	288	117.78	11.97	98.99	149.51
Fiscal Revenue per capita	258	7.24	9.19	0.43	52.11

Table 2.4 *Regression results*

	Dependent variable					
	(1)	(2)	(3)	(4)	(5)	(6)
	Investment	Investment	Investment	Investment	Investment	Investment
Adj	**-0.067*** **	**-0.065*** **	**-0.063*** **	**-0.084*** **	**-0.067*** **	**-0.065*** **
	(0.013)	**(0.022)**	**(0.015)**	**(0.030)**	**(0.013)**	**(0.022)**
GDP per capita		0.021		3.175		0.021
		(0.819)		(2.446)		(0.819)
CPI		-0.001		-0.002		-0.001
		(0.002)		(0.004)		(0.002)
Government revenue per capita		0.002		-0.011		0.002
		(0.007)		(0.013)		(0.007)
Fixed Effects/Random Effects	No	No	City and Time Fixed Effects	City and Time Fixed Effects	City and Time Random Effects	City and Time Random Effects
Observations	291	249	291	249	291	249

Robust standard errors in parentheses.
*p<0.1, **p<0.05, ***p<0.01.
Source: CEIC China Premium Database

Table 2.5 *Placebo test*

	Dependent variable					
	(1)	(2)	(3)	(4)	(5)	(6)
	Investment	Investment	Investment	Investment	Investment	Investment
Water_Tariffs	-0.063*	-0.011	**-0.068*** **	-0.063*	**-0.032** **	-0.011
	(0.037)	(0.020)	**(0.023)**	(0.037)	**(0.015)**	(0.020)
GDP per capita	2.034	0.057		2.034		0.057
	(2.480)	(0.895)		(2.480)		(0.895)
CPI	-0.005	-0.005***		-0.005		-0.005***
	(0.004)	(0.002)		(0.004)		(0.002)
Government revenue per capita	-0.005	0.001		-0.005		0.001
	(0.013)	(0.007)		(0.013)		(0.007)
Fixed Effects/ Random Effects	No	No	Prefecture and Time Fixed Effects	Prefecture and Time Fixed Effects	Prefecture and Time Random Effects	Prefecture and Time Random Effects
Observations	245	245	286	245	286	245

Robust standard errors in parentheses.

*p<0.1, **p<0.05, ***p<0.01.

3

Compensation for Legal Transition and China's Hierarchical Protection of Private Enterprises

Currently, some studies have acknowledged the significant role of law in explaining the prevalence of SOEs. Milhaupt and Zheng posit that the weak legal protection afforded to private enterprises in China accounts for the dominance of SOEs (Milhaupt and Zheng, 2014, p. 692). Many Chinese scholars also advocate for enhancing the protection of private enterprises (Zhou, 2014). While this perspective holds merit, it does not readily explain why SOEs are more prevalent in certain sectors than others or why strengthening legal protections for private enterprises has been challenging in China. This chapter seeks to demonstrate that the legal protection of private enterprises in China is hierarchical; the strength of protection varies across different circumstances due to the varying levels of regulatory costs. Consequently, this approach provides a more nuanced understanding of the sectoral distribution of SOEs in China.

Before we delve into the comparison of legal protection of private enterprises, it is important to note a methodological difficulty: It is usually difficult to measure the strength of legal protection for private enterprises. For instance, suppose a government policy is changed to require Company A to upgrade its equipment to reduce pollution. Meanwhile, a national law is amended, forcing Company B to be shut down as a result. Which company receives a weaker protection? This may depend on a series of factors, including the profits Company A and Company B would generate if the government taking does not occur the degree to which the two companies could anticipate the policy or legal changes, and the level of compensation offered to them. In addition, when a policy has been imposed on a private enterprise, it may receive some benefits in the future in exchange. These benefits may take many forms. Some companies may obtain land at low costs, while others may receive a license to operate in a special industry. Additionally, measuring and comparing these benefits can be challenging.

This chapter attempts to overcome this methodological challenge by examining disclosed judicial judgments related to a particular rule – Article 8 of *China's Administrative License Law* (hereinafter referred to as Article 8) – which stipulates that the government can withdraw an administrative license for the public interest when the relevant laws or regulations have been amended or when circumstances have changed. Paragraph two of Article 8 provides that if a license is withdrawn, the government must compensate the private enterprise for the losses. This rule serves as a legal basis for compensation when a new regulation adversely affects the property interests of an enterprise. The level of compensation thus measures the strength of property protection offered to enterprises in the event of a policy change.

This particular legal issue is selected for analysis for several reasons. First, changes in the law are a major source of regulatory costs. Regulatory costs here arise mainly due to the incompleteness of the law. The state may frequently change laws or regulatory policies in order to cope with new circumstances or to exercise extralegal control, which negatively affects the property interests of private enterprises. Legal protection for private enterprises is stronger when the law is relatively more complete, and consistent with the state's developmental goals. However, legal protection for the property interests of private enterprises is especially weak when it runs into conflicts with certain governmental goals. Such conflicts are more common in some sectors than others. As a result, law is more frequently "bent" in these sectors, granting greater discretions to the government, which can be exercised opportunistically, leading to higher regulatory costs. This theory can be applied in China's context to explain why SOEs remain prevalent in China's economy, particularly in sectors with incomplete law and high regulatory costs.

Second, this question is of particular importance in the context of China. As Frank Upham notes, in a society undergoing transition, "structural changes" to society inevitably affect existing property rights. Law and development studies should therefore focus more on "how institutions can render these transformations more efficient and less socially disruptive" (Upham, 2008, p. 551; Upham, 2018, p. 134). Since China adopted the economic reform and opening up policy in 1978, Chinese laws have been changing drastically. In the late 2000s, many private enterprises were ordered to be closed down or nationalized by the governments, a trend referred to by some scholars as the "advance of the state, retreat of the investment" (Chen, 2012). During this period, some private coal corporations invoked the *China's Administrative License Law* (ALL) to protect their interests. It thus offers a precious opportunity to analyze the pattern of legal protection for private enterprises in China.

How the state protects private enterprises against harms caused by legal transitions remains a fundamental and universal question in law, in development, and in property law. Whether to compensate enterprises during legal transition is essentially the question of when a regulation constitutes a regulatory taking. There is a substantial amount of literature on whether compensation should be provided when a new regulatory rule negatively affects property interests (Kaplow, 1986; Rose, 2000; Rose-Ackerman and Rossi, 2000; Shaviro, 2000; Dana and Merrill, 2002). In some countries, such as the United States, such decisions may constitute regulatory takings and may thus constitute the just compensation requirement under the Constitution of the United States, although such cases are relatively rare. Private enterprise property interests are usually protected through political channels.

China's case is different in that changes are much more drastic. In addition, China at times adopts new laws that fundamentally deprive the property interests of private enterprises, which is a phenomenon that is seldom seen elsewhere. For example, China has promulgated a large number of state regulations on air pollution, which led to the closure of many high-polluting private enterprises, reducing the value of their assets to almost zero. The legal transition constitutes a significant intrusion on private property and may deter investment. While state ownership of enterprises incurs higher ownership costs, it may address the underinvestment problem in areas with significant policy changes and legal uncertainty. In areas where legal transitions are frequent, SOEs are likely to be more prevalent. Assessing how China protects private property during legal transitions deepens our understanding of the development of both private enterprises and SOEs in China.

Nevertheless, it should be noted that the method employed here still has some drawbacks and limitations. First, it focuses only on one particular issue–the withdrawal of administrative licenses and the compensation awarded to private enterprises. In practice, many governmental decisions that harm the property interests of private enterprises are not regarded as "withdrawal of administrative license" and hence are not regulated by that framework. Second, the analysis focuses primarily on judicial protection and does not fully assess the level of protection awarded by the government to private enterprises. Those private enterprises who resort to ALL to protect their interests are presumably those that cannot gain adequate protection from the government in the first place. Despite these limitations, the empirical studies offered here still provide interesting and important insights into the legal protection of private enterprises. This chapter aims to provide concrete illustrations of the constraints imposed by the Chinese courts on governmental actions that might potentially infringe upon the property interests of private enterprises, with a particular focus on the local level.

I. Legal Transition and Judicial Protection of Private Enterprises: Article 8 of Administrative License Law in China

In China, ALL does not specify the methods for calculating the compensation. The Supreme People's Court (SPC) of China has provided a judicial interpretation that courts should generally determine the amount of compensation based on the value of assets invested by the enterprise. However, in practice, courts sometimes award higher or lower compensations than the value of invested assets. During a legal transition, private enterprises bear the costs arising from the incompleteness of the law to the extent that their losses are not fully compensated. In theory, all private enterprises face the risk of potential legal changes that may lead to losses. However, lower compensation notably weakens the protection of private enterprise's property interests. This can then discourage future investments in the same sector or related industries. Consequently, low compensation can serve as an indicator of high regulatory costs in these sectors.

When governments enact new laws or adopt new policies in response to societal changes, the values of existing properties may be negatively affected. The question then arises as to whether the government should compensate the property holders for the decrease in property value caused by the negative impact (Michelman, 1967; Kaplow, 1986; Rose-Ackerman and Rossi, 2000). The *Chinese Constitution* also includes a general provision for protecting private property. Article 13 of the *Chinese Constitution* provides that "[t]he state may, for the public interest, expropriate or take over private property of citizens for public use, and provide compensation in accordance with the law." However, unlike the United States, Chinese courts rarely invoke the Constitution when making such determinations. The requirements of compensation must instead be found in specific laws.

Additionally, Article 8 provides that when there is a change in law or circumstances, the government may withdraw administrative licenses, provided that it pays compensation to the licensees. This creates a legal basis for compensating the rights affected by the legal transitions. Published judicial judgments in China show that this rule has been applied frequently in recent years. China has recently made a commitment to achieve carbon neutrality within forty years, necessitating significant economic reform. To fulfill its promise, China would need to undergo significant legal transitions to amend its environmental and energy regulatory rules, which would inevitably affect the existing enterprises heavily reliant on coal. The enactment of national laws on environmental protection, energy efficiency, and safety regulation in recent decades has already given rise to a significant number of legal disputes. Apart from the legal transitions initiated by the national government, the local governments have also made changes to the law or policies, including many zoning regulations that affected existing property rights.

Article 8 applies when the government withdraws an "administrative license." In China, courts have adopted a broad interpretation of the concept, viewing it to include not only specific licenses to operate in particular industries (such as the licenses of mining and exploration of coal, safety production license, and environmental license) but also more general licenses such as a business permits which are required of all enterprises.

The second key question arising under Article 8 is whether the governments' decision constitutes a "withdrawal" of administrative licenses. Courts generally interpret this in a broad sense. For example, in the case of *Su Yaohua v. the Boluo County People's Government of Guangdong Province* (the *Su Yaohua case*), which was selected as one of the ten significant administrative cases of environmental protection issued by the SPC in 2014, the plaintiff started operating a stud farm in Luofu Mountain Modern Agricultural Technology Exhibition Zone starting from 2006. The animal farm obtained the "tax registration certificate," "permit to emit pollution," and "Business License of Individual Business." Later, the local government decided that operating the stud farm in the zone emits pollution to the water, which affects the operation of the agricultural zone. It thus issued the "*Circular on the Designation of Luofu Mountain National Modern Agricultural Science and Technology Demonstration Park into the Scope of Breeding-Prohibited Areas*" (hereinafter referred to as the Circular), requiring the stud farm, in the park, operated by Su Yaohua to move out. The Boluo County People's Government argued that the Circular did not constitute a withdrawal of the administrative license, and that although Su Yaohua had obtained the licenses to operate, Su Yaohua is still required to comply with all the laws and regulations. The court held that the Circular was essentially equivalent to the withdrawal of the stud farm's "pollutant discharge permit," "individual industrial and commercial business permit," and other licenses; therefore Su Yaohua's rights were protected by Paragraph two of Article 8. The *Su Yaohua case* demonstrates that even without a decision to directly withdraw the administrative license, as long as the new regulatory rules or decisions make it impossible for an enterprise to continue to operate, the business permit and other administrative licenses of the enterprise can be deemed to have been withdrawn due to the legal transition. This is true even when the administrative authority did not make a formal decision to directly withdraw the administrative licenses.

Based on these interpretations of the provision, if a private enterprise is compelled to close due to a new regulatory policy that makes it impossible for the enterprise to continue operating it may seek compensation from the government for the losses stemming from withdrawal of permit. This establishes an important legal recourse for enterprises adversely impacted by legal transitions. The application of Article 8 extends to a broad range of cases, offering an opportunity to investigate the impact on private enterprises during such legal transitions.

It is important to note that in such cases, private enterprises have limited alternative remedies available to them. One relevant recourse is the *Chinese State Compensation Act* (*guojia peichang fa*), which typically applies when the government unlawfully encroaches upon the property interests of private enterprises. According to Article 4 of this Act, an administrative organ is required to provide compensation if it engages in the following acts while exercising its functions and powers: (1) unlawfully imposing administrative sanctions such as fines, license revocation, production suspension orders, or property confiscation; (2) unlawfully implementing compulsory administrative measures such as property sealing, distraint, or freezing; (3) unlawfully expropriating or requisitioning property; or (4) engaging in other illegal acts that cause property damage. However, it should be noted that when legal changes result in the closure of private enterprises, such closure is not considered an unlawful governmental act and therefore falls outside the scope of the State Compensation Act. Another relevant legal basis is the *Property Law* (*wuquan fa*), which pertains to state expropriation of tangible properties. For instance, when the government exercises eminent domain to acquire land or buildings, the *Chinese Property Law* may provide a remedy. However, in cases where the government forces private enterprises to shut down without expropriating tangible property, Article 8 usually remains the only statutory basis for obtaining compensation.

Under Article 8, the withdrawal of an administrative license by the government needs to meet two requirements. Firstly, there must be a revision, abolition, or major change in the laws, or certain changes in the circumstances. In practice, situations that trigger the application of Article 8 include the revision of national laws, the promulgation of administrative regulations by the State Council, as well as the promulgation of some local regulations, local government rules, meeting minutes, and the administrative decisions by local governments. This provision also applies even if the foundation for the government decisions is not authorized by statute or regulation at the national or local level.

Secondly, the government's withdrawal of administrative licenses must be in the public interest. Currently, the courts generally support the government's decision to withdraw administrative licenses, without substantially reviewing whether the government's decisions are in the public interest. This is consistent with the current findings that courts are reluctant to review whether governmental decisions are in the public interest in China (Mao and Qiao, 2021). Only in a few cases did the courts rule to revoke government decisions to withdraw the administrative license, generally on the grounds that the decisions violated legal procedures. In most cases, the court permits the government to withdraw administrative licenses following the relevant procedures, allowing licensees to seek compensation only in accordance with Paragraph two of Article 8. Compensatory protection of private properties is the main remedy for licensees and the focus of this chapter.

As for the amount of compensation, the outcomes of cases vary significantly in practice. Article 15 of *Judicial Interpretation of the Supreme People's Court on the Trial of Administrative Licensing Cases* (hereinafter referred to as the SPC's Interpretation) stipulates that when an administrative license is withdrawn, the court should generally determine the amount of compensation based on the "actual losses." If the administrative license is for "the development and utilization of limited natural resources, allocation of public resources, and limiting market access to specific industries directly related to the public interest," the SPC's Interpretation states that the courts should generally determine the amount of compensation according to the value of the assets invested by the licensee. Even in cases where the license is not for these purposes, courts generally calculate actual losses based on the actual investment of the licensee. For example, in *Tumote Left Bannar Tengda Fireworks Manufacturing Co., Ltd. v. the Hohhot People's Government and Tumote Left Bannar People's Government* (hereinafter referred to as the *Tengda Fireworks case*), the Hohhot Government issued the *Reply of*

Hohhot City on Approving of the Complete Withdrawal from Production of the Fireworks Industry (Hu Zheng Pi Zi [2010] No. 9), following the shutdown of Tumote Left Bannar Tengda Fireworks Manufacturing Co., Ltd. (Tengda Company). Consequently, the Safety Supervision Bureau of the government expropriated the fireworks and revoked the safety production license held by Tengda Company. Unlike a mining license, the safety production license does not regulate certain natural resources or entry to certain regulated markets. The government paid Tengda Company a compensation of 23.8 million RMB for the closure of the enterprise, which was below the value of the actual investments of Tengda Fireworks Company. The court finally determined that Tengda Company shall be compensated by the actual investment based on an evaluation report. In another example, *Yueyang Lantian Metallurgical Building Materials Co., Ltd. (Lantian Company) v. Yueyang Environmental Protection Bureau*, the Environmental Protection Bureau ordered Lantian Company to stop smelting in accordance with the "*Decision of the State Council on Several Issues Concerning Environmental Protection.*" In this case, the courts also decided to compensate Lantian Company for the whole of its investments even though the license withdrawn was not about the regulation of natural resources.

In many cases, courts set the compensation level at or above the value of assets invested by the licensee, as the SPC's interpretation requires. This chapter refers to these outcomes as a "high" compensation. Some courts use the original value of the investment. For example, in a recent case, a company obtained a mining license in 2014 through an auction. In 2019, the Luxi County Natural Resources Bureau found that the mining area overlapped with the local nature reserve and required the mining company to close down. According to a policy adopted by the Hunan Province, the People's Government of Luxi County decided to give the licensee an appropriate compensation of 6 million RMB. The court finally decided that the administrative agency should compensate about 6.5 million RMB based on the value of the investment made by the licensee. Some courts also consider the future cash flow of the assets. For example, in the case of *Zhoushan Red Star Stone Co., Ltd. v. Jintang Management Committee of the Zhoushan Islands New Area in Zhejiang Province* (hereinafter referred to as the *Zhoushan Red Star case*), Red Star Stone Co., Limited (Red Star Company) engaged in stone quarry and sales activities. In 2008, the People's Government of Dinghai District of Zhoushan made the decision in the *No.7 Meeting Minutes in 2008* to close the stone quarry. The court held that the government should compensate the licensee for its loss of future profits.

In contrast, in some cases, the compensation amount is set below the value of the licensee's original investment, which can be deemed as "low" compensation to the licensees. These instances typically involve the government unilaterally determining the compensation amount since it usually has the incentive to keep a compensation amount lower than the investment value. For example, in the case of *Du Huihua v. the Wudang District People's Government of Guiyang City*, the court held that the plaintiff had a factual and legal basis to request the defendant to compensate for its investment. However, the court ruled that the amount of compensation should be determined at the discretion of the administrative authority and it is not proper for judicial powers to intervene. Since the SPC's interpretation only guides the courts' calculation of the compensation but not the governments' decision to compensate, the compensation standards set by the government can be lower. In practice, the compensation offered by the governments usually falls below the value of the assets invested by the licensees. Thus, the protection of investors' interests is weaker than what is provided in Article 15 of the SPC's Interpretation. For example, in the case of *Lipingxian Huafeng Yeyan Zhenkong Jizhi Zhuanchang Deng v. Lipingxian Renmin Zhengfu Buchang An*, the plaintiff argues that he invested 9 million RMB to build a brick factory, and the county government only compensated the plaintiff with 1.6 million RMB. The plaintiff was dissatisfied with the compensation and filed a lawsuit. Another example is the case of *Zeng Chuangao v. the People's Government of Lizhou District of Guangyuan City and the Coal Industry Administration Bureau of Lizhou District of Guangyuan City*, where Zeng Chuangao claimed that he invested 53.3 million RMB in Zhanghuajing Coal Mine and demanded compensation from the government for its decision to shut down the coal mine. The Lizhou District Government of Guangyuan calculated the amount of compensation to be 10.8 million RMB based on the coal mine's production capacity. The court held that the compensation plan was in line with the provincial, municipal, and district policies for coal mine closure and compensation and ultimately dismissed Zeng Chuangao's claim.

II. An Empirical Analysis of the Application of Article 8

While Article 8 provides protection to enterprises, it remains unclear how courts enforce this rule in practice. In China, courts usually refrain from providing detailed reasoning or explanations in their judgments. It is thus necessary to conduct a statistical analysis of the various factors that might affect the court's decisions to decipher the logic underlying their decisions.

A. *Overview of Case Outcomes*

A study of Article 8 can thus yield insight into the threat of legal changes faced by enterprises in different sectors. I used "Article 8 of the Administrative Licensing Law" as the keyword to search the *China Law and Reference* database for all cases related to Article 8 as of January 30, 2023. After excluding court judgments that were not related to Paragraph two of Article 8 and cases in which the court did not rule on the merits, 438 cases were selected. Sometimes a single government's policy may affect multiple enterprises, resulting in several lawsuits. Counting these cases separately may bias the analysis. Thus, I have only included one of these cases arising out of the same legal transition in the dataset. I also excluded cases that are clearly irrelevant to Article 8 although the court considered the application of Article 8 and rejected the claim of the plaintiff. Excluding these cases does not change the major conclusion of the below findings.

Among these 438 cases, the courts dismissed the plaintiffs' claims and offered *no* compensation in 74 cases. Courts sometimes refused to grant compensation on legal or factual grounds. For example, courts may reject claims because the government's decision did not constitute a withdrawal of licenses or because the license had expired. Courts may also believe that plaintiffs have failed to prove the actual loss or that the evidence does not support their claims. For example, in the case of *Ren Laifu v. The Government of Pinglu County*, the court held that Ren Laifu's claim of coal mine compensation from the Pinglu County People's Government had a legal basis and should be supported. However, Ren Laifu's request for compensation of 2 million RMB was not supported because he did not provide direct evidence of the actual loss of his property. Whether the court's determination of facts was proper is difficult to tell based on the information in the judicial decision. In 364 cases, the court ruled that the government needed to compensate the plaintiff, offering low compensation in 203 cases, and high compensation in 161 cases. Table 3.1 presents the number of cases over time, while Table 3.2 provides the number of cases with different outcomes.

B. *Factors That May Affect the Outcome*

To analyze the decision patterns of courts, several factors that could influence the case's outcomes were collected. The first factor considered was the type of plaintiffs involved. In practical cases, plaintiffs can be individuals, sole proprietorship enterprises (SPEs), or partnerships, as well as limited liability companies and joint-stock companies. The

Table 3.1. *Yearly distribution of cases*

Year	Frequency	Percent
2004	1	0.2
2005	1	0.2
2007	2	0.5
2010	1	0.2
2011	2	0.5
2012	2	0.5
2013	8	1.8
2014	8	1.8
2015	32	7.3
2016	37	8.5
2017	32	7.3
2018	69	15.6
2019	126	28.8
2020	97	22.2
2021	18	4.1
2022	2	0.5
Total	438	100

Source: China Law and Reference database

Table 3.2 *Number and proportion of cases with different outcomes*

	Number	Proportion (percent)
No compensation	74	16.9
Low compensation	203	46.3
High compensation	161	36.8
Total	438	100

Source: China Law and Reference database

information on plaintiff types was gathered and categorized accordingly. Table 3.3 illustrates that when the plaintiff is an individual or an SPE, there is a higher proportion (26 percent) of cases where courts provide no compensation compared to cases involving companies (8 percent). This suggests that the courts tend to offer stronger protection to plaintiffs that are companies. Additionally, the proportion of cases with high compensation (27 percent) is much lower when the plaintiff is an individual or an SPE, in contrast to cases involving companies (46 percent).

Table 3.3 *Plaintiff and outcome*

Plaintiff	No compensation	Low compensation	High compensation	Total	No compensation (percent)	Low compensation (percent)	High compensation (percent)
Company	18	100	102	220	8	45	46
Individual or SPE	56	103	59	218	26	47	27
Total	74	203	161	438	17	46	37

Source: China Law and Reference database

In practice, the defendants may be the governments at various levels. According to Article 30 of the *Constitution of the People's Republic of China*, the administrative authorities in China include the provincial-level, county-level (*xian ji*), and township-level (*xiang ji*) governments. In practice, China has developed a fourth level of prefectural level which is lower than the provincial level and higher than the county level. Therefore, there are four levels of local government authorities (in order of increasing authority): township level, county level, prefectural level, and provincial level. In addition, the *Organic Law of the People's Republic of China on the Local People's Congresses and Local People's Governments* stipulates that the subordinate government departments are under the leadership of the corresponding level of people's government. Table 3.4 presents the number of cases that involve different levels of the government.

The level of the court can be another factor that influences the decisions made. According to the Organic Law of the People's Courts of the People's Republic of China, the Supreme People's Court holds the highest authority, while local courts are categorized into three judicial levels: Higher-Level People's Courts, Intermediate-Level People's Courts, and Basic-Level People's Courts.

In Table 3.5, I have compiled the statistics regarding the court levels and their pattern of decision making. It is observed that Basic-Level People's Courts provided no compensation in 40 percent of cases. In comparison, Intermediate-Level People's Courts, Higher-Level

Table 3.4 *Defendant information*

Level of the administrative authorities	Number of cases	Percentage (%)
Township Governments	12	2.74
Subordinate Departments of County Government	104	23.74
County Government	183	41.78
Subordinate Departments of Prefectural Government	37	8.45
Prefectural Government	79	18.04
Subordinate Departments of Provincial Government	19	4.34
Provincial Government	4	0.91
Total	438	100

Table 3.5 *Court level and outcome*

Court level	No compensation	Low compensation	High compensation	Total	No compensation (percent)	Low compensation (percent)	High compensation (percent)
Basic-Level	28	19	23	70	40	27	33
Intermediate-Level	29	114	84	227	13	50	37
Higher-Level	16	66	45	127	13	52	35
Supreme People's Court	1	4	9	14	7	29	64
Total	74	203	161	438	17	46	37

Source: China Law and Reference database

People's Courts both had a lower rate of no compensation, both at 13 percent, while the Supreme People's Court had an even lower rate at 7 percent. Additionally, Basic-Level People's Courts offered high compensation in only 33 percent of cases, the lowest among the different court levels. Intermediate-Level People's Courts and Higher-Level People's Courts provided high compensation in 37 percent and 35 percent of cases, respectively, while the Supreme People's Court offered high compensation in 64 percent of cases. These figures generally suggest that higher-level courts tend to provide stronger protection.

The withdrawal of administrative licenses may be caused by different types of legal transitions, including national and local legal transitions. Many national policy changes may affect the interests of licensees, although these changes must first be implemented by local governments. These legal transitions are categorized as "national legal transitions." Meanwhile, legal transitions are initiated by local governments subject to their discretion; they are referred to as "local legal transitions." It should be noted that if a local government is authorized by a national statute to exercise discretion in adjusting the policies, for the purposes of this chapter, we will treat such cases as national legal transitions.

Table 3.6 presents data on cases triggered by different legal transitions. Among these cases, there were 223 instances related to national legal transitions. Within these cases, the court provided high compensation in 61 cases (27 percent), low compensation in 125 cases (56 percent), and rejected the claim for compensation in 37 cases (17 percent). In contrast, there were 163 cases involving local legal transitions. In these cases, the court awarded high compensation in 84 cases (52 percent), low compensation in 52 cases (32 percent), and no compensation in 27 cases (17 percent). Therefore, while the proportion of cases where no compensation was offered was similar between national and local transitions, they tend to provide high compensation more frequently in cases stemming from local legal transitions compared to those resulting from national ones.

To assess which of the factors affect the outcome of compensations, this chapter considers the above factors in a multivariate ordered logistic regression. The dependent variable, ***Compensation***, denotes "0" if the court rejected the claim of compensation, "1" if it offered low compensation, "2" if offered high compensation. Cases in which the court did not rule on the merits were excluded, and the cases in which the claims of the licensees were dismissed. Several factors serve as independent variables in the analysis. ***Individual*** denotes "1" if the plaintiff is an individual or an

Table 3.6 *Type of legal transitions and outcome*

Type of regulation	No compensation	Low compensation	High compensation	Total	No compensation (percent)	Low compensation (percent)	High compensation (percent)
Local legal transition	27	52	84	163	17	32	52
Provincial legal transition	8	26	12	46	17	57	26
National legal transition	37	125	61	223	17	56	27
Total	72	203	157	432	17	47	36

Source: China Law and Reference database

SPE and "0" if the plaintiff is a company. ***Government_level*** is coded according to Table 3.7.

Court_level is coded as "1" if the court adjudicating the case is a Basic-Level People's Court, "2" if the court is an Intermediate-Level People's Court, "3" if the court is a Higher-Level People's Court, and "4" if it is the Supreme People's Court. ***National_transition*** equals "2" if the dispute was caused by a national legal transition, "1" if was caused by a provincial legal transition, and "0" if caused by a local legal transition. ***Year*** denotes the year of the case decision. The summary statistics are stated in Table 3.8.

To examine which factors affect the compensation outcomes, I ran a multivariate ordered logistical regression with ***Compensation*** being the dependent variable and the other factors as independent variables. I included both year-fixed-effects and sector-fixed-effects as control variables. Table 3.9 presents the results of the regression. Columns 1 shows that among these variables, the coefficient of ***Individual*** is statistically significant and negative, suggesting that courts are more

Table 3.7 *Levels of government*

Level of the sued administrative authorities	Code
Township Governments	0
Subordinate Departments of County Government	1
County Government	2
Subordinate Departments of Prefectural Government	3
Prefectural Government	4
Subordinate Departments of Provincial Government	5
Provincial Government	6

Source: China Law and Reference database

Table 3.8 *Summary of statistics*

Variable	Observations	Mean	Std. Dev.	Min	Max
Compensation	438	1.20	0.71	0	2
Individual	438	0.50	0.50	0	1
Government level	438	2.32	1.26	0	6
Court level	438	2.19	0.74	1	4
National transition	432	1.14	0.94	0	2
Year	438	2,018.06	2.32	2,004	2,022

Source: China Law and Reference database

Table 3.9 *Regression results*

	Compensation					
Variables	(1)	(2)	(3)	(4)	(5)	(6)
Individual	**−0.993*****				**−1.022*****	**−1.101*****
	(0.187)				**(0.207)**	**(0.255)**
Government_Level		−0.100			**−0.240*****	−0.126
		(0.071)			**(0.082)**	(0.097)
Court_Level			**0.367*****		**0.381*****	**0.366****
			(0.128)		**(0.147)**	**(0.168)**
National_transition				**−0.366*****	**−0.368*****	**−0.270****
				(0.100)	**(0.106)**	**(0.126)**
Year-fixed-effects	No	No	No	No	Yes	Yes
Sector-fixed-effects	No	No	No	No	No	Yes
Observations	438	438	438	432	432	432

Robust standard errors in parentheses.
*** $p<0.01$, ** $p<0.05$, * $p<0.1$.

likely to grant lower compensation when the plaintiff is an individual or an SPE, as opposed to a company. The coefficient of ***Court_level*** is statistically significant and positive, indicating that a higher-level court is likely to grant a higher compensation. The coefficients for ***National_transition*** are highly statistically significant and negative, meaning that compensation is lower when the dispute was caused by a national legal transition. Column 6 shows the result of a multivariate regression, where coefficients of ***Individual***, ***Court_level*** and ***National_transition*** remain statistically significant.

C. *Plaintiff's Sector*

The cases collected also provide a chance to observe the extent to which changes in the law or policy affect private enterprises in different sectors as well as whether the level of compensation varies across sectors. Table 3.10 presents the distribution of cases across sectors.

There is a significant disparity in the level of compensation provided to different types of enterprises. To illustrate this, we can compare the compensation offered to the mining sector and the manufacturing sector.

Table 3.10 *Plaintiff's sector*

Plaintiff's sector	Number	Percent
Mining of nonmetal ores	134	30.59
Manufacture	70	15.98
Livestock farm	48	10.96
Transportation	43	9.82
Nonbusiness Sectors	36	8.22
Coal mining	24	5.48
Real estate	21	4.79
Catering service	14	3.2
Hydropower Generation	12	2.74
Advertisement	9	2.05
Slaughterhouse	8	1.83
Textile	6	1.37
Agriculture	5	1.14
Garbage treatment	5	1.14
Mining of metal ores	3	0.68
Total	438	100

Among the twenty-four cases initiated by coal enterprises, the court rejected claims for compensation in three cases (13 percent), provided low compensation in sixteen cases (67 percent), and high compensation in five cases (21 percent), as shown in Table 3.11. A similar pattern can be observed in the mining of nonmetal ores. Out of the 134 cases related to the mining of other natural resources, the court rejected claims in 26 cases (19 percent), offered low compensation in 70 cases (52 percent), and high compensation in 38 cases (28 percent).

In contrast, the compensation provided to manufacturing enterprises tends to be relatively higher compared to the mining sector. Among the 70 cases involving manufacturing enterprises, the court rejected claims for compensation in only two cases (3 percent), which is significantly lower than the rejection rate in the mining sector. Additionally, the court provided high compensation in 44 cases (63 percent), considerably higher than the compensation offered in mining cases.

Table 3.12 presents the findings of a multivariate ordered logistic regression, which includes dummy variables for various sectors. In this analysis, coal mining serves as the baseline sector. The coefficient associated with the manufacturing sector is statistically significant and positive. The results presented here indicate that if the plaintiff's business belongs to the manufacturing sector, there is a higher probability of receiving higher compensation compared to those in the coal mining sector.

D. *Potential Selection Biases*

It should be noted that the above findings rely on the published judicial judgments and are subject to a selection bias problem since not all cases have been disclosed. However, several reasons suggest that the selection bias is unlikely to significantly affect the findings.

First, studies show that in certain years, the disclosure rate is fairly high. Statistics show that in 2017 and 2018, the proportion of disclosed cases amounted to 70 percent (Yang et al., 2019). I failed to find evidence of a correlation between the case outcomes and the year in which the decision was made. This shows that as courts are forced to disclose a larger proportion of cases, the average level of compensation offered to the licensees does not change significantly over time, implying that courts likely make similar decisions in unpublished cases. During these years, uploading cases was the default option for judges in Chinese courts, and a failure to upload requires interpretation and review by a supervisor. Studies have also shown that courts are more likely to refuse to disclose

Table 3.11 *Type of legal transition and outcome*

Type of regulation	No compensation	Low compensation	High compensation	Total	No compensation (percent)	Low compensation (percent)	High compensation (percent)
Coal mining	3	16	5	24	13	67	21
Mining of Nonmetal Ores	26	70	38	134	19	52	28
Manufacture	2	24	44	70	3	34	63

Table 3.12 *Regression results*

Variables	Compensation
Individual	**−1.124***** **(0.237)**
Court level	**0.490***** **(0.163)**
National transition	**−0.258**** **(0.118)**
Government level	**−0.189**** **(0.088)**
Advertisement	−0.315 (0.806)
Agriculture	1.510 (1.438)
Catering service	−0.574 (0.712)
Garbage treatment	0.677 (1.271)
Hydropower generation	1.077 (0.786)
Nonbusiness sector	**1.651***** **(0.583)**
Livestock farm	−0.369 (0.509)
Manufacture	**1.476***** **(0.497)**
Mining of ferrous metal ores	−0.581 (1.103)
Mining of nonmetal ores	−0.073 (0.447)
Real estate	**1.808**** **(0.737)**
Slaughterhouse	−1.029 (0.847)
Transportation	0.351 (0.523)
Textile	−0.778 (0.980)
Observations	432

Standard errors in parentheses.
*** $p<0.01$, ** $p<0.05$, * $p<0.1$.

sensitive criminal cases that would have a wide social influence, such as cases involving adolescents, divorce, settlement, and national security (Yang et al., 2019). The cases examined in this study do not easily fall into any of these categories (Mao and Qiao, 2021).

Second, in an unpublished regression analysis, the cases where the plaintiff received no compensation were also excluded. The results remained similar. Regardless of whether the plaintiff receives low or high compensation, the plaintiff is considered to have won the case, which may be viewed by some as detrimental to the reputation of the administrative authorities. Therefore, it is unlikely that courts would be more inclined to disclose one type of case over another. Since Article 8 fails to specify the means of determining compensation, courts enjoy wide discretion in adjudicating these disputes. It is thus unlikely that courts would face pressure in publishing cases in which the compensation is low. Consequently, there are reasons to believe that the selection bias does not systematically affect the conclusion of this chapter.

One may also be concerned with the selection bias caused by settlements between the parties. Parties may settle some disputes prior to trial, or the government may choose to compensate licensees to prevent lawsuits. However, the cases examined in the above study adhere to the *Administrative Litigation Procedural Law*, where the litigation fees are relatively low; even if plaintiff loses, the litigation fee is only 50 RMB (Chang and Klerman, 2021). Moreover, the licensees whose licenses have been withdrawn are in an "end game" with the government since they are required to cease operations. They thus are less likely to worry about maintaining a healthy, long-term relationship with the government. Consequently, the plaintiffs lack incentives to settle with the government. In addition, even if some cases are settled before the court ruling, as long as settlement decisions do not correlate with the timing of the investment and the types of legal transitions, the empirical results of this study remain valid. Since the application of Article 8 largely remains unclear, parties are likely to litigate the case to its conclusion. It is therefore reasonable to conclude that the selection bias caused by the settlement is not severe.

E. *Explaining the Courts' Approach*

1. Regulatory Costs and Alternative Explanations

The above empirical analysis shows that the extent of compensation for private enterprises varies across sectors. Why would courts offer relatively lower compensation to enterprises in some sectors than others?

This chapter contends that this phenomenon arises due to the courts' tendency to provide weaker protection when there is a clash between the objective of safeguarding property and the state's other legitimate goals, such as environmental preservation. As various sectors are subject to diverse regulations, and in those sectors where conflicts between disparate goals are more acute, the demarcation between public power and private property becomes more difficult and they may face elevated regulatory costs.

For instance, in the context of coal mining, the central government may adopt a more expansive regulatory approach, aimed at promoting environmental sustainability, enhancing safety regulations, and ensuring a stable energy supply. Such regulations are frequently perceived as reasonable and justifiable. These regulations might also be seen as a redefinition of property boundaries rather than a direct infringement of property rights. Distinguishing between legitimate regulation for public benefit and opportunistic actions becomes more complicated in such a sector. Courts would tend to award lower compensation when these regulatory measures affect the property interests of private enterprises to allow more flexibility for the government to implement its policies. Consequently, the government is granted more discretion, which could potentially be abused. Private enterprises operating within this industry, therefore, confront an augmented likelihood of opportunistic government behavior and higher regulatory costs.

By contrast, certain industries demonstrate a higher degree of clarity concerning the state-enterprise relationship due to the narrower scope of regulation. Take, for example, manufacturing companies, which are subject to health and safety as well as environmental regulations, but typically with less magnitude. Similarly, real estate enterprises may encounter land-use regulations and safety standards, but it is unlikely for the government to issue closure orders without clear legal authority. In these sectors, the courts can more readily demand greater compensation from the government when there is a clear violation of the property interests of these private entities. Courts can also determine the scope of losses of the enterprise more easily. This facilitates the identification of any opportunistic actions taken by the government and offers precise protection to private enterprises.

The coefficient associated with the real estate sector is also statistically significant. This finding can be attributed to the fact that the property interests affected in these cases were mostly tangible property rights in urban areas, which can be easily evaluated and compensated. Moreover, in most of these cases, the real estate companies were not completely shut down; instead, only part of their assets was affected. In addition, unlike environmental regulation, some of the regulations and government policies affecting the property interests of the real estate corporations are harder to justify as a necessary and legitimate exercise of government power for the public interest.

For instance, in the case of *Fushun Shunrong Real Estate Development Company v. Fushun County People's Government, and Fushun Dongzhou District People's Government*, Fushun Shunrong Real Estate Development Company (Fushun Shunrong) entered into an agreement with Fushun County Urban Construction Bureau on February 20, 2001, to construct several residential buildings. Fushun Shunrong was responsible for the demolition, relocation, and compensation within the relocation area. Following the agreement, Fushun Shunrong obtained the investment license for the fixed asset investment project. Four residential buildings were constructed, and the corresponding infrastructure supporting projects in the planned area was completed. On November 27, 2004, the jurisdiction of the area containing Fushun Shunrong Real Estate Development Company's projects was transferred from one district to another – specifically, to the Dongzhou District Government of Fushun. This jurisdictional transfer granted the new district government the authority to sell the land to another property developer.

The court held that the Government of Dongzhou District had the power to withdraw the licenses due to changes in the circumstances but should compensate the real estate company for the losses. Since the real estate company's investment was relatively clear and verifiable, the court compensated for the losses suffered by the real estate company, including the expenses of demolition, resettlement, backfilling, and leveling of the land. This case illustrates that it is usually easier to compensate real estate companies for their losses when the government withdraws their licenses to develop certain properties. In addition, the policy changes also do not provide clear benefits to the public. Thus, courts may believe these regulations are less justified and hence offer stronger protection for property interests.

The difficulty of distinguishing government opportunism and legitimate regulation has long been recognized in the literature. Scholars have proposed various theories about whether the government should offer compensation to a party whose property interests are affected by legal transitions (Kaplow, 1986; Rose-Ackerman and Rossi, 2000; Shaviro, 2000; Dana and Merrill, 2002). Legal transition can generate uncertainty for investors, which will cause the problem of underinvestment and adversely affect economic development. This theoretical analysis is in line with the theory of new institutional economics proposed by Nobel Laureate Douglass North and others – that there is a close connection between the protection of property rights and economic development (North, 1990). Max Weber similarly argues that the functioning of markets depends on the support of a legal system that yields predictable outcomes (Trubek, 1972a; Laffont and Tirole, 1993; Tirole, 1994). However, an excessively high level of compensation granted by the courts during legal transitions may potentially undermine investor incentives to anticipate and plan for future regulatory changes and result in over-investment in certain sectors (Kaplow, 1986, p. 529). The difficult choice faced by courts in determining the appropriate compensation to private enterprises during legal transition stems from the inherent incompleteness of the law.

An alternative explanation for the court's approach is that their decisions may be driven by political economy factors. Scholars have proposed various theories to explain the factors that may affect the decisions of courts (Pei et al., 2010; Liebman, 2011; He and Su, 2013; Li, 2017). While some argue that courts, as professional institutions, are largely independent (Pei et al., 2010), others present evidence that courts in China are often under political influence and pursue the government's policies while adjudicating disputes (Liebman, 2011). Currently, many scholars studying Chinese courts have embraced the theory of "haves" and "have-nots," which suggests that the outcome of cases often depends on whether the parties have rich financial resources or strong political connections (Pei et al., 2010; He and Su, 2013; Li, 2017). Others believe that judicial decision-making can be influenced by the relative power of not only the disputants but also the court (Li, 2017). The theories of judicial behavior may explain the above empirical findings that the identity of plaintiffs correlates with the outcome. Generally speaking, individuals or SPEs have fewer financial resources than companies. Meanwhile, this theory can also explain the correlation between the court level and the level of compensation. Lower-level courts are more susceptible to influence by local governments and tend to rule in their favor compared to higher-level courts. Thus, courts may favor the haves in their rulings (Li, 2017). This theory can also explain why courts generally offer a lower compensation when the defendant is a higher-level government.

The theory of haves and have-nots, however, cannot fully explain why the compensation level is affected by the types of legal transition (national or local) and the types of business. This empirical finding supports the LTS theory. It shows that courts can help curb opportunistic behaviors of the government in certain cases, especially where the local government is involved, although their strength of protection is weakened when the legal transition is initiated by higher-level governments. Under China's particular political structure, local governments may be more likely to act as predatory entities against private properties compared to the central government. As Donald Clarke notes, "the threat of arbitrary expropriation in China today does not come from the central government; it comes from local government. It is local government that is the most closely acquainted with a firm's financial health and that has the greatest incentive and ability to loot it" (Clarke et al., 2008). Scholars have observed that local government officials are in a "promotion tournament" (Zhou, 2007). They compete to increase the local GDP growth in order to impress the party committee at the higher level and, ultimately, receive a promotion (Guo, 2009). Driven by a motivation to spur local economic development, local governments may give key support to large enterprises that can promote employment rate and economic growth, thus ignoring the interests of small businesses since they are incentivized o pursue GDP growth. Local governments thus may adjust regulatory rules that infringe upon private property rights. For example, in the *Zhoushan Red Star case*, the government forced the closure of the Zhoushan Red Star Company due to the need for the reclamation and construction of the northern Jintang area. The local government might have believed the development of the northern Jintang area would generate more GDP growth and then decides to sacrifice the interests of the Zhoushan Red Star Company. LTS can thus explain the different attitudes of courts toward legal transitions initiated by local and central governments in China.

2. Regulatory Costs in Sectors Subject to Environmental Regulation

To further understand the legal protection offered to private enterprises, it would be helpful to consider sectors subject to the national policy of environmental protection. The tendency of Chinese courts to award lower compensation in cases involving polluting enterprises can be explained by the concern of implementing the state's environmental policies (Zeng, 2022). As China has made environmental protection one of its national policies, different levels of courts in China have organized meetings to study these policies and promote the concept of green development in recent years, which may have affected the court's decisions on compensation.

It is important to point out that elevating compensation levels in sectors with stricter regulations would impede the state's capacity to implement policies that serve the public interest. While providing higher compensation to affected parties during legal transitions may mitigate the uncertainty faced by investors and prevent underinvestment, it can also lead to the unintended consequence of overinvestment. When right holders receive high compensation, their incentive to anticipate and adjust their investment decisions in response to legal transitions weakens. For instance, in cases where environmental protection laws change and noncompliant enterprises are compelled to cease operations, if the government compensates these enterprises adequately for their losses, it may inadvertently encourage them to disregard the risks associated with legal transitions and invest excessively in hazardous industries. Meanwhile, enterprises that proactively anticipate the evolving trends of environmental protection policies and make prudent investments do not receive corresponding competitive advantages. Consequently, compensating enterprises in such situations may not foster healthy competition among businesses to achieve regulatory goals. It is crucial to consider the potential negative effects of compensation on balanced competition and alignment with regulatory objectives.

In a few cases, courts explicitly noted that the protection of property interests will be weaker if it conflicts with these state goals. For example, in *Zhuzhou Shenzhou Transportation Service Co. Ltd. v. Zhuzhou City Police Bureau Transportation Police Branch* (hereinafter referred to as *Zhuzhou Shenzhou case*), the court held that:

> The law does not require full compensation for the losses of the licensees ... In the situation where protecting the environment has become a basic national policy, the prevention and control of air pollution will naturally affect the interests of some groups ... The Implementing Measures set the compensation standard, and give compensation based on vehicle type and registration time. There may be a certain gap between the amount of compensation and the actual losses of the plaintiff, but it is a price that must be paid to curb the continuous pollution of the atmosphere.

In practice, many of the cases were driven by the government's policy of getting rid of the outdated production capacity (*taotai luohou channeng*). Some sectors are affected more significantly by the legal changes than others. These sectors include coal, iron, and steel. This explains why a trend of "the advance of the state, retreat of the private sector" has been observed in these sectors.

For instance, various notices and circulars have been issued by the State Council to strengthen the regulation of coal mines since the 1990s. In June 2005, the State Council issued a reply approving policy measures for the sustainable development of the coal industry in Shanxi. It mandated the continued rectification and closure of coal mines and the requirement for integrated mines to maintain a minimum annual production scale of 300,000 tons, with newly constructed mines ideally exceeding 600,000 tons per year. The State Council also granted the Shanxi government the authority to develop more detailed plans to promote the coal sector's sustainable development.

In response, the local government of Shanxi Province issued the "Implementation Opinions on Accelerating the Merger and Reorganization of Coal Mining Enterprises." This policy specified that by the end of 2010, coal mining enterprises within the province should have a minimum scale of 3 million tons per year, and the number of mines should be limited to 1,500. The goal was to establish 2–3 super-sized coal conglomerates with an annual production capacity of billions of tons and 3–5 large coal enterprise groups with an annual production capacity exceeding 50 million tons. This restructuring was intended to ensure that the coal production controlled by these large conglomerates accounted for over 75 percent of the province's total output.

In April 2009, the Shanxi provincial government issued a notice to further accelerate the merger, reorganization, and integration of coal mining enterprises. This notice specified the maximum number of mines that each prefecture within Shanxi province could retain. Under this plan, Taiyuan Prefecture could retain up to 50 mines; Datong Prefecture, 71 mines; Yangquan Prefecture, 50 mines; Changzhi Prefecture, 95 mines; Jincheng Prefecture, 118 mines; Shuozhou Prefecture, 65 mines; Xinzhou Prefecture, 63 mines; Jinzhong Prefecture, 110 mines; Lvliang Prefecture, 100 mines; Linfen Prefecture, 127 mines; and Yuncheng Prefecture, 18 mines. Additionally, the key state-owned coal conglomerates would retain a total of 133 mines.

The analysis above highlights the significant role played by Chinese central and local governments in implementing the state's policy of consolidating coal enterprises. The fate of each enterprise is heavily influenced by the decisions of the government. Moreover, the maximum number of mines allocated to each prefecture appears to be arbitrary and inflexible, with a lack of clear standards. The primary objective of seems to be reducing the number of firms with the assumption that consolidation eases regulatory challenges. This regulatory approach could be subject to criticism as it places regulatory burdens on private enterprises, although it also generates the potential benefit of enhanced compliance.

In pursuing environmental and energy policies, local governments have been granted substantial power in regulating related sectors. The regulatory authority of local governments in the coal mining sector is arguably broader and more influential compared to their authority in other sectors. This may help explain the dominance of the state in the coal sector, as private enterprises face significant regulatory costs stemming from the local government's potential abuse of power.

The above analysis suggests that while courts offer relatively weak protection to the property interests of private enterprises, strengthening the protection by offering these enterprises higher compensation does not always lead to desirable outcomes. For example, in the case of *Wang Zhigang v. Taigu xian People's Government,* Wang Zhigang established a Building Material Factory (Junyou Factory) on May 6, 2008, which engaged in the production and the sale of clay bricks. The State Council issued the *Notice of the General Office of the State Council on Further Promoting Wall Material Innovation and Promoting Energy-saving Architectures* in 2005. The Safety Regulatory Department of the State Council later issued the *Notice of the State Administration of Safety Supervision and Other Departments on the Opinions on Implementing the Rectification of Metal and Non-metal Mines* in 2012, under which the local government forced the closure of plaintiff's factory. In this case, the State Council issued a regulation on the promotion of energy-saving materials in 2005, which was not fully implemented until 2012. If the court offered higher compensation to the private enterprises, it would incentivize investors to invest excessively in this sector, which would be contrary to the goals of the state which is the implementation of the new energy-saving standards.

III. Summary

To summarize, the legal protection of private enterprises in China exhibits significant variation across sectors, as evidenced by differing compensation levels. It is a misconception to assume that private enterprises uniformly encounter weak legal protections. Chinese law does provide a certain degree of protection to private enterprises; the government cannot overtly breach legal provisions or expropriate private property without facing legal consequences. However, in some sectors, courts typically refrain from curtailing governmental powers due to concerns that such actions could impede the state's regulatory objectives. Private enterprises may refrain from investing, leading to an overall higher proportion of SOEs in these sectors. The complexities in defining the boundaries between public power and private property in these sectors lead to relatively high regulatory costs, which cannot be easily reduced as readjusting compensation level results in a transfer of wealth rather than a reduction of the total social costs associated with regulation.

Some may perceive the above explanation as essentially a political theory, given that judges may be influenced by the state's political decisions to pursue regulatory goals. For instance, in the context of regulating the coal mining industry, the court's decision to offer lower compensation could be construed as aligning with the state's political objective of curbing environmental pollution. However, it is important to recognize that this theory diverges significantly from the prevailing political theories of SOEs as proposed by certain scholars or as is commonly understood (Wang, 2014). Here, the influence of politics over state ownership is more nuanced and indirect. Instead of the state making explicit decisions to privatize or retain SOEs, it establishes a legal framework that provides hierarchical legal protections, thereby affecting the ownership structures of enterprises within specific sectors. Furthermore, this analysis acknowledges that the decision to privatize or retain SOEs is not solely determined by the government, but also by private investment decisions to a certain extent.

Some may question the necessity of state regulations in these sectors and challenge whether such regulations are warranted at all. Indeed, many contend that excessive government intervention in the Chinese market impedes efficiency. However, determining the optimal intensity of these regulations is complex and beyond the scope of this book. Assuming that a certain level of regulation is inevitable, it is probable that the associated regulatory costs will hinder the growth of private enterprises in specific sectors. In such contexts, SOEs may be necessary to fulfill market demand, thereby maintaining market stability and ensuring the provision of essential services.

4

Enforcement of Public-Private Partnership Contracts and the Distribution of State Ownership in China's Infrastructure Projects

In recent years, China has actively promoted numerous public-private partnership (PPP) projects, facilitating investor participation in the construction of infrastructure projects, including transportation and utility projects, which were traditionally provided by the state. According to a report by the World Bank in 2017, there were more investment commitments in Asia in infrastructure projects than all other regions. Most of the investments were made in China and Indonesia (The World Bank, 2017). Statistics show that more than 15 trillion RMB worth of investment has been made in PPP projects in China since 2014. In 2021, 1.1 trillion RMB was invested in the PPP market, whereas the investment in new shares issued in the Chinese stock market in 2021 was only about 0.5 trillion RMB. Scholars have noted that the investment in infrastructure has contributed significantly to China's economic rise (Zhang et al., 2007). A notable phenomenon in China's PPP market is the substantial involvement of SOEs. Despite the commonly held notion that SOEs are inefficient, they continue to make up a majority of the investors participating in China's PPP market.

Currently, scholars have mainly employed political economy theory and political theory to explain the prevalence of SOEs in China, focusing on the supply side of state ownership. They largely presume that privatization is exogenously determined by the political decisions made by the government. However, this supply-side analysis does not fully account for the enduring prominence of SOEs in the PPP market, where the government has openly conveyed its intention to attract private investment for infrastructure development.

This chapter employs a demand-side analysis to explain the prevalence of SOEs in the PPP market. It argues that there is a substantial demand for the goods or services provided by SOEs, while private enterprises are unable to meet the market's demand on equal terms. The objective is to illustrate that state ownership is, at least in part, determined endogenously by market forces and the legal institutions within a state, which tend to change gradually (Peerenboom, 2002). Consequently, in a competitive market where the government aims to privatize SOEs and attract private investment, these SOEs might persistently maintain a significant portion of market share, potentially outcompeting private firms.

While SOEs may incur higher ownership costs because of the "soft budget constraint" problem and their relatively weaker incentives to pursue profit (Megginson and Netter, 2001), they alleviate the concern for government opportunism, which is a major source of regulatory costs. In situations where regulatory costs are excessively high, private enterprises may refrain from investing or only do so when high returns are anticipated. If these regulatory costs remain high, a lack of participation by SOEs could lead to the underinvestment problem. This chapter tests this theory by examining China's PPP market, where SOEs and private firms coexist and compete with each other.

It is important to highlight that the analysis of state ownership presented here places greater emphasis on the transactional dynamics between enterprises and the government, which slightly diverges from the aforementioned cases. In the context of infrastructure investment, the government typically engages in contractual agreements with enterprises. This might give the impression that state ownership primarily serves to reduce transaction costs between the enterprise and the government, rather than to minimize regulatory costs. However, it should be noted that the social costs incurred in the PPP context are not entirely the same as transaction costs arising between two private entities. As the subsequent sections of this chapter will illustrate, the state often fails to fulfill its obligations under the contract in pursuit of public interest objectives. As a result, the inherent risk faced by enterprises still stems from government opportunism based on its regulatory power. Furthermore, the government may enact legislation that renders it impossible for them to honor the contract, thereby leading to breaches or terminations. Hence, despite the contractual nature of the government-enterprise relationship, the government retains regulatory authority over the contract. Therefore, regulatory costs can explain the prevalence of state ownership in this sector and shed light on its evolving nature over time.

This chapter first presents an empirical study of the legal enforcement of PPP contracts, showing that courts generally offer weak protection for private investors (He and Su, 2013; He, 2016; Li, 2017; Qin et al., 2020). The government may act opportunistically after investors make a specific investment by terminating or nationalizing the projects (Williamson, 1985, 1996; Levy and Spiller, 1994; Che and Qian, 1998; Trebilcock and Iacobucci, 2003).

This chapter then considers whether the power of local courts affects the level of privatization in the PPP market. Drawing on a judicial reform that phased in gradually in different areas of China after 2014, this chapter presents evidence showing that a more powerful judiciary system leads to a higher degree of privatization of infrastructure projects. The findings suggest that SOEs are prevalent in certain markets because legal institutions offer relatively weak protection for private investors. Enhanced legal protection could instill confidence, thus increasing their market share and promoting the level of privatization.

I. The Development of Public-Private Partnership Projects in China

The diverse nature of PPP projects makes it challenging to provide a precise definition. However, they all share certain fundamental characteristics. These projects invite investment from business firms, including private firms and state-owned firms, to enter into agreements with the government and to invest in public infrastructure traditionally provided by the government, such as highways, bridges, and utilities (Custos and Reitz, 2010, p. 555). Like elsewhere, PPP projects in China have also extended to a broad array of government services such as hospitals and education (Custos and Reitz, 2010, p. 555). Consequently, they can be viewed as a form of privatization of social provision, similar to the trend observed in the United States during the late 1990s and early 2000s (Minow, 2003). Typically, a PPP project company is established, wherein investors contribute assets in exchange for shares. Subsequently, this PPP project company enters into a contract with the government, mutually agreeing on the services and goods to be provided and specifying the rights and duties of the government. The payment for the provision of goods or services rendered by the PPP project company can be sourced from the government, the public consumers, or both. Figure 4.1 illustrates the simplified structure of a typical PPP project.

China has enacted a set of regulatory rules to govern the PPP projects. When the government initiates a PPP, it must first develop a project plan and request an assessment of the fiscal capabilities of implementing the plan from the finance bureau responsible for overseeing public expenditure at the relevant level. Local governments lacking sufficient fiscal capabilities are prohibited from participating in PPP projects. Upon approval of the PPP project by the finance bureau, the government would proceed to conduct an auction to invite investors and engage experts to

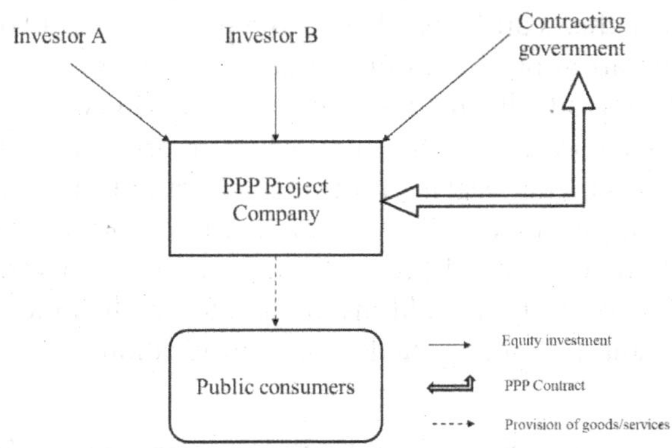

Figure 4.1 Structure of PPP.

evaluate and score each bidder. In cases where open bidding is unsuitable, methods like invited bidding or competitive negotiation may be employed. Subsequently, a negotiation panel is formed to engage with the bidders, prioritizing them based on their combined scores, to finalize a detailed agreement that specifies the proportion of shares between investors and the contracting government (Qin et al., 2020, pp. 22–23; Yin, 2020). The contracting government may hold the shares through an SOE. Notably, throughout the negotiation process, the core contract terms cannot be renegotiated or modified. The core terms include the technological and economic indicators (such as the investment size and duration), the right to use the land, PPP mode (BOT, TOT or others), the scope of the contract, the ownership structure of the project company, the ownership of the assets, the allocation of risks, the revenue mode (whether the fees would be paid by the government or the users), the price and price-adjustment mechanisms, and the standards of construction and the maintenance (Qin et al., 2020, pp. 22–23; Yin, 2020, p. 81). The fiscal expenditure will be incorporated into the government's fiscal budget and requires endorsement from the legislative body. Winning investors typically establish a PPP project company and invest in it to carry out the project plan.

China has decided long ago to introduce private investment in this market. Back in the late twentieth century, China had already initiated a few PPP projects, most notably in the sectors of energy, water utilities, and transportation (Wang et al., 2018, p. 594). For example, in 1984, the Shenzhen government introduced Hong Kong investors to build the Shajiao B power plant (Cheng et al., 2016). Similarly, in 1990, private investment was involved in the construction of Guangzhou Northern Ring Road (Wang et al., 2018, p. 589, 600). Over time, the scope of PPP market gradually extended to encompass other sectors such as waste management. However, SOEs still play a large role in the PPP market. A prime instance is the China Communications Construction Company, a company owned by Chinese central government, recognized as one of the largest state-owned corporations in China, particularly active in the realm of highway construction.

The prevalence of SOEs in this market thus raises some interesting theoretical questions. Scholars have long noted that SOEs are less efficient than private firms because of the lack of incentives to cut costs and innovate, as well as the "soft budget constraint" problem (Vickers and Yarrow, 1991; Hart et al., 1997). According to this theory, SOEs are expected to be outperformed by private firms in fair competition, relying on governmental subsidies or other preferential treatment to sustain their operations. In light of this, why do certain Chinese SOEs continue to hold a significant market share in the infrastructure sectors, despite the state's intent to introduce private investment? Could the contracting governments be influenced or captured? Alternatively, could these SOEs possess genuine competitive advantages over private firms?

Numerous empirical studies have aimed to examine whether SOEs are indeed less efficient, employing various methodologies. In analyzing the efficiency of SOEs, researchers have employed methods such as cross-sectional statistical analysis, comparing the performance of SOEs with that of private firms, and time series analysis to examine firm performance before and after privatization. Many of these studies demonstrate enhanced performance post-privatization. However, some studies provide evidence supporting the market failure hypothesis, suggesting that in sectors characterized by significant market failures requiring government intervention, privatization yields adverse effects (Megginson and Netter, 2001).

In the context of China, researchers have conducted studies comparing the performance of SOEs to that of private firms. For example, Bai et al. (2006b) utilized panel data to scrutinize the shifts in performance observed within privatized firms. Their findings indicate that privatized SOEs exhibit superior financial performance. However, it is worth noting that privatization may also lead to negative social impacts; some find that privatized firms are more prone to tax evasion and tend to reduce employment levels (Bai et al., 2006b, pp. 11–12).

However, the existing empirical studies encounter notable methodological limitations. First, many of them rely on cross-country data without adequately acknowledging the substantial variations in PPPs within each country (Hammami et al., 2006; Sabry, 2015). To illustrate, in China, a considerable number of investors engaged in PPP projects are themselves state-owned. When measuring the size of the private investment in PPP markets, current studies have failed to distinguish them from truly private investors (Wang et al., 2018). In addition, a number of studies regard regulations and the legal system as exogenous. They draw comparisons between the performance of regulated private enterprises and public enterprises within a given state, ultimately concluding that the private enterprises demonstrate superior efficiency (Davies, 1971). This situation could potentially be explained by considering that these states have already established mature regulatory institutions. Regulated private enterprises are more efficient in regions with developed and sophisticated regulatory institutions. There are many omitted variables associated with each country, stemming from their distinct economics, historical, political, and cultural differences, making it difficult to draw conclusions. It is imprudent to assert, based solely on this evidence, that privatization is universally beneficial, regardless of the specific institutions existing within a given state. While some researchers argue that, in the absence of sophisticated legal institutions, especially in corporate law, privatized firms may become susceptible to managerial expropriation (Stiglitz, 1999a, p. 26, 33; Black et al., 2000; Nellis, 2002). The difficulties linked to establishing effective regulatory institutions subsequent to privatization have not been given ample emphasis.

Second, within China, the cross-sectional analysis also encounters endogeneity issues since private firms and SOEs operate in distinct markets and possess substantial differences. Consequently, it becomes challenging to identify private firms that are comparable to SOEs for meaningful comparison. Similarly, time series or panel data analysis faces endogeneity concerns due to the nonrandom selection of firms designated for privatization by the government. These selected firms may possess certain inherent characteristics that differentiate them from those not subjected to privatization.

Third, while some studies focus on one particular country, the dependent variable usually does not measure private investment directly. Some studies measure private investment by the type of contract or the service production mechanism (such as internal production versus outsourcing) (Brown and Potoski, 2005), while others rely on survey data (Ameyaw et al., 2017). Finally, while a few studies consider the level of private investment, they have failed to differentiate the identity of the investors

(SOEs or private firms) (Wang et al., 2018). This chapter seeks to overcome some of these methodological challenges by investigating the factors that account for the variation of the level of state ownership across PPP projects.

II. Government Opportunism in Public-Private Partnership Projects

This chapter posits that SOEs indeed possess a competitive edge: their capability to mitigate instances of government opportunism. Theoretically, PPP projects face the daunting challenge of opportunism (Williamson, 1985; Wang and Jin, 2016; Smith, 2020; Zeng, 2023). Chinese local governments have incentives to act opportunistically to promote GDP growth. Scholars have noted that officials of local governments are under a "performance tournament" and thus are incentivized to promote GDP growth (Zhou, 2007). While some argue that such interregional competition spurs local governments to protect private property in order to attract investments (Clarke et al., 2008), the performance tournament arrangement also stimulates government officials to act opportunistically, as such behavior boosts the local GDP.

Chinese government officials have also clearly recognized the threat of government opportunism in PPP projects, noting its disproportionate impact on private enterprises compared to SOEs. For example, On July 21, 2017, the Legislative Affairs Office of the State Council, in collaboration with the National Development and Reform Commission and the Ministry of Finance, issued the "*Regulations on Cooperation between Government and Social Capital in the Field of Infrastructure and Public Services (Draft for Soliciting Opinions).*" The Legislative Affairs Office of the State Council particularly explains that:

> [This document] embodies two principles for the implementation of cooperative projects ... The second principle is to emphasize keeping promises and strictly fulfilling the cooperative project agreement, especially by strictly restraining government behavior and focusing on eliminating the worries of social capital parties, particularly **private** investors. The consultation draft stipulates that the government and social capital parties should keep promises and fulfil the obligations stipulated in the cooperative project agreement comprehensively (Article 20). At the same time, to address the concerns of social capital parties about fair treatment, reasonable returns, and government changes to the agreement or disregard for prior commitments, the draft clearly stipulates: ... the implementation of the cooperative project agreement is not affected by

> adjustments to administrative divisions, changes of government, adjustments of government departments or functions, or changes in personnel in charge. (Article 20, Paragraph 2)

From the perspective of the government, one of the most typical types of opportunistic action would be to refuse to honor an agreement when it is no longer in its favor. For example, if a government could improve local GDP growth by diverting resources to other purposes after breaching a PPP contract, it might choose to do so. Given the government's control over local courts, private investors may find it difficult to enforce the contract. A potential solution would be to tighten the legal or political constraints on the government regarding the enforcement of PPP contracts. To illustrate, consider the case of Xinyuan Minjiang No.4 Bridge (鑫远闽江四桥). Initially, the Fuzhou Prefectural People's Government assured investors of the bridge's exclusivity, serving as the primary entry point into downtown Fuzhou from the south (Zhang, 2017). However, the government later reneged on its commitment and introduced new projects diverting traffic away from the bridge, resulting in reduced revenue.

A more challenging problem involves the government's power to amend or terminate PPP contracts. This issue essentially arises from the regulatory costs between the government and PPP project investors. Investors in PPP projects tend to prioritize profit maximization, which can lead to a reduction in the quality of goods and services, particularly when quality is difficult to measure (Schultz, 2018, pp. 189, 205). Thus, the government needs to retain effective control to ensure project quality and to amend or terminate contracts when unforeseen circumstances arise (Minow, 2003). These challenges are not much different from the transaction costs encountered in private transactions. Making credible commitments would be easier if the government were not required to exercise control or adjust contracts in response to changing circumstances (Custos and Reitz, 2010, p. 575; Dannin, 2011, pp. 58–60). Allowing the government to change the administrative contracts unilaterally may be viewed as necessary to ensure that the government can react when new circumstances arise.

For example, in *Fuzhou Kehuan Gaoxin Environmental Protection Co. Ltd. v. Xianyou County People's Government*, the Xianyou township government and the contracting party entered into a PPP contract to construct and operate a garbage treatment project divided into two phases. After the completion of the first phase, the Environmental Protection Bureau of the Putian prefectural government issued a notice to the Xianyou township government that the garbage treatment facilities caused significant water pollution and public complaints. Pursuant to Article 24 of the *Environmental Impact Law*, if circumstances change that lead to significant pollution in the local area after the approval of a construction project, the project needs to be reapproved. The court found that the agreement on the second phase project was contingent on approval by the environmental regulatory authority, making it unenforceable. However, given the wide discretion of the contracting government to terminate administrative contracts, there's a risk of this power being misused to benefit government officials under the guise of public interest. This raises the question of whether the courts can effectively curb the opportunistic behavior of the governments while allowing them to terminate the contracts when they genuinely serve the public interest.

The occurrence of government opportunism in PPP projects is influenced by a range of factors, among which project duration stands out significantly. In practice, it is widely acknowledged that one of the major risks faced by PPP projects in China is the government's potential failure to uphold its commitments (Su et al., 2021, pp. 81–85). Sun Xiaoxia, a government official affiliated with the Ministry of Finance, has highlighted private investors' particular concern regarding the reliability of local government officials in maintaining their commitments, especially in long-term PPP projects where officials may change over time (Chen, 2016), perhaps because some officials may be reluctant to honor the promises made by their predecessors (Chen et al., 2021, pp. 10–14).

Another factor impacting the likelihood of opportunism is the sector of the project. Research indicates that governmental intervention, which poses a significant risk in PPP projects, varies in intensity and frequency across different sectors (Chan et al., 2015). For example, transportation projects often face a higher risk due to potential competitive initiatives by the government, especially when demand is increasing. By contrast, sectors like water, electricity, or natural gas utilities, characterized by regional monopolies, generally experience lower competition risks. Furthermore, some scholars argue that PPP projects in the water utilities sector tend to be more complex and require greater specialized expertise, making them less susceptible to predatory government actions (Wang et al., 2018, p. 601). They note that water utilities exhibit a higher level of "irreplaceability," which fosters "a sense of investment security for private investors" (Wang et al., 2018, p. 601). Thus, government opportunism is less severe in water utilities projects.

The significance of these factors can be illustrated through an examination of PPP projects that have encountered disputes. To identify relevant cases, I employed the China Academic Journals and the China Core Newspapers Database provided by CNKI, conducting extensive searches encompassing media and journal reports. A total of sixteen projects were identified, and their relevant information, such as the ownership structures, duration, sector, and level of the contracting government, is presented in Table 4.1 of the Appendix (Liu et al., 2016).

These cases exhibit several notable characteristics. The majority of PPP projects that triggered disputes exhibited a protracted duration, averaging over twenty-five years. Many of these projects were initiated during China's early developmental phase. For instance, the Hangzhou Bay Cross-Sea Bridge, approved in 2002 and completed in 2008, encountered direct competition in 2013 with the construction of the Jiashao Bridge. As projects continue over an extended period, unforeseen circumstances may arise. The longer the project persists, the greater the potential for unexpected changes and government's opportunistic behavior.

Out of the sixteen projects examined, six were related to water utilities, six were in the transportation sector, and four were associated with electricity utilities, indicating a higher prevalence of PPP projects in these sectors. Notably, all six PPP projects in the water utilities sector that experienced disputes and renegotiations ultimately had their ownership interests repurchased, either by the government or by other private investors. This trend can be attributed to the substantial bargaining power held by private water utilities, as they can threaten to cease services to the public. In contrast, investors in numerous transportation projects suffered more significant losses, as the government established competing projects that adversely impacted their revenue streams. An illustrative instance is Fujian Xinyuan Minjiang No.4 Bridge project, which initially enjoyed government guarantees of exclusivity for a specified period. However, subsequent approval of a competing project by the government led to direct competition, resulting in substantial revenue reductions (Jiang, 2016).

Beyond issues of opportunism, PPP projects in China may face other challenges. Another major concern is that relevant government officials may not serve the public interest and might even collude with the project company to pursue their own interests at the expense of the public (Solomon and Zaring, 2018). To address this concern, the Ministry of Finance has developed a platform on which all PPP contracts must be uploaded and subject to public scrutiny. Thus, although some scholars worry that contracting out public services may negatively affect the quality due to the opaque nature of administrative contracts (Solomon and Zaring, 2018), the PPP contracts in China are more transparent than ordinary contracts entered into between nongovernmental parties. This chapter focuses mainly on the problems of opportunism, which are pivotal for the success of a PPP market.

III. The Enforcement of Public-Private Partnership Contracts

The above analysis suggests that government opportunism is a major challenge for PPP projects. This section considers whether the existing legal institutions can enforce the PPP contracts and protect investors from opportunism in practice.

While government opportunism is a concern globally in PPP projects (Levy and Spiller, 1994; Che and Qian, 1998; Trebilcock and Iacobucci, 2003), it is particularly acute in China. Current studies have already shown that courts in China tend to favor the "haves" over the "have-nots" and are often influenced by politically powerful parties (He and Su, 2013). It is thus possible that courts may tend to rule in favor of the government over the contracting parties.

The concern of government opportunism further intensifies if one considers the treatment of PPP contracts under Chinese law, which confers significant power on the government. Under Chinese law, a PPP contract is usually referred to as a concession contract (*texu jingying xieyi*) (Yu, 2017), which belongs to the category of "administrative contract" (*xingzheng xieyi*) in China. These contracts are similar to ordinary civil contracts (*minshi hetong*) with some special characteristics. Currently, the Chinese Administrative Litigation Law amended in 2014 allows private contracting parties to an administrative contract to bring an administrative lawsuit against the contracting government. The SPC issued the "*Interpretation on Several Issues Concerning the Application of the Administrative Litigation Law*" in 2015 (hereinafter referred to as the *2015 SPC Interpretation*). Article 15 of this document allows the government to make unilateral amendments or terminate the administrative contract provide, with the condition of providing compensation to the counterparty of the agreement. This provision was later replaced by Article 16 of the "*Provisions of the Supreme People's Court on Several Issues Concerning the Trial of Administrative Agreement Cases*" promulgated in 2019 (hereinafter referred to as the *2019 SPC Interpretation*), which stipulates the same rule. Theoretically, the government's power to terminate the administrative contract can be viewed as a form of taking, although the right to be expropriated is a contract right rather than a property right. Since the government can avoid default after it unilaterally terminates the contract and hence would not be liable for damages, the rights of the project company under the PPP contract can be considered weaker than those under an ordinary contract. In accordance with the *Civil Code of China*, which governs ordinary contracts, if one party defaults under an ordinary contract, it would be liable for expectation interests, which include the benefits it would have obtained had the contract been performed.

This does not imply that the interests of the contracting party are entirely unprotected because the government can only exercise such power for the public interest and with compensation. While the level of compensation is theoretically lower than contract damages, the extent to which courts can regulate the government's decision remains uncertain. While parties can agree on a higher compensation, it cannot exceed the losses incurred by the affected party. Whether these losses include the expected interests remains unclear.

To examine how well courts offer judicial protection against the termination of administrative contracts, this chapter presents an empirical study using the data from the PKU law database. It first collects cases where the government amended or terminated the administrative contracts by searching for cases in which the court cited Paragraph Three of Article 15 of the *2015 SPC Interpretation* and Paragraph One of Article 16 of the *2019 SPC Interpretation* by May 31, 2021. After filtering out irrelevant cases, a total of forty-one cases related to concession contracts were found. It should be noted that the above forty-one cases do not represent the entirety of disputes arising from PPP projects. In practice, some courts apply contract law to resolve disputes related to PPP projects instead of citing the *2015 SPC Interpretation* or the *2019 SPC Interpretation*. These cases are not included in the above dataset. This chapter further conducts a search for cases in which the court mentioned "PPP" and "concession contracts" and finds over 300 cases. Some of these cases involve breaches by either the government or the PPP project company. This chapter concentrates on analyzing the implementation of the *2015 SPC Interpretation* and *2019 SPC Interpretation* as they are cited in cases where the government wields the most unrestrained power. By scrutinizing these rules, the potential for government opportunism can be demonstrated.

Table 4.2 of the Appendix presents the outcomes of cases involving concession contracts. In only six cases (15 percent), the court mandated that the government continue performing the contracts. In 20 cases (49 percent), the government was allowed to terminate the contract provided it compensated the contracting party. In nine cases (22 percent), the court held that the government could modify or terminate the contract without compensation. In five cases (12 percent), the court decided that the government could modify or terminate the contract and did not mention whether the government should compensate the private enterprise. In one case, the concession contract was deemed void. The outcomes of cases involving concession contracts differ significantly from those involving compensation contracts. One of the reasons is that the performance of many concession contracts is believed to affect the public interest. Consequently, the government needs to adjust the contract or terminate the project when new circumstances arise. By contrast, many compensation contracts have relatively short terms, and the government was more likely to act opportunistically when it attempted to terminate the contract. Only in a few cases involving PPP projects did the court require the government to continue to perform the concession contract.

In addition, while the above analysis focuses on a small number of cases where the government terminated the PPP contracts compared to the total number of projects, government opportunism is still likely a major challenge for PPP projects in practice. Currently, many projects are in their incipient stage and may be subject to government opportunism later, perhaps during an economic downturn. In addition, even if few projects have been terminated, the government could have employed its power to terminate the contract as a bargaining chip to compel the project company to obey various government orders. Many practitioners regard government intervention as the most significant risk in PPP projects (Qin et al., 2020; Cheung and Chan, 2011).

Certainly, a higher proportion of cases where the court supported the governments' attempt to amend or terminate administrative contracts do not necessarily indicate weak protection for the rights of the contracting party. It is thus necessary to examine the circumstances under which courts allowed governments to terminate administrative contracts. In practice, courts allow governments to amend or terminate administrative contracts for a variety of reasons.

First, a change in legal rules or regulations might lead to the closure of a project. For example, in *Shijiazhuang Prefecture Natural Resources* and *Planning Bureau v. Pingshan County Hengxin Guishichang*, the administrative contract that granted a firm the license to extract minerals was terminated because of a national initiative to address air pollution.

Second, the court may also allow the government to terminate an administrative contract when the firm fails to meet the local demand.

For example, in *Changyang Huoshaoping Water Co. Ltd. v. Changyang Tujiazu Autonomous County People's Government*, a firm obtained the license to supply water to a local township. The township government believed that with the local development, the firm failed to meet the demand and contracted with another firm for water supply. The court allowed for the termination, believing that doing so was in the public interest.

Third, the government can decide to construct a new project for the public interest in the region where a prior project is situated. For example, in *Sanya Honghao Real Estate Development Co. Ltd v. Anding County National Land Resources Bureau*, the court also allowed the government to terminate an administrative contract because they needed to construct a new water reserve in a region where the sand extraction project was situated.

Judicial protection against the termination of PPP contracts in China is relatively weak compared with other states. For example, in the United States, if the government adjusts its policies in a way that leads to violation of its contractual commitments, the decision will be subject to court review. Courts in the United States developed the doctrines of sovereign act defense and unmistakability defense in the nineteenth century. These doctrines typically shielded the government from liability for breach of contract unless it has made a promise to be bound "in unmistakable terms" (Freeman, 2000). Courts usually deferred to the decision of the government under these doctrines (Freeman, 2000). However, in the case of *United States v. Winstar Corp.*, the Supreme Court narrowed the scope of these two doctrines, stating that the government could be held liable for breach of contract even if its actions were justified by the public-oriented reasons (Freeman, 2000). China's approach, which allows the government to terminate the concession contract under a wide variety of circumstances, generally places PPP project company at a greater risk of opportunism compared to the United States.

While the courts impose minimal restriction on the government when it attempts to terminate the contract, there remains a question about whether the court would offer fair compensation as adequate protection. It is thus necessary to further examine the level of compensation offered by courts. Among these eighteen cases involving concession contracts where the government must compensate the contracting party, the compensation level also differs significantly.

A further empirical study is conducted to examine the level of compensation offered in these cases. Table 4.3 of the Appendix presents the statistics. In ten out of the eighteen cases (56 percent), the court awarded an amount that was less than the value of the investment or decided that the government had the discretion to set the compensation amount. In two cases (11 percent), the court set the compensation amount at the same value as the investment. Only in six cases (33 percent) did the court set the compensation at the market value of the firm or at least considered some of the firm's profits in the calculation. These statistics suggest that investors cannot easily recover their investment, let alone obtain profits.

It should be noted that many cases in China are undisclosed (Liebman et al., 2023). However, the disclosed cases still provide meaningful information. It is very likely that courts have incentives not to disclose cases where political pressure influenced their decisions. Given that local governments are usually the politically powerful parties in these disputes, the results of the undisclosed cases are more likely to favor the local governments. Hence, in undisclosed cases, courts may offer even lower compensation to private investors. The results shown in this chapter offer an optimistic estimate of compensation for investors in PPP projects.

IV. State Ownership of Public-Private Partnership Projects

The above analysis shows that Chinese courts usually do not substantively review the government's decision to terminate administrative contracts, offering relatively weak protection. This part conducts a micro-examination of PPP projects to illustrate how the concern of opportunism impacts the level of state ownership in the PPP projects.

Given the inadequate protection for investors, privatization could face challenges, as potential investors may be hesitant to invest. This chapter proposes a hypothesis that privatization attempts are likely to fail, leading to significant state ownership in projects where government opportunism is a prominent concern. In other words, state ownership arises as a consequence of insufficient investment from private investors, rather than it being solely the government's intentional choice. To be more precise, state ownership can manifest in two forms: partial privatization and public-public partnerships.

A first possible approach to address government opportunism is partial privatization – the contracting government can hold a proportion of shares in the PPP project company (Grossman et al., 1986, pp. 691–719; Hart & Moore, 1990, pp. 1119–1158). This would reduce the chance of opportunistic government behavior because the government would also bear investment losses if the project company fails to achieve expected investment return. The contracting government would likely only amend or terminate the contract, exercise its control rights, or build a competitive project only if the increase in public interests outweighs at least some of the losses incurred by the project company (Yi and Li, 2023).

Nevertheless, this arrangement places a fiscal burden on the contracting government and results in partial privatization, rather than complete privatization, of the projects. Local governments, constrained by tight budgets and aiming to maximize resource utilization for GDP growth, would be reluctant to invest in shares of the PPP project company unless doing so would attract investment Another potential concern is that the contracting government may seek to acquire information by holding a significant number of shares and appointing directors to the project company's board. However, in practice, the contracting government is usually the minority shareholder and hence lacks effective control over the appointment of directors or the managers of the project company. In addition, considering that the government can employ alternative methods, such as negotiating contractual rights of inspection, this concern is unlikely to be the primary motive behind the government's shareholding. Thus, the contracting government would probably not agree to invest unless it is necessary to attract investment. Partially privatized PPP projects where the contracting government holds a large proportion can be regarded as less successful compared to fully privatized ones.

State ownership of investors of PPP projects may also address the concern of government opportunism. In China's PPP market, many investors are themselves state-owned. These projects are thus better called "public-public partnerships." If the investors themselves are SOEs, they may enjoy stronger property protection from local governments (Che and Qian, 1998, pp. 467, 471; Clarke, 2003). For example, a provincial state-owned company could leverage its position to compel compliance from prefecture-level (*shi ji*) governments. Practitioners in the PPP market generally acknowledge that SOEs are adept at handling disputes with local governments (Huang and Ma, 2018). This does not discount the political sway private firms may wield. As scholars have noted, private firms may also capture the government (Milhaupt and Zheng, 2014). However, the government may act opportunistically after the investment has been made, and the ability of private firms to influence the government is likely to be more limited. As a result, when bidding for the PPP project, these investors may accept a lower rate of return for their investment and hence gain a competitive advantage over private investors.

One of the major purposes of contracting out public services to PPP project company is to enhance efficiency – private firms driven by profit motives can lower the costs of providing goods or services traditionally supplied by the government. SOEs, on the other hand, have historically grappled with inefficiencies and higher operational costs due to weaker profit incentives and the "soft budget constraint" problem. In projects where concerns about government opportunism are prominent, SOEs may play a more significant role as they possess the capacity to restrict government actions. However, their involvement tends to be less prominent in projects with a lower risk of opportunism as their management inefficiencies make them less competitive.

The theory that state ownership mitigates government opportunism is supported by the scarcity of legal disputes involving SOEs. Out of the sixteen projects examined from newspapers and journals, only one was exclusively developed by SOEs, whereas fifteen (94 percent) involved private investment. Additionally, eleven projects were solely developed with private investment, suggesting that projects with SOE investors are less prone to disputes, or that SOEs may have informal channels for resolving conflicts with the government, which remain undisclosed to the public.

In addition, among the PPP projects that triggered legal disputes, none involved SOEs. Table 4.4 illustrates the characteristics of twenty-two PPP projects extracted from the forty-one cases discussed above where the government terminated or amended PPP contracts. The number of projects is smaller than the number of cases because the same project might have given rise to multiple judicial decisions. All investors involved in these cases are private investors, with no involvement of SOEs in any lawsuits. Several factors may contribute to this observation. SOEs may prefer to resolve disputes with the contracting governments through informal means. They may also possess informal influence over the contracting government, making them less susceptible to government opportunism.

V. Judicial Reform and Privatization: An Empirical Study

A. *Hypothesis*

This chapter hypothesizes that the lack of powerful legal institutions plays a significant role in hindering the privatization of PPP projects. While private enterprises generally exhibit better performance, they also face an elevated risk of government expropriation. Investment in infrastructure is vulnerable to such expropriation for several reasons.

Firstly, these projects often involve substantial long-term fixed investments, making them especially susceptible to government opportunism. Secondly, the PPP contracts may not be strictly enforced because the government stands as one of the contracting parties and may influence the decisions of the courts (He and Su, 2013). Chinese local courts often face pressure to align their rulings with governmental objectives. This dynamic can result in courts permitting the government to terminate PPP contracts, often providing only modest compensation to private investors. In such scenarios, private investors could be deterred from investing altogether or might opt to invest only under terms that sufficiently offset the risks linked to government opportunism.

Considering the substantial discretionary powers vested in the court, a more powerful judicial system plays a crucial role in offering protection to the PPP investors. When courts maintain independence from local government influence, they are better positioned to fairly enforce PPP contracts and grant more substantial compensation to the project company when the contracts are terminated. This could promote private investments and reduce the government's stake in the PPP project company. This theory suggests that enhanced judicial power could promote privatization by boosting investors' confidence.

China's judicial reform provides an opportunity to investigate how judicial enhanced judicial power impacts the privatization process. The initiative emerged from the Third Plenary Session of the 18th Central Committee of the CPC in 2013, which introduced a judicial reform aimed at centralizing the administration of personnel and funding for courts below the provincial level. Prior to this reform, the financial resources and staffing decisions of local courts were subject to the influence of local governments. Notably, local governments held considerable sway over personnel decisions within local courts, including the appointment of the president of the court. The budget of local courts, including the salaries of the judges and clerks, also needs to be approved by the local governments. Local courts thus tend to follow the orders of local governments in the adjudication of disputes.

The judicial reform centralizes all decisions related to personnel changes and budget matters at the provincial level. The intention behind it was to sever the influence exerted by local governments over the courts and strengthen their power (Chen, 2014; Zhang and Ginsburg, 2019, p. 334). The head of the Office of the Leading Group for Central Judicial System Reform explicitly stated that "the unified management of personnel and assets of courts and procuratorates below the provincial level is to eliminate improper local interference" (Yang, 2014). China's court system is currently structured across four tiers: SPC, High People's Courts at the provincial level, Intermediate People's Courts at the prefectural level, and Basic People's Courts at the township level. As a result of this reform, the degree of control wielded by both prefectural and township governments over Intermediate People's Courts and Basic People's Courts would experience a notable reduction. Currently, different scholars hold different opinions as to the actual effects of the reform. Chen (2014) and Zhao and Zhang (2022) note that such a reform has a significant impact on the independence of local courts in China. However, Wang argues that the implementation of the reform was limited in some regions and faced difficulties (Wang, 2019, p. 551), providing interview data indicating that the successes of the judicial reform are inconsistent across different areas (Wang, 2021). Nevertheless, the empirical findings suggest that courts which have adopted the judicial reform are more likely to exhibit an increased level of judicial power compared to those that have not. The reform still made some progress toward developing courts independent from local governments (Wang, 2019, p. 550).

In the context of PPP disputes, when a contracting government decides to terminate or breach a PPP contract, the PPP project company can initiate legal proceedings against the contracting government. According to Chinese law, the trial would typically take place within the jurisdiction of the defendant government. For instance, consider a scenario where the environment bureau of a township-level government engages in a PPP contract aimed at enhancing local environmental conditions. The Court of First Instance would usually be the Basic People's Court situated within the township, unless the case was considered significant and complicated. Alternatively, if a government department at the prefectural level is a party to the PPP contract, the case would be heard by the Intermediate People's Court located in the prefectural jurisdiction.

Commencing in 2014, the reform was initially piloted in six provinces/municipalities: Jilin, Qinghai, Hubei, Shanghai, Guangdong, and Hainan. These areas were thoughtfully chosen to encompass the eastern, western, southern, northern, and central parts of China, thereby accounting for the various social and economic distinctions across the nation (Peng, 2014). Each province or municipality was granted the flexibility to conduct pilot experiments within specific prefectures or townships before scaling the reform across the entire province. Subsequently, the reform was extended to other provinces. Table 4.5 of the Appendix presents the number of provinces that had completed the judicial reform at the beginning of each year. In a recent study utilizing a difference-in-difference approach, it was discovered that the judicial reform had a significant positive impact on the success rate of plaintiffs in administrative lawsuits against government authorities (Zhao and Zhang, 2022). This judicial reform can be viewed as an exogenous factor that has affected various courts, making it suitable for causal impact analysis (Li, 2022; Zhao and Zhang, 2022). However, existing research has not explored how this judicial reform might influence the privatization process.

The judicial reform in China offers an opportunity to study how enhanced judicial power affects privatization. The theoretical prediction is that in regions where the judicial reform has been implemented, private investors are likely to hold a larger proportion of shares in PPP project companies, leading to a decrease in the proportion of shares held by SOEs and governmental entities. The validity of this theory remains uncertain from an a priori perspective. As discussed earlier, current studies have mainly focused on the political and political economy theories in explaining the prevalence of SOEs. According to these theories, enhanced judicial power would not affect the prevalence of SOEs or the level of private investment. Furthermore, it remains unclear to what extent the law is important in curbing the opportunistic behavior of the government. Some may argue against the "legal-centric view," suggesting that private investors might rely on informal mechanisms like reputation or long-standing personal relationships to mitigate the government's opportunistic behavior and protect their investment. This concept has been referred to as "finance without law" or "order without law" by certain scholars (Macaulay, 1963; Ellickson, 1991; Pistor and Xu, 2005; Qiao, 2023b).

B. *Model Specification and Variable Definitions*

The estimated equation in this empirical study takes the following form:

$$\begin{aligned}
&\boldsymbol{Gov_share_i(Private_share_i)}\\
&= \begin{aligned}[t]&\boldsymbol{\beta * Reform_{j,k} + Duration_i + Investment_size_i}\\
&\boldsymbol{+ Gov_level_i + Revenue_mode_i + Deal_process_i}\\
&\boldsymbol{+ Sector_i + GDP_per_capita_k}\\
&\boldsymbol{+ Net_Fiscal_balance_k + \theta_j + \lambda_p + \epsilon_i}\end{aligned}
\end{aligned}$$

Table 4.6 of the Appendix presents the definition of the variables. The dependent variables under consideration include $\boldsymbol{Gov\_share_i}$, representing the combined share proportion held by governments or SOEs in PPP project company *i*, and ***Private_share***$_i$, denoting the combined share proportion owned by private investors. The primary independent variable of interest is ***Reform***$_{j,k}$, which takes a value of 1 if the court at prefecture *j* of the PPP project in prefecture *k* where project *i* was initiated had undergone reform at the time of the project, and zero otherwise.

Several control variables are introduced. ***Duration***$_i$ refers to the length of project *i*. This variable may affect the dependent variables because projects with a longer duration may be subject to heightened risk of opportunism. ***Investment_size***$_i$ quantifies the magnitude of the total investment in project *i*. It may also affect the dependent variables because SOEs may have an advantage in obtaining financing, especially in large projects. ***Gov_level***$_i$ refers to the level of the government initiating the PPP project. It takes the value of 3 if it is at the provincial level, 2 if it is at the prefectural level, and 1 if it is at the township level.

Revenue_mode$_i$ categorizes each observation based on the specific revenue mode it falls under. Each PPP project may adopt one of three distinct revenue modes. The project's funding structure can involve payments originating from the public consumers, the government, or a combination of both consumer payments and government subsidies. A set of three dummy variables is utilized to represent the ***Revenue_mode*** variable. When an observation is associated with a particular revenue mode, the corresponding dummy variable takes the value of 1; otherwise, it takes the value of zero.

Deal_process$_i$ consists of dummy variables related to the deal-making process. The PPP projects can take five different deal-making processes. Most PPP projects underwent an *open bidding* process. In some cases, projects followed an *invitation-only bidding* process, wherein the government selects more than three qualified investors from a preapproved list to bid on the project. *Competitive negotiation* involves the government directly inviting more than three investors to engage in negotiations and subsequently make a selection. *Competitive consultation* entails initial negotiations with potential bidders regarding the terms, followed by the government's decision. Lastly, the deal-making process can also involve *single-source procurement*, typically employed when circumstances hinder the feasibility of a bidding process. The dummy variable takes a value of 1 when a specific deal-making process is employed and zero otherwise.

Sector$_i$ includes dummy variables representing each sector. The sector classification utilized in this research aligns with the categorization established by the PPP center under the Ministry of Finance. This classification system divides all PPP projects into nineteen broad categories. Additionally, the study includes the control variable ***GDP_per_capita***$_i$, representing the GDP per capita of the specific prefecture where project i is located in the year of the project initiation, to account for regional economic development. The variable ***Net_fiscal_balance***$_i$ is derived by subtracting fiscal expenses from fiscal revenues for the prefectural government of project i's initiation in the corresponding year. $\boldsymbol{\Theta}_j$ are year-fixed effects and $\boldsymbol{\lambda}_p$ accounts for the province-fixed effects.

C. Data

The data utilized in this study are sourced from the China Public-Private Partnership Center, which operates under the Ministry of Finance. Chinese law mandates that comprehensive details of PPP projects be publicly disclosed. By the end of 2020, the China Public-Private Partnership Center contained the information of 4,024 PPP project companies. For each project company, the Tianyancha platform, which aggregates enterprise data from China's National Enterprise Credit Information Publication System, is used to identify shareholder names, their respective share proportions, and the ultimate controller (government or private investor). This chapter treats an investor ultimately controlled by a central or local government authority as state-owned and those ultimately controlled by a private business entity or individual as privately owned. Sometimes the ultimate controller of the investor is difficult to be categorized as a government or a private investor. Thus, the sum of ***Gov_share*** and ***Private_share*** sometimes does not equal to one. Due to some missing information about the project companies, the empirical study ultimately focuses on 3,511 PPP project companies.

Table 4.7 displays the various revenue modes adopted by the projects. In Table 4.8, an overview of the deal-making processes utilized is provided. Table 4.9 offers a detailed description of project distribution across various sectors. Tables 4.10 and 4.11 present the distribution of projects across time and provinces/municipalities. The numbers of projects in 2019 and 2020 are relatively small because, by the end of 2020, most of these projects had not entered the execution stage and, and hence, the project companies had not been established. Table 4.12 presents the summary statistics. On average, governments and SOEs own 55 percent of the shares of PPP project companies, while private investors hold 42 percent. The sum of the two figures is below 100 percent because the ultimate controllers of some investors are difficult to identify.

D. Results

The results are presented in Table 4.13. The statistical significance of the coefficients of ***Reform*** persists regardless of the inclusion of control variables. These coefficients maintain their statistical significance even when employing cluster standard errors at either the provincial or the prefectural level. On average, these findings indicate the implementation of the judicial reform resulted in a reduction of approximately 8 percent in the government's ownership stake in the project company. They thus suggest that enhanced judicial power leads to an increase in the private investors' proportion of shares.

The coefficients of ***Gov_level*** are also positive and statistically significant, which suggests that the proportion of shares held by SOEs is higher in PPP projects initiated by a higher-level government. This might be attributed to the notion that the courts generally possess a comparatively lesser ability to curb opportunistic behavior demonstrated by higher-level governmental entities. To illustrate, the decisions of a High People's Court may not restrain the opportunistic behavior of the provincial government because the court is subject to the government's control. In contrast, the opportunistic behavior of a department within a prefectural government would face more stringent restraints imposed by the court. While the Intermediate People's Court might encounter some influence from the prefectural government, its decisions would be subject to review by the High People's Court during the second-instance trial. This review process would be more difficult for the prefectural government to sway.

Table 4.14 displays the regression outcomes with ***Private_share*** as the dependent variable. As previously noted, the identification of ultimate controllers for certain investors can be difficult, leading to slight variations in the coefficients of the independent variables compared to those showcased in Table 4.13. Nevertheless, the findings persist in their similarity, thereby indicating that judicial reform continues to influence the extent of privatization in PPP projects.

E. Robustness Checks

To test the robustness of the findings, this chapter further engages in several regression analyses. First, instead of using the proportion of shares held by SOEs and the government, it is possible to conduct a logistic regression analysis using a dependent variable ***SOE***, which denotes 1 if at least one of the investors is an SOE or a government authority and zero if all investors are private. Column 1 of Table 4.15 presents the outcome. The coefficient of ***Reform*** remains statistically significant and negative after controlling for other control variables and using clustered standard errors at the prefectural level. This result suggests that judicial reform reduces the likelihood that SOEs being investors in PPP projects.

One potential concern regarding the identification strategy in this chapter is the nonrandom selection of courts for implementing the judicial reform. However, this concern would only impact the conclusion if the reasons behind selecting certain regions for the reform systematically biased the results. One possible scenario is that the reform triggered broader economic changes that increased the returns of PPP projects, which might raise the proportion of private investments. Nonetheless, this scenario seems unlikely, given that the reform exclusively targets the judicial system and has not significantly influenced the operation of the government or the PPP market directly.

Another scenario that might introduce bias into the findings is the possibility that increased levels of private investment in PPP projects could have spurred the local regions to implement the reform. This situation represents a classic case of "reverse causality." To address this concern, a second robustness check is conducted to investigate the effects of the judicial reform on PPP projects initiated by different levels of government. If the hypothesis that increasing private investments in PPP projects can drive legal reforms holds true, the judicial reform is likely to have a greater impact at the township level. When a department of the township-level government signs a PPP contract and breaches it, the PPP project company could sue the government authority at the Basic People's Court at the township level. If the plaintiff is dissatisfied with the court's decision, it could appeal to the Intermediate People's Court at the prefectural level. The judicial reform would affect both the courts of first instance (the Basic People's Court) and the second instance (the Intermediate People's Court). By contrast, investors of a PPP project initiated by a department of the prefectural government can initiate a lawsuit at the Intermediate People's Court and appeal to the High People's Court. The judicial reform only affects the Intermediate People's Court. Hence, the judicial reform would have less of an impact on PPP projects at the prefectural level than at the township level.

However, if we were to consider the possibility of reversed causality – that is, private investments in PPP projects prompting judicial reforms – we would not necessarily observe the same effects. In this case, there is no inherent reason why the increased private investment in PPP projects would be more evident at the township level than at the intermediate court level.

To test this hypothesis, an interaction term, ***Reform**Gov_level***, has been introduced. The findings are displayed in Column 2 of Table 4.15. The coefficient of ***Reform*** retains its negative sign when the dependent variable is ***Gov_share*** and achieves a notable level of statistical significance at the 1 percent threshold. Moreover, the interaction term's coefficient exhibits a positive sign and demonstrates statistical significance at the 1 percent level. This suggests that as the government level increases, the magnitude of the negative impact associated with the judicial reform experiences a reduction, which is consistent with the theoretical prediction presented above.

An additional consideration involves the potential impact of corruption on the bidding process in certain regions, which could consequently influence bid outcomes. To address this potential effect, another variable, labeled as ***Not_corrupt***, is introduced. The scores for this variable are obtained from the National Academy of Development and Strategy at Renmin University of China (NADS). These scores, available since 2017, are derived from data provided by market participants and Baidu, a prominent online search engine in China. A higher value for this variable indicates a lower likelihood of corruption among government officials. The data is available at the prefectural level, though there are instances where certain prefectures lack a corresponding score. Notably, these scores have been assigned since 2017. In cases where projects were initiated before 2017, the data from 2017 is utilized as a substitute. Column 3 of Table 4.15 presents the results. The coefficient of ***Not_corrupt*** is negative, indicating that in regions where the government officials are less likely to be corrupt, SOEs hold a smaller proportion of shares of PPP projects. The coefficient of ***Reform*** remains statistically significant, suggesting that even after taking into account the likelihood of the corruption in the bidding process, the results persist.

Furthermore, a placebo test was conducted in which the timing of judicial reforms in each region was intentionally shifted backward by one year. The results are presented in Column 4 of Table 4.15. The coefficient of ***Reform*** becomes insignificant. The lack of significant effects on investment subsequent to this modified judicial reform timeline signifies that the initial study findings were not likely to be driven by mere coincidence.

Another potential omitted variable is the level of private investments in these different regions. Local governments and courts in regions selected for judicial reform may possess a greater capacity to promote private investments or are simply more keen on attracting private investment. To address these concerns, this study incorporates a set of prefecture-level control variables aimed at controlling for changes in both direct equity investments and indirect investments through the banking system. These control variables, together with GDP per capita and net fiscal balance, control for the other changes in the economic environment associated with the judicial reform at the prefectural level.

Column 5 of Table 4.15 introduces the results of the regression analysis after including two variables that account for prefecture-level direct investments, the monthly fixed-asset investments and the number of firms in each year for each prefecture. The coefficient for ***Gov_share*** becomes highly statistically significant and negative. Furthermore, in Column 6 of Table 4.15, the analysis incorporates two additional variables that control for prefecture-level indirect investments, including the monthly loans generated by commercial banks and monthly deposits in each prefecture. Since the data for certain prefectures are missing, the total sample size is reduced. However, the regression results remain consistent with those previously observed, which suggests that after controlling for the potential impacts of the reform on the overall investment environment, there was still a significant change in the ownership structure of PPP projects.

Another concern pertains to the fact that the dependent variables mentioned above only measure the proportion of shares held by the government and private investors in PPP projects, without considering the overall investments made by different parties in a given region. In theory, it is plausible that private investors might increase their investment in smaller projects while reducing their investment in larger ones. This chapter addresses this concern by aggregating the amount of equity investment made by private investors at the prefectural level. The dependent variable is replaced by ***Agg_Gov_share***, which represents the ratio of aggregate equity investments made by governments to the aggregate equity investments made by all investors (public and private) in a prefecture. This empirical design reduces the total sample size because there are only over two hundred prefectures. Table 4.16 presents the results, which indicate that the coefficient of the ***Reform*** variable is negative and statistically significant when controlling for monthly fixed-asset investment and the number of firms in the prefecture. When controlling for the amount of loans and deposits at the prefectural level, the sample size becomes even smaller because of the missing data with regard to these two variables. However, the coefficient of ***Reform*** remains marginally statistically significant. These findings suggest that the reform led to a general reduction in the proportion of the aggregate government investment in the PPP market.

Finally, it should be noted that province-fixed effects are used in the above studies. In an unpublished regression, I also employ prefecture-fixed effects. The coefficient for ***Reform*** remains negative, although it is not statistically significant. Province fixed effects are employed because the primary variation in judicial reform is at the provincial level, and there is significant uniformity within most provinces regarding policy adoption and its impact.

VI. Discussions and Implications

This chapter shows that the legal protection for private investors in China's PPP market remains relatively weak. Under China's context, it is very unlikely that courts would strictly enforce a contract between the government and an enterprise if the government truly wants to act opportunistically. The contracting government can unilaterally terminate the PPP contract and offer low compensation for the affected parties. As a result, private investors are likely to demand the contracting government to hold a proportion of shares before they participate in the PPP project. They would also demand a higher rate of return to compensate for the risk of opportunism. SOEs thus have a comparative advantage in PPP projects due to their ability to influence the contracting government. This chapter presents evidence that the level of state ownership in different PPP projects correlates with the possibility of government opportunism. Judicial reform that enhances power of the courts and alleviates the concern of government opportunism can promote privatization. Meanwhile, some evidence suggests that SOEs also incur higher ownership costs. Alternative theories, such as the political and political economy theories, cannot fully explain the pattern of state ownership in this market.

The findings of this study generate several important implications. Firstly, they suggest that judicial reform could play an important role in facilitating the privatization of infrastructure. It indicates that bolstering judicial power has the potential to diminish the influence of SOEs and facilitate a gradual process of privatization within competitive markets.

Secondly, it should also be noted that enhancing judicial power carries significant social costs. The judicial reforms in China, aimed at diminishing local government influence over local courts, encounter numerous challenges. The current reform strategy involves centralizing control over the financial and personnel resources of local courts. Rather than granting autonomy to local courts, this strategy shifts oversight from local to higher-level governments. This reflects a hesitancy to fully empower courts, possibly due to fears of judicial corruption. Moreover, this centralized approach can face challenges when higher-level governments lack intimate knowledge of local court needs and operations (Wang, 2021). The necessary collaboration between local governments and courts for many governmental functions further complicates this approach (Wang, 2021). Additionally, this reform can disrupt established interests, particularly in wealthier areas where courts have more specialized judges. Centralizing resources can adversely affect these interests, which are difficult to compensate (Wang, 2021). Consequently, the reform faces resistance and could lead to instability. Considering the challenges of promoting judicial power at lower levels, advancing it at higher levels becomes even more daunting. While these costs are not insurmountable, it is necessary to recognize that privatization of SOEs and promotion of private enterprises essentially involves developing legal institutions that can delineate the boundaries between public power and private property. Therefore, from a public policy perspective, the decision to promote privatization through judicial reform hinges on weighing the reform costs against the potential benefits of reducing SOE dominance in the market.

Thirdly, this analysis contributes to the debate on privatization. It exploits a judicial reform in China to establish a causal relationship between law and privatization. At present, there is a notable scarcity of direct empirical evidence demonstrating the impact of law on privatization. This chapter provides evidence that exogenous variations in the organization of the judicial system, influencing the degree of independence of local courts, have an impact on the level of privatization. It lends additional support to the incremental reform approach by showing that without strong institutions, the extent of privatization would be limited even where the government intends to privatize and introduce private investment. If China could further develop powerful and competent courts, the regulatory costs between private firms and the governments might be reduced and governments may be able to fully privatize more infrastructure projects. Before strong legal institutions could be developed, this chapter suggests that ensuring a level playing field for SOEs and private firms, rather than a full privatization approach is more appropriate for developing the PPP market.

Fourthly, this chapter presents a nuanced view of the role of law in promoting private enterprises and economic development. The conventional wisdom of law and development suggests that strong property protection and contract enforcement promote private investment and contribute to economic development (Trubek, 1972a; North, 1990, p. 138; Clarke, 2003; La Porta et al., 2008; Acemoglu and Robinson, 2013, pp. 437–438). However, many have noted that China's economy developed without a strong rule of law. Clarke (2003) points out that China's economic expansion gained momentum during its initial developmental phase driven by the economic activities of TVEs. These enterprises, with their financial interests intimately intertwined with local governments, received substantial protection, thereby contributing to the nation's economic progress. Similarly, Pistor and Xu argue that "formal legal governance structures are not the exclusive way of governing newly emerging stock markets in transition economies" (Pistor and Xu, 2005, p. 185). Qiao (2022) also challenges "the necessity of law to developing impersonal and sophisticated financial markets."

In contrast, this chapter introduces a more nuanced viewpoint. On one hand, the presence of a strong rule of law might not be an immediate necessity for economic development because SOEs or enterprises with close ties to the government could leverage informal channels to safeguard their property interests and enforce the PPP contract, thus overcoming the underinvestment problem. On the other hand, a robust rule of law, particularly an impartial judicial system, indeed contributes to economic development, although the mechanism is more complex than the one portrayed in current studies. Enhancing judicial power promotes economic efficiency by mitigating the dominance of SOEs in the market. With SOEs typically incurring higher ownership costs due to their inferior management performance, heightened judicial power encourages the development of private enterprises by protecting their rights, allowing them to leverage their managerial superiority, enabling the cost-effective provision of social goods or services and thereby enhancing efficiency overall.

Last but not least, the findings presented above suggest that privatization of SOEs without first developing strong legal institutions is likely to incur certain social costs. Such a move disregards the intrinsic advantages that SOEs possess in effectively navigating government relations. If SOEs fail to bridge the market demand gap resulting from private investors' lack of confidence, PPP projects are likely to suffer from underinvestment. Thus, while the political economy theory suggests that SOEs may have adverse consequences, this chapter suggests that state ownership can at least alleviate the concern for government opportunism and address the underinvestment problem. While the analysis so far focuses primarily on the impacts of regulatory costs, it is crucial to recognize that SOEs may incur higher ownership costs. This can occur because SOE managers may not be as concerned about budget constraints and might invest in wasteful projects. This chapter does not posit that the current level of SOEs is optimal. It merely seeks to lay out the underlying forces affecting the prevalence of SOEs in this area.

Appendix

Table 4.1 *PPP projects resulting in conflicts or disputes collected from newspapers*

Project name	Initial investor	Project duration	Project sector	Government level	Outcome
Fujian Citong Bridge	Private investor and the contracting government	30 years	Transportation	Prefecture	Competing projects developed
Changchun Huijin Wastewater Treatment	Foreign investor	20 years	Water utilities	Prefecture	Government repurchased ownership
Shanghai Da Chang Water Factory	Foreign investor	20 years	Water utilities	Municipality	Government repurchased ownership
Fujian Xinyuan Minjiang No.4 Bridge	Hong Kong private investor	28 years	Transportation	Prefecture	Competing projects developed
Beijing No.10 Water Factory	Foreign investor	23 years	Water utilities	Municipality	Foreign investors transferred the ownership to domestic investors
Lianjiang Sino-France Water Supply Factory	Foreign investor	30 years	Water utilities	County	Government repurchased ownership
Sichuan Zizhong County Toll Station	Private investor	25 years	Transportation	County	Experienced losses due to lower than anticipated traffic.
Shandong Zhonghua Electricity Factory	SOEs and private investors	20 years	Electric utilities	Province	Government changed the policy of price regulation, resulting in losses of the project company

Shenyang No.8 Water Factory	Foreign investor	30 years	Water utilities	Prefecture	Government repurchased ownership
Qingdao Veola Wastewater Treatment Factory	Foreign investor	25 years	Water utilities	Prefecture	Government repurchased ownership
Xingjin Garbage Electricity Factory	Private investor		Electric utilities	County	Government constructed a road for garbarge transportation
Tianjin Shuanggang Garbage Electricity Factory	SOEs	30 years	Electric utilities	Municipality	Project generated pollution that caused public criticisms
Beijing No.4 Subway Line	SOEs and Hong Kong private investor	30 years	Transportation	Municipality	Government agreed to subsidize the project after renegotiation
Nanjing Changjiang No.3 Bridge	SOEs and private investor	30 years	Transportation	Prefecture	Project suffered losses; government extended the license for operation for five years
Wuhan Changjiang No.3 Bridge	SOEs and foreign investor	Unclear	Transportation	Prefecture	Competing projects developed
Shenzhen Shajiao B Electricity Factory	SOEs and foreign investor	10 years	Electric utilities	Prefecture	Project suffered losses; government agreed to extend license for three years

Table 4.2 *Outcome of cases involving concession contracts*

	Number	Proportion (percent)
Government should continue to perform the contract	6	15
Government can terminate/modify the contract with compensation	20	49
Government can terminate/modify the contract without compensation	9	22
Government can terminate/modify the contract (unclear whether compensation is necessary)	5	12
Contract is void or voidable	1	2
Total	41	100.0

Table 4.3 *Compensation awarded to the contracting party*

	Number	Proportion (percent)
Amount below the value of investment or to be determined by the government	10	50
The value of investment	2	10
The market value or the discounted value of some of the future profits	6	30
Compensation to be decided in the future	2	10
Total	20	100

Table 4.4 *PPP projects extracted from the judicial judgments*

Case name	Investor ownership	Project duration	Project sector	Government level
Pingxiang Guihong Environmental Protection Technology Co., Ltd. v. Pingxiang People's Government First Instance Administrative Judgment	Private		Garbage treatment	County
Jinan Hanyang Solid Waste Disposal Co., Ltd. v. Jinan People's Government and Other First Instance Administrative Judgments	Private	25	Garbage treatment	Prefecture
Changyang Huoshao Ping Water Supply Co., Ltd. v. Changyang Tujia Autonomous County Huoshao Ping Township People's Government Special Water Supply Franchise Agreement Case	Private		Water utilities	Township
Gansu Xingguo Hydropower Development Co., Ltd. and Gansu Xiahe County People's Government First Instance Administrative Ruling	Private	70	Hydropower generation	County
Haicheng People's Court First Instance Administrative Judgment on the Case of Plaintiff Xiuyan Manchu Autonomous County Jiahe Motor Vehicle Inspection Co., Ltd. Disputing the Failure of Xiuyan Manchu Autonomous County Environmental Protection Bureau and Xiuyan Manchu Autonomous County Motor Vehicle Exhaust Management Office to Fulfill the Government Franchise Agreement as Agreed	Private	10	Pollution detection	County

Table 4.4 (*cont.*)

Case name	Investor ownership	Project duration	Project sector	Government level
Xiuyan Manchu Autonomous County Jiahe Motor Vehicle Inspection Co., Ltd. v. Xiuyan Manchu Autonomous County Environmental Protection Bureau Second Instance Administrative Judgment on Administrative Agreement	Private	10	Pollution detection	County
Hanzhong Xinxing Luqiao Investment Co., Ltd. v. Hanzhong People's Government, Hanzhong Transportation Bureau, and Shaanxi Hanzhong Highway Management Bureau Second Instance Administrative Compensation Ruling	Private		Public highway	Prefecture
Yabang Group Co., Ltd. v. Longyan Housing and Urban-Rural Development Bureau and Longyan Environmental and Sanitation Management Office Other First Instance Administrative Judgment on Urban-Rural Construction Administration	Private	Until the closure of the project	Garbage treatment	Prefecture
Pan Xiaoping, Majian Town People's Government of Lanxi City, and Zhejiang Xindao Agricultural Technology Co., Ltd. and Other First Instance Administrative Judgments	Private	45	Water utilities	County
Yanshan Hecreate Environmental Protection Technology Co., Ltd. and Yanshan County People's Government First Instance Administrative Judgment	Private	30	Garbage treatment	County
Hebei Qianqiu Family Real Estate Development Co., Ltd. and Pingxiang County People's Government Other Judgments	Private		Real estate development	County
Guizhou Huazhong Long Energy Development Co., Ltd. and Guanling Buyi and Miao Autonomous County Water Affairs Bureau Second Instance Administrative Judgment	Private		Hydropower generator	County

Tonghai Tonglu Gas Co., Ltd. v. Tonghai County People's Government Urban and Rural Construction Administration: Other (Urban Construction) Second Instance Administrative Ruling	Private	30	Natural gas supply	County
Huizhou Tianju Advertising Co., Ltd. v. Huizhou Housing and Urban-Rural Development Bureau and Huizhou Urban and Rural Management and Comprehensive Law Enforcement Bureau Other Administrative Management First Instance Administrative Judgment	Private	8	Advertising infrastructure development	Prefecture
Linhai Comprehensive Administrative Law Enforcement Bureau and Zhejiang Hengtai Biotechnology Co., Ltd. First Instance Administrative Judgment on Administrative Contract	Private		Waste management and disposal	Prefecture
Jiande Liguo New Energy Technology Co., Ltd. v. Jiande City Management Bureau Civil Administration (Civil Affairs) First Instance Administrative Judgment	Private		Waste management and disposal	County
Wuzhou Xinghua Investment Co., Ltd. and Shenzhen Oufu Chuangzhan Investment Co., Ltd. First Instance Administrative Judgment	Private		Real estate development	Prefecture
Shouyang County New Idea Advertising Production Department v. Shouyang County Urban and Rural Environmental Sanitation Management Center Health Administration (Health) First Instance Administrative Judgment	Private	10	Advertising infrastructure development	County
Nanxian Natural Resources Restoration Affairs Center, Nanxian Natural Resources Bureau v. Hunan Dongfang Construction Co., Ltd., Nanxian Dongjian Drought-to-Water Project Co., Ltd. Second Instance Administrative Judgment on Illegal Change of Land Administrative Agreement	Private		Land development	County

Table 4.4 (*cont.*)

Case name	Investor ownership	Project duration	Project sector	Government level
Shandong Twenty Degrees Smart Heating Co., Ltd. and Junyuan County People's Government Industry and Commerce Administration (Industry and Commerce) Second Instance Administrative Ruling	Private		Heat supply	County
Baoting China National Petroleum and Gas Co., Ltd. v. Baoting Li and Miao Autonomous County People's Government Other Administrative Licensing and Administrative Compensation	Private	30	Natural gas supply	County
Case of China National Oil and Gas Company in Yingde v. Yingde People's Government of Guangdong Province, etc.	Private	30	Natural gas supply	County

Table 4.5 *The number of provinces/municipalities that had completed the judicial reform*

The beginning of	Number
2015	2
2016	5
2017	13
2018	20
2019	21
2020	21

Table 4.6 *Definition of variables*

Variable	Definition
Gov_share	The combined proportion of shares held by the governments and state-owned investors
Private_share	The combined proportion of shares held by private investors
Agg_Gov_share	The ratio of the aggregate equity investments made by the governments to the aggregate equity investments made by all investors in a prefecture
Reform	Whether the court in the location of the contracting government at the corresponding level has been reformed
Duration	The length of the project
Investment_size(billion RMB)	The size of the investment
Gov_level	The level of the contracting government
Revenue_mode	The mode of revenue of the PPP project company
Bidding	The type of the deal-making process
Sector	The sector of the project
GDP_per_capita	The GDP per capita of the prefecture where the contracting government is situated
Government_Budget (billion RMB)	The fiscal revenue minus fiscal expenditure of the prefectural government where the project is situated in the corresponding year
SOE	Whether at least one of the investors of the PPP project company is ultimately state-owned
Not_corrupt	The likelihood of corruption of the prefectural government where the project is situated in the corresponding year; sourced from NADS since 2017.

Table 4.7 *Revenue mode*

Revenue_mode	Frequency	Percent
Payments by public consumers	158	4.50
Payments by public consumers with government subsidy	1,872	53.32
Payments by contracting government	1,481	42.18
Total	3,511	100.00

Table 4.8 *Deal-making process*

Deal-making process	Frequency	Percent
Open bidding	2,671	76.08
Competitive consultation	736	20.96
Single-source procurement	49	1.40
Competitive negotiation	35	1.00
Invitation-only bidding	19	0.54
Unknown	1	0.03
Total	3,511	100.00

Table 4.9 *Distribution of projects across sectors*

Sector	Frequency	Percent
Prefectural Infrastructure	1,472	41.93
Transportation	521	14.84
Ecological Construction and Environmental Protection	316	9.00
Urban Development	229	6.52
Water Conservancy	180	5.13
Education	165	4.70
Tourism	96	2.73
Healthcare	93	2.65
Government Facilities	72	2.05
Affordable Housing	58	1.65
Culture	58	1.65
Technology	57	1.62
Other	45	1.28
Energy	42	1.20
Sports	33	0.94
Elderly Care	29	0.83
Agriculture	18	0.51
Forestry	17	0.48
Social Security	10	0.28
Total	3,511	100.00

Table 4.10 *Yearly distribution of the PPP projects*

Year	Frequency	Percent
2009	1	0.03
2010	1	0.03
2011	1	0.03
2012	9	0.26
2013	20	0.57
2014	89	2.53
2015	778	22.16
2016	1,175	33.47
2017	1,186	33.78
2018	211	6.01
2019	39	1.11
2020	1	0.03
Total	3,511	100.00

Table 4.11 *Distribution of the PPP projects across provinces/municipalities*

Province/Region	Number	Percent
Shandong	355	10.11
Yunnan	259	7.38
Zhejiang	234	6.66
Hebei	222	6.32
Sichuan	217	6.18
Jiangsu	217	6.18
Henan	210	5.98
Anhui	189	5.38
Hunan	182	5.18
Guangdong	149	4.24
Hubei	134	3.82
Fujian	132	3.76
Inner Mongolia	130	3.70
Xinjiang	124	3.53
Guizhou	117	3.33
Shaanxi	107	3.05
Jiangxi	83	2.36
Jilin	82	2.34
Shanxi	73	2.08
Guangxi	65	1.85
Gansu	43	1.22
Liaoning	37	1.05
Beijing	35	1.00
Heilongjiang	34	0.97
Hainan	27	0.77
Ningxia	19	0.54
Qinghai	12	0.34
Tianjin	11	0.31
Chongqing	11	0.31
Shanghai	1	0.03
Total	3,511	100.00

Table 4.12 *Summary statistics*

Variable	Obs.	Mean	Std. Dev.	Min	Max
Project-level variables					
Gov_share	3,511	0.55	0.44	0	1
Private_share	3,511	0.42	0.43	0	1
Reform	3,511	0.26	0.44	0	1
Duration	3,511	18.90	7.39	5	50
Gov_level	3,511	1.27	0.47	1	3
Investment_size (billion RMB)	3,511	1.684	3.938	0.008	88.600
Prefecture-level variables					
GDP_per_capita (ten thousand RMB)	3,070	5.70	2.88	1.12	17.30
Net_fiscal_balance (ten billion RMB)	3,083	−2.03	1.08	−10.75	1.67
Monthly fixed-asset investment (billion RMB)	2,517	132.56	132.35	0.04	940.42
Monthly loans (billion RMB)	1,529	605.56	700.88	30.61	3,947.12
Monthly deposits (billion RMB)	1,522	777.87	874.51	37.15	6,705.38
Number of firms	2,746	1,714.82	1,518.18	52.00	10,476.00

Table 4.13 *Regression results*

	(1)	(2)	(3)	(4)	(5)	(6)
Variables	***Gov_ share***	***Gov_ share***	***Gov_ share***	***Gov_ share***	***Gov_ share***	***Gov_ share***
Reform	**−0.058****	−0.050*	**−0.058****	**−0.078*****	**−0.078****	**−0.078****
	(0.027)	(0.026)	**(0.026)**	**(0.028)**	**(0.028)**	**(0.030)**
Duration		0.000	0.002	0.001	0.001	0.001
		(0.001)	(0.001)	(0.001)	(0.002)	(0.001)
Investment_size		**0.006*****	0.001	0.001	0.001	0.001
		(0.002)	(0.002)	(0.003)	(0.003)	(0.003)
Gov_level		**0.095*****	**0.075*****	**0.086*****	**0.086*****	**0.086*****
		(0.016)	**(0.016)**	**(0.018)**	**(0.025)**	**(0.022)**
Deal_process			Yes	Yes	Yes	Yes
Revenue_mode			Yes	Yes	Yes	Yes
Sector			Yes	Yes	Yes	Yes
GDP_per_capita				Yes	Yes	Yes
Net_fiscal_balance				Yes	Yes	Yes
Year-fixed effects	Yes	Yes	Yes	Yes	Yes	Yes
Province-fixed effects	Yes	Yes	Yes	Yes	Yes	Yes
Observations	3,511	3,511	3,511	3,070	3,070	3,070

Robust standard errors in parentheses in Columns 1–4, clustered standard errors at the provincial level in parentheses in Column 5, clustered standard errors at the prefectural level in parentheses in Column 6.

*** $p<0.01$, ** $p<0.05$, * $p<0.1$.

Table 4.14 *Regression results (Private_share)*

	(1)	(2)	(3)	(4)	(5)	(6)
Variables	***Private_ share***	***Private_ share***	***Private_ share***	***Private_ share***	***Private_ share***	***Private_ share***
Reform	**0.055****	0.047*	**0.055****	**0.075*****	**0.075****	**0.075****
	(0.026)	(0.026)	**(0.026)**	**(0.028)**	**(0.030)**	**(0.031)**
Duration		−0.000	−0.002	−0.002	−0.002	−0.002
		(0.001)	(0.001)	(0.001)	(0.002)	(0.001)
Investment_size		**−0.006*****	−0.002	−0.001	−0.001	−0.001
		(0.002)	(0.002)	(0.003)	(0.003)	(0.003)
Gov_level		**−0.103*****	**−0.083*****	**−0.096*****	**−0.096*****	**−0.096*****
		(0.016)	**(0.016)**	**(0.018)**	**(0.022)**	**(0.022)**
Deal_process			Yes	Yes	Yes	Yes
Revenue_mode			Yes	Yes	Yes	Yes
Sector			Yes	Yes	Yes	Yes
GDP_per_capita				Yes	Yes	Yes
Net_fiscal_balance				Yes	Yes	Yes
Year-fixed effects	Yes	Yes	Yes	Yes	Yes	Yes
Province-fixed effects	Yes	Yes	Yes	Yes	Yes	Yes
Observations	3,511	3,511	3,511	3,070	3,070	3,070

Robust standard errors in parentheses in Columns 1–4, clustered standard errors at the provincial level in parentheses in Column 5, clustered standard errors at the prefectural level in parentheses in Column 6.

*** $p<0.01$, ** $p<0.05$, * $p<0.1$.

Table 4.15 *Robustness checks*

	(1)	(2)	(3)	(4)	(5)	(6)
Variables	***SOE***	***Gov_ share***	***Gov_ share***	***Gov_ share***	***Gov_ share***	***Gov_ share***
Reform	**−0.520****	**−0.199*****	**−0.074****	−0.035	**−0.089*****	**−0.106****
	(0.222)	**(0.059)**	**(0.033)**	(0.033)	**(0.033)**	**(0.048)**
Duration	−0.019*	0.001	0.001	0.001	0.002	0.000
	(0.010)	(0.001)	(0.002)	(0.001)	(0.002)	(0.002)
Investment_	−0.001	0.001	0.003	0.001	−0.001	−0.002
size	(0.023)	(0.003)	(0.003)	(0.003)	(0.003)	(0.004)
Gov_level	**0.361****	**0.063****	**0.086*****	**0.087*****	**0.075*****	**0.072****
	(0.155)	**(0.025)**	**(0.024)**	**(0.023)**	**(0.024)**	**(0.033)**
Reform*		**0.100****				
Gov_level		**(0.042)**				
Not_corrupt			−0.001			
			(0.001)			
Monthly fixed-asset investment					Yes	Yes
Number of firms					Yes	Yes
Monthly loans						Yes
Monthly deposits						Yes
Date						
Other control variables	Yes	Yes	Yes	Yes	Yes	Yes
Observations	3,054	3,070	2,846	3,070	2,517	1,426

Clustered standard errors at the prefectural level in parentheses.
*** p<0.01, ** p<0.05, * p<0.1.

Table 4.16 *Robustness checks with another dependent variable*

	(1)	(2)	(3)
Variables	***Agg_Gov_share***	***Agg_Gov_share***	***Agg_Gov_share***
Reform	−0.081*	**−0.107****	−0.130*
	(0.044)	**(0.051)**	(0.067)
Monthly fixed-asset investment		Yes	Yes
Number of firms		Yes	Yes
Monthly loans			Yes
Monthly deposits			Yes
GDP_per_capita	Yes	Yes	Yes
Net_fiscal_balance	Yes	Yes	Yes
Year-fixed effects	Yes	Yes	Yes
Province-fixed effects	Yes	Yes	Yes
Observations	779	656	355

5

The Corporate Form and State Ownership in China

The preceding chapters have extensively explored how LTS accounts for the development of SOEs and private firms across various sectors. Building on this foundation, this chapter shifts the focus exclusively to SOEs that have not been fully privatized, aiming to show how LTS can also effectively explain the evolution of their legal forms.

In the 1990s, China embarked on a strategy of corporatizing SOEs, transforming them into modern corporate entities while retaining a majority shareholding and consequent control rights. Similar approaches have been adopted by other nations featuring a substantial number of SOEs, such as Vietnam, India, and Brazil. However, Chinese SOEs have not undergone complete corporatization and occasionally manifest characteristics inconsistent with the corporate form adopted by private business enterprises. Notably, the state continues to furnish implicit guarantees for the debts of certain SOEs, thereby deviating from the fundamental principles of limited liability. Additionally, the Party has demanded certain SOEs to establish a Party organization, which changes the internal governance structure of SOEs.

This chapter employs LTS to provide a theoretical explanation for the corporatization of SOEs in China. It posits that modern corporations and public-oriented SOEs confront inherent institutional conflicts. The corporatization of SOEs serves to transform them into profit-driven entities, thereby alleviating ownership costs. However, this transformation can also engender augmented regulatory costs, as it somewhat diminishes the state's control. Hence, an inherent trade-off between ownership and regulatory costs arises for SOEs that do not primarily use the corporate form to secure financing. The state possesses the flexibility to choose from various institutional arrangements that strike different balances between these two costs.

I The Corporatization of SOEs in China

Since the 1978 reform, China has been changing its legal regimes governing SOEs. In 1983, the State Council issued the "*Interim*

Regulations on State-Owned Industrial Enterprises," which mandated the implementation of a system of manager responsibility under the leadership of the Party Committee. These enterprises were guided by principles such as collective leadership, democratic management by workers, and administrative command by managers, although they were not required to establish a board of directors. Even within this regulation, the state expressed its intention to strengthen the autonomy of the SOEs.

In addition, in 1983, the State Council adopted the reform of *li gai shui* (transforming profit-sharing into taxation), which alleviated the "soft budget constraint" problem that usually characterizes SOEs. It promulgated the "*Implementation Measures for the Transformation of State-Owned Enterprises' Profit-Sharing into Taxation*" (*guanyu guoying qiye li gai shui shixing banfa*), which mandated that all profitable large and medium-sized SOEs pay income tax at a rate of 55 percent based on realized profits. After paying income tax, a portion of the remaining profits must be turned over to the state, while another portion is retained by the enterprise. The retained profits can be used for purposes such as new product trial production, production development, reserves, employee welfare, and employee incentives. This measure aims to "establish a fixed distribution relationship between enterprises and the state." "Well-managed enterprises can gain more, while poorly managed ones receive less." It more clearly demarcates the boundaries between the governments and the SOEs. By allowing the SOEs to retain profits, they can be incentivized to perform better, potentially decreasing the ownership costs.

In 1984, the Central Committee of the CPC made a decision on economic system reform, aiming to transform SOEs into independent economic entities responsible for their own profits and losses. Starting from the mid-1980s, China initiated the transformation of SOEs into joint-stock companies, aiming to strengthen their autonomy. In 1988, the National People's Congress enacted the "*Law on Industrial Enterprises Owned by the Whole People,*" which changed the legal designation of SOEs to "enterprises owned by the whole people." Although these enterprises did not possess all the characteristics of modern corporations, the law included provisions that granted certain autonomy to the SOEs. For example, Article Seven stipulated that the managers would be responsible for the operation of the SOEs. Article 23 granted enterprises the right to request adjustments to nonessential planned supplies and sales arrangements, while Article 24 allowed enterprises to independently sell their products beyond the planned scope, with some exceptions set by the State Council. Article 33 also affirmed the enterprises' right to refuse resource allocations from government departments. The purpose of this law aimed to address concerns about high ownership costs by preventing government departments from assigning tasks to the enterprises without bearing the responsibility for any resulting losses.

In 1993, China introduced the *Company Law*, which played a pivotal role in further facilitating the corporatization of SOEs. Subsequently, in 1999, the Central Committee of the CPC issued a decision on the reform and development of SOEs, which emphasized the maintenance of large SOEs in sectors related to national security, natural monopolies, the provision of important public products and services, as well as key backbone enterprises in strategic and high-tech industries. In contrast, other industries and sectors could undergo asset restructuring and structural adjustments to enhance the overall quality of the state-owned economy while encouraging and guiding the development of nonpublic ownership, such as individual and private enterprises. A significant step in supervising SOEs came with the establishment of State Asset Supervisory and Administrative Committee (SASAC) in 2003. This development coincided with the public listing of several large SOEs and the introduction of strategic investors to state-owned banks. Many SOEs began to accumulate significant profits in their operations.

In 2013, the Third Plenary Session of the 18th Central Committee of the CPC made the decision to pursue mixed ownership reform. The decision called for SOEs to increase the proportion of market-oriented selection for managers, reasonably determine, and strictly regulate the levels of management personnel's salaries, job benefits, official expenses, and business expenses. Furthermore, the *Opinions of the State Council on Development of an Economy of Mixed-Ownership of State-Owned Enterprises*, promulgated in 2015, provided several measures for the mixed-ownership reform. These measures included introducing private and foreign investors in SOEs, utilizing of PPP for financing infrastructure projects, exploring the possibility of using preferred shares in SOEs, and conducting experiments on employee-owned shares in SOEs. The Central Committee of the CPC and the State Council have also issued guiding opinions on deepening the reform of SOEs, with a strong emphasis on enhancing the corporate governance structure. The primary objective was to promote the establishment of a board of directors and establish a decision-making and supervisory mechanism. Importantly, these reforms stress the necessity for the board of directors to exercise their rights in major decision-making, personnel appointments, salary distribution, and other critical matters. This ensures the autonomy of the management team's operations and prohibiting any unauthorized intervention by government departments. Moreover, it is mandated that external directors should constitute the majority of the board. These reforms have aligned certain SOEs more closely with the characteristics of modern corporations.

Scholars in China widely acknowledge that improving corporate governance is a crucial approach to enhancing the performance of SOEs. Studies conducted by Zheng and Wang (2000), Clarke (2003), and Liu (2013) have revealed that Chinese SOEs face several deficiencies in their internal governance structures, in addition to the common corporate governance issues faced by modern enterprises. Firstly, some argued that SOEs encounter the challenges of having "no owners." Although these enterprises are nominally owned by the state, the actual exercise of principal powers by citizens is limited during the operation process. This lack of a genuine principal gives rise to insider control (Liu, 2013). Consequently, the absence of real owner results in a lack of accountability for managerial selections and an inability to establish an effective mechanism for appointing qualified managers. Secondly, many argue that the complex layers of delegation and agency relationships within SOEs contribute to efficiency losses. The lengthy delegation-agency chains contribute to high agency costs within SOEs. Thirdly, the corporate governance structure of SOEs is considered flawed as it fails to establish effective checks and balances among the board of directors, management, shareholders, and other stakeholders. In some cases, these mechanisms are superficial and fail to be implemented. All of these deficiencies significantly impact the performance of SOEs. Existing literature generally suggests that SOEs face substantial challenges in terms of corporate governance (Liu, 2013).

However, the extent to which corporatization can effectively address these problems remains unclear. Firstly, while current studies recognize that SOEs have "no owners," transforming them into modern corporations may not readily resolve this issue. The SASAC has been established to exercise shareholder rights, but its actual control over SOEs is sometimes questioned in practice. Additionally, even private corporations in developed countries often face the separation between ownership and control, as identified by Berle and Means in the early twentieth century (Berle and Means, 1932). Thus, private corporations can also be considered as having "no owners" effectively monitoring their performance. Secondly, corporatization does not necessarily reduce the layers of ownership. In fact, many SOEs are owned by multiple layers of other SOEs, ultimately leading back to the government. Hence, agency costs persist even after corporatization. Thirdly, while corporatization may introduce checks and balances within SOEs, the effectiveness and potential side effects of such arrangements require further discussion. Lastly, while many criticize the dominance of state ownership in China's economy, corporatization does not necessarily lead to privatization. In fact, the Chinese government once embraced the concept of corporatization without privatization (Howson, 2017). Therefore, whether corporatization itself improves corporate governance warrants further examination and discussion.

II What Does the Corporatization of SOEs Really Achieve?

The adoption of the corporate form in SOEs by China is a complex decision influenced by multiple factors. While many studies assume the inherent superiority of the corporate form, it is essential to delve deeper into the reasons behind this choice.

The decision made in the 1999 document titled "*The Central Committee of the Communist Party of China's Decision on Several Major Issues Concerning the Reform and Development of State-owned Enterprises*" sheds some light on the rationale behind the corporatization of SOEs. It emphasizes the implementation of standardized corporate reforms in large and medium-sized SOEs, considering the corporate form as an effective organizational structure in modern enterprises. According to the understanding revealed by this decision, the core of the corporate form lies in its governance structure, wherein the shareholders' meeting, board of directors, supervisory board, and management team are assigned specific responsibilities. This structure aims to ensure accountability, coordination, effective checks and balances, and the ultimate control rights of the owners over the enterprises. The board of directors bears the responsibility of safeguarding the rights and interests of shareholders and is accountable to the shareholders' meeting. It makes decisions regarding the company's development goals and significant operational activities, appoints executives, and evaluates their performance.

However, notwithstanding these rationales, the underlying benefits of corporatization remain somewhat elusive. Some assert that it enables a clear demarcation between government and business activities, while others argue that it engenders managerial incentives (Zhu, 1998). For instance, the provision of stock options to managers can serve as a catalyst for heightened motivation and diligence. Nevertheless, these perspectives fall short of grasping the fundamental essence of the corporate structure. In alternative organizational frameworks, such as partnerships, managers can also be incentivized through profit-sharing arrangements, which generate managerial incentives to pursue profits.

This chapter seeks to explain the corporatization of SOEs by considering the essential characteristics of the corporate form. The corporate form exhibits five crucial features that enable access to diverse external financing sources. In the following section, we will explore these characteristics and evaluate the level of corporatization within Chinese SOEs. It is crucial to understand the reasons why complete corporatization has not been fully embraced by SOEs, as the benefits of these features may not always outweigh the associated costs. While the corporate form can effectively mitigate ownership costs, it can also give rise to conflicts with the principles of state ownership.

A *Limited Liability*

The principle of limited liability has long been recognized as a fundamental pillar of corporate law, offering numerous significant advantages. One notable benefit is the reduction in information costs for creditors and shareholders. Limited liability relieves potential creditors from the burden of assessing the financial status of numerous individual investors, allowing them to focus solely on the corporation's overall financial health. This leads to a decrease in the information costs incurred during transactions with the company, as creditors can concentrate on evaluating the company's assets and liabilities. In contrast, under a joint and several liability regime, creditors would need to assess the assets of each individual shareholder when seeking payment from them in the event of the company's failure to pay. Similarly, when shareholders bear joint and several liability for the company's debts, they would have to consider the payment abilities of other shareholders, as it would impact their own share of the payment in the event of the company's bankruptcy.

Limited liability plays a crucial role in facilitating the transfer of control and the trading of corporate shares, making the process independent of the individual wealth of buyers and sellers. In the absence of limited liability, the valuation of corporate shares would be contingent on the financial status of the shareholders. Specifically, a shareholder close to insolvency would place a higher value on the same share compared to a financially secure shareholder, due to the reduced likelihood of being called upon to cover additional debts if the corporation face insolvency. This principle underscores the significance of limited liability in standardizing share value across shareholders, irrespective of their individual economic circumstances. Limited liability also alleviates the burdens associated with bankruptcy proceedings, as the court would not need to involve all shareholders in the process. This is particularly significant considering that some corporations have thousands of investors, resulting in substantial cost reduction in bankruptcy proceedings.

However, the advantages of limited liability are most pronounced in corporations with a large, diverse shareholder base. This scenario typically does not apply to SOEs, where the government often acts as the controlling or sole shareholder. For instance, in an SOE wholly owned by the government, the distinction between limited and unlimited shareholder liability becomes negligible. If the SOE operates under limited liability, a creditor's assessment would focus on the enterprise's assets and creditworthiness. If, however, limited liability is not in place, the creditor's evaluation would extend only slightly further to include the government's financial resources. Therefore, the complexity of assessing the financial capacity of numerous shareholders, a typical challenge in privately owned corporations, is largely absent in the context of SOEs.

To be sure, one might argue that assessing the creditworthiness of a government shareholder could be more challenging than evaluating that of a private entity. For instance, if the shareholder is a local government in China, uncertainties may arise regarding the possibility of the local government bankruptcy and whether the central government would intervene with a bailout if limited liability does not apply. Creditors must therefore consider the government's track record and secure further information before entering into transactions with SOEs, potentially increasing information costs. Furthermore, the government's ability to transfer its equity stake in an SOE to private investors adds another layer of complexity. Consider a scenario where a bank provides a loan to an SOE under the assumption that the government will offer additional support if the enterprise faces financial difficulties. If the government subsequently transfers its shares to a private investor who may not support the bailout, this could significantly undermine the creditor's interests. Corporatization could mitigate these risks by imposing limited liability on the government, thereby simplifying the creditors' assessments to focus solely on the financial health of the corporatized SOE, rather than the broader governmental backing.

However, the corporatization of SOEs does not guarantee the attainment of limited liability. Limited liability serves merely as a default provision under corporate law and does not preclude a government shareholder from electing to guarantee the corporation's debts. Conversely, even in a regime where unlimited liability is standard, nothing precludes a potential creditor and a government shareholder from negotiating an agreement that absolves the shareholder of liability. Additionally, creditors have the option to create contractual safeguards to address scenarios where an SOE's ownership is transferred to private entities, ensuring that their interests are protected regardless of the ownership structure.

In practice, Chinese governments often provide further support to SOEs to bail them out when they face insolvency even after they are corporatized. When the government undertakes a bailout of a SOE, it may inject capital into the firm, effectively assuming liability for the SOE's debts as a shareholder. Chinese governments, particularly local governments, frequently intervene to provide financial support to SOEs. As a result, the credibility of these SOEs becomes closely intertwined with the credibility of their government owners. This can be observed notably, in China, where many local government financial vehicles (LGFVs) issue debt instruments without explicit government guarantees for repayment. However, there exists a general expectation that local governments may step in to rescue these LGFVs in case of default. Consequently, the credit risk associated with these debts is perceived to fall under the responsibility of the local government. Failing to support these LGFVs would damage the reputation of the local government, making it more challenging to raise funds through LGFVs in the future. Thus, corporatization of SOEs does not necessarily lead to the adherence to the limited liability principle.

The adoption of limited liability is often considered to have another important function – mitigating the "soft budget constraint" problem commonly associated with SOEs (Vickers and Yarrow, 1991; Hart et al., 1997). The "soft budget constraint" problem arises when the government provides various forms of support to the SOEs, preventing them from facing bankruptcy. As a result, SOE managers may not experience the financial pressures that their counterparts in private sector do when facing losses or potential insolvency, which in turn reduces their motivation to improve efficiency and performance. Furthermore, some SOEs maintain monopolistic positions in the market, enabling them to generate excess profits without significant incentives to enhance managerial performance. By establishing a clear separation between SOEs and governmental support, limited liability could prevent the government from routinely rescuing SOEs in financial distress, thereby motivating SOE managers to reduce costs and enhance operational efficiency. Thus, the emergence of "soft budget constraints" depends largely on how shareholder liabilities are structured and managed.

While SOEs are usually associated with the "soft budget constraint" problem, this theory faces several challenges. Firstly, even if an SOE operates under a "soft budget constraint," this does not preclude the state from penalizing managers responsible for financial mismanagement. The government may still hold the option of replacing managers before rescuing the troubled enterprise. It is also entirely feasible for the state to reward managers for strong financial performance irrespective of any subsidies provided to the SOE, incentivizing them to improve the financial performance of the SOEs. The critical factor in promoting efficiency appears to be the internal incentive structures driving better performance of the managers, rather than the arrangement of "budget constraint."

Secondly, private corporations can also experience government bailouts. For example, to mitigate the systemic risks of a bank failure, the government might elect to support failing private banks. However, this is not typically perceived as indicative of a "soft budget constraint," since directors and managers of private banks remain subject to robust corporate governance standards and are expected to enhance performance, even potentially in anticipation of government rescue efforts. In addition, the occasional bailouts of private firms indicate that the existence of "soft budget constraints" is not exclusively tied to ownership type. Instead, whether a bailout is deemed necessary often reflects broader public policy considerations.

Furthermore, the extent to which the problem of "soft budget constraints" can be mitigated through corporatization also hinges on specific institutional designs. Lin et al. (1998) contends that certain SOEs are tasked with carrying out policy mandates and implementing government strategies. Consequently, these SOEs might not be viable without state subsidies and support. Simply converting these SOEs into corporate entities does not inherently confer limited liability, nor does it guarantee enhanced corporate performance. Therefore, the potential benefits of corporatization in alleviating "soft budget constraints" are not assured.

The above analysis largely suggests that if the purpose of corporatization is to introduce the arrangement of limited liability to SOEs, the benefits of such a transformation remain ambiguous. Meanwhile, to the extent that limited liability enhances managerial performance and thus reduces ownership costs, LTS indicates that it may also lead to increased regulatory costs. The withdrawal of government support for SOEs under strict limited liability can have profound implications. Firstly, it may lead to the cessation of operations by the SOEs, resulting in certain externalities that impact society. SOEs often fulfill specific governmental functions and receive substantial subsidies from the government. Without government support, these SOEs may struggle to sustain themselves (Lin et al., 1997). In such cases, the SOEs may face insolvency, leading to bankruptcy or their acquisition by private investors. However, in regulated industries, the government may be reluctant to allow private investors to take over because it may then lose internal control over these firms. As a result, the government may feel compelled to step in with a bailout, although it contradicts the principle of limited liability. Thus, the decision to withhold support from SOEs carries the risk of compromising the government's control and regulatory authority. Secondly, limited liability creates strong incentives for managers to pursue profits, as losses would lead to company bankruptcy and personal financial losses for the managers themselves. Unfortunately, this may also incentivize managers to exploit their power to circumvent laws and regulations, increasing regulatory costs.

A case in point is the inclination of shareholders in commercial banks to engage in risky behavior, with the expectation that the government will extend a bailout in the event of failure. The "too big to fail" predicament looms large over numerous SOEs. The bankruptcy of these entities could potentially lead to economic instability, particularly when considering the contagion effect of financial risks. SIFIs serve as a prominent illustration, as their collapse may trigger a financial crisis given the highly transmissible nature of such risks. Such defaults can result in substantial losses for counterparties, thereby setting off fire sales of assets and a sharp depreciation in asset prices. This, in turn, would have a detrimental impact on other financial institutions harboring comparable assets. Considering the often-substantial leverage of financial institutions, the failure of one entity can catalyze a chain reaction leading to the downfall of other institutions. During the 1990s Asian financial crisis, many state-owned banks in China faced substantial nonperforming loans. Despite this predicament, the state refrained from selling off these banks to private investors. Theoretically, one option could have been to sell equity stakes to foreign investors, allowing the banks to continue their operations. However, such an approach carries the risk of diluting the state's regulatory control over the financial institutions.

Nonfinancial firms may also receive government bailout given that the services they provide are essential for the public interest and alternative options, such as allowing private firms to take over, may lead to regulatory concerns. A notable example is seen in the case of infrastructure, such as water utilities. In China, there have been instances where local state-owned water utility companies encountered financial difficulties and potential insolvency as a result of tariff regulation measures. As water utilities are essential public services, governments continue to provide subsidies to ensure their ongoing operation. Despite operating as corporations, water utilities typically retain the characteristic of unlimited liability, with government owners assuming responsibility for their continued functioning. While complete corporatization of state-owned water utilities could potentially enhance management performance by placing managers under greater pressure to perform well and to prevent bankruptcy, this approach may also lead to increased regulatory costs. Managers may be incentivized to manipulate revenues and inflate costs to justify more frequent adjustments to water prices. Hence, complete corporatization of state-owned water utilities could undermine the substantial advantage of reduced regulatory costs associated with state ownership.

In conclusion, the process of corporatization in SOEs does not fully realize the benefit of limited liability enjoyed by shareholders in private corporations, as long as the government maintains an implicit guarantee for bailouts. Consequently, limited liability that follows corporatization of SOEs can be perceived as largely illusory. If the government maintains the discretion to provide a bailout to an SOE, true corporatization cannot be deemed fully realized in the context of China. Instead, it remains a case of partial corporatization. For SOEs deemed crucial by the government, the nature of the enterprise remains unchanged despite the transition to a corporate structure.

B Entity Shielding

Another important aspect of corporatization is entity shielding. While limited liability safeguards shareholders of a corporation from being pursued by creditors for payment, entity shielding safeguards the corporation's assets from the creditors of its shareholders. Entity shielding encompasses two crucial elements: priority and liquidity protection (Hansmann and Kraakman, 2000). It ensures that the corporation's assets are utilized first to settle debts owed to creditors before being returned to shareholders. Additionally, it guarantees that the bankruptcy of a shareholder does not impede the corporation's functioning.

Entity shielding holds significant importance for several reasons. Firstly, it diminishes information costs. In the absence of entity shielding, prospective investors would need to assess the financial standing of other shareholders prior to investing in a corporation or acquiring shares from existing shareholders. Similarly, creditors of a corporation would have to consider the potential withdrawal of investment by shareholders. Secondly, entity shielding safeguards the continuity of the corporation's operations. Without entity shielding, a shareholder could withdraw its capital investment at any time to repay debts, thereby disrupting the corporation's functioning.

Scholars have acknowledged that entity shielding holds greater significance in comparison to limited liability. This is because parties have the potential to negotiate and agree upon limited liability even in the absence of legal provisions. Simply put, in a legal framework lacking explicit limited liability, shareholders can still enter into contractual agreements with the corporation to include clauses that exempt them from the corporation's liabilities. If both parties agree, shareholders can benefit from this protection. However, entity shielding is harder to achieve through contract if the law does not provide this arrangement. Considering that a corporation may have multiple shareholders involved in various contracts, it becomes challenging for the corporation to ensure that each shareholder includes a clause in their individual contracts absolving the corporation from liabilities arising from those contracts. Moreover, monitoring the actions of shareholders under such circumstances would also present difficulties.

The aforementioned theory posits that corporatization plays a significant role in the reform of SOEs. However, within the specific context of SOE reform, the impact of corporatization is likely to be more limited due to certain factors. The shareholder in most cases is the government, and the number of investors is limited. Governments typically have few creditors and their likelihood of bankruptcy is minimal in China's context. Therefore, it is highly uncommon for an SOE to face claims from creditors of its government owner. Moreover, for many SOEs that pursue public objectives, the government typically retains ownership and does not transfer it to other investors. Hence, even without entity shielding, significant information costs are not likely. Additionally, the going concern value of SOEs is usually well safeguarded, even in the absence of entity shielding. As mentioned earlier, the bankruptcy of an SOE entails substantial social costs, prompting the government to actively prevent such scenarios from occurring.

In the process of corporatizing SOEs, there are instances where the owner of an SOE is not the government itself, but another SOE controlled by the government, or multiple SOEs owned by different levels of governments in various regions. In such cases, the shareholder SOE(s) may have additional creditors who could potentially assert claims against the subsidiary SOE. In this scenario, entity shielding is effective in safeguarding the subsidiary SOE's assets and facilitating its day-to-day operations when dealing with its own creditors. However, considering the close relationship among the shareholders, they can easily monitor each other's financial status. The information costs would still be limited. Consequently, entity shielding does not play as significant a role as it does within private corporations.

When SOEs seek financing from the public, entity shielding becomes a crucial arrangement. The adoption of the corporate form plays a vital role in attracting public finance for these SOEs. By transforming an SOE into a corporation and issuing shares, the government owner can offer some of these equity shares to the general public. Without entity shielding, there is a risk that the public may be apprehensive about the possibility of the government easily transferring the core assets of the SOEs to another entity or utilizing them to settle the government owner's debts to other parties. Entity shielding effectively partitions the assets of the SOEs from the government owner's other assets. However, it is important to note that for SOEs that do not intend to obtain finance from private investors, the benefits of corporatization are limited. Chinese law, in some instances, does not mandate entity shielding and may even "reverse pierce" the corporate veil of a state-owned corporation, diminishing the protection it offers (Zeng, 2021a).

Entity shielding can also enhance managerial performance by enabling the measurement of managers' effectiveness. By separating the assets of an entity from its shareholders, the performance of managers in each SOE can be evaluated through an examination of the profits generated by that particular SOE on an annual basis. As demonstrated in Chapter 4, SOEs owned by the central and local governments often compete for projects. In some cases, even different branches of the same SOE may bid for the same project. Through the segregation of assets into distinct pools, the corporate structure allows for intragovernmental competition. SOEs owned by various government entities with different fiscal constraints may compete in their performance, which reduces ownership costs. However, intense competition among government entities also raises concerns regarding its potential negative impact on public interests and the possible increase in regulatory costs. In such scenarios, different branches may engage in competition that compromises regulatory rules or exploits loopholes in their application in order to maximize profits.

C Delegated Management

A third important characteristic of the corporate form is delegated management. Corporations typically entrust the authority to act on their behalf to a board of directors, which possesses certain distinct features. Firstly, the board operates independently from the managers. In theory, the board of directors is responsible for monitoring the performance of the managers. This is particularly relevant in the case of Chinese SOEs, where a major issue identified in their governance was managers engaging in self-serving activities that benefited themselves at the expense of the SOEs (Qian, 1995). It is important to note, however, that monitoring by the board of directors is not the sole solution to the agency costs between the SOEs and the managers. Another significant channel is the Party's control over the appointment of senior managers. As highlighted by Yingyi Qian, during China's initial development phase, the Party retained control over senior managerial appointments, thereby mitigating the agency costs problem (Qian, 1995).

Secondly, the board of directors exercises the authority of the corporation, although certain decisions require shareholders' approval. This arrangement helps reduce decision-making costs, particularly in corporations with numerous shareholders holding diverse interests, whose active involvement can be costly. However, SOEs often do not incur significant decision-making costs unless they are partially privatized since they have a controlling government shareholder rather than a large group of equity holders with heterogeneous interests. In addition, alternative arrangements, such as the legal representative (*fading daibiaoren*), may also achieve similar goals. The SOE could designate a certain person to act on its behalf, thereby reducing decision-making costs.

Lastly, the board can function as a bulwark for protecting the rights of minority shareholders. Directors, with a personal stake in the success of the corporation, invest not only financial capital but also their expertise and reputation. Consequently, their motivations generally coincide with the collective interests of the shareholders. Delegating decision-making authority to the board of directors can help mitigate the inherent conflicts of interest between controlling and minority shareholders, particularly in corporations with a dispersed ownership structure.

Moreover, in the majority of SOEs, the government assumes the role of the controlling shareholder, exerting significant influence over the decision-making process. Consequently, the board of directors often fails to function as a safeguard for the interests of minority shareholders. In Chinese SOEs, the composition of the board predominantly comprises insiders closely associated with the government. Many of these individuals have a background in government service and may be reassigned to other governmental positions after their tenure in the SOEs. Their allegiance to the government and inclination to comply with its directives make them unlikely to act as strong advocates for the interests of external minority shareholders. It is crucial to acknowledge that this argument primarily applies to corporations with a notable presence of dispersed minority shareholders.

In China, one of the primary objectives of SOE corporatization is to enhance the autonomy of these enterprises and provide managers with greater operational flexibility, freeing them from the influence of various government departments. Prior to the SOE reforms, multiple government entities frequently interfered in the affairs of these enterprises, leading to a phenomenon known as "management of the water by nine dragons" (*jiulong zhishui*). By consolidating managerial authority under the SASAC, the process of corporatization can mitigate the associated decision-making costs to some extent.

However, it is important to note that these advantages do not derive from the establishment of the board of directors within the SOEs. Let us consider a scenario where the government possesses complete ownership of a corporatized SOE. Whether the exercise of control is vested in directors or members of the Party committee holds little significance. The government retains the ability to appoint directors, who subsequently nominate managers, or it can directly make decisions through the Party committee. The manner in which the government wields its power within an SOE is fundamentally an internal management matter.

In the process of implementing mixed-ownership reforms in Chinese SOEs, the state has imposed a requirement that a majority of the board of directors should be external members. This strategic move is intended to facilitate the monitoring of SOE managers by outsiders, potentially resulting in a reduction of ownership costs. The inclusion of outside directors, who have weaker connections with the insiders of the SOEs, can establish a system of checks and balances and elevate the pressure on managers to deliver effective performance.

However, while enhancing the autonomy of corporatized SOEs can yield benefits, it also carries the risk of diminishing governmental control. For instance, if a majority of the board of directors consists of external directors who are not subject to stringent government or regulatory oversight, their decision-making may prioritize interests other than those of the government. This could undermine the government's control over the SOEs and potentially lead to an increase in regulatory costs.

D *Transferrable Shares*

The corporatization of SOEs also affects the freedom of share transferability, yielding two distinct benefits. Firstly, it grants the state the ability to sell a portion or the entirety of its shares, providing access to cash when needed. This facilitates partial privatization, thereby fostering corporatization. Secondly, the corporatization and securitization of SOEs create a liquid stock market wherein share prices reflect managerial performance. Consequently, the state can use stock prices to monitor managerial conduct.

However, it is crucial to recognize that these benefits are confined to SOEs that the state intends to privatize or those whose primary objective is to optimize profits and generate investment returns for the state. For SOEs dedicated to serving governmental goals, the advantages of transferable shares are limited. For instance, the SASAC has explicitly stated its intention to maintain a dominant position in certain types of SOEs. The state may seek to preserve its controlling stake to ensure compliance with its directives and prohibit the sale of shares in these enterprises.

Moreover, while the share price generally reflects the performance of corporatized SOEs, the government may encounter difficulties discerning whether the underperformance of an SOE stems from managerial inadequacy or the policy burdens imposed by the state. This quandary is commonly known as the "problem of two masters" (Bainbridge, 1993; Choudhury, 2008). In private corporations, directors and managers typically strive to maximize shareholders' welfare. A major argument against them considering the interests of other stakeholders is that demanding a servant to serve two masters can impede the monitoring and evaluation of their performance. However, SOEs often need to pursue diverse state objectives, resulting in plural purposes. Consequently, assessing the performance of managers in an SOE with multiple objectives becomes exceedingly challenging.

E *Investor Ownership*

Modern corporations are predominantly owned by investors, and this ownership structure is widely regarded as efficient for several reasons. Firstly, shareholders provide vital long-term capital investment, which is essential for the sustained growth of corporations. Without obtaining residual control rights and financial rights, shareholders may face the risk of managerial opportunism. Secondly, shareholders primarily pursue profit and tend to have aligned interests, resulting in lower decision-making costs compared to alternative ownership arrangements.

For those SOEs primarily focused on profit generation without aiming for public objectives, corporatization can transform the state's role into one resembling that of a private investor. This process might also lead to the partial privatization of SOEs. When the interests of the state and private investors align, SOEs have the potential to operate more efficiently. Yet, for SOEs tasked with public duties and governmental aims, corporatization does not alter the underlying reality that the state remains in control, leveraging this influence to achieve public goals. Under these conditions, the impact of corporatization is minimal. When an SOE undergoes corporatization and partial privatization but still acts as a vehicle for government policies, a significant conflict of interest can emerge between the state as owner and private investors. This conflict is especially intense for SOEs saddled with heavy policy mandates (Howson, 2017). In these scenarios, corporatization and partial privatization might not necessarily enhance efficiency.

F Summary: The Finance and Governance Functions of the Corporate Form

The discussion above illustrates two principal functions served by the corporate form in the corporatization of SOEs. First, it helps secure finance from a broad base of investors who are strangers to each other (Zhang and Morley, 2022). Second, it enhances corporate governance of SOEs.

The corporate form stands as a cornerstone for financing, facilitating SOEs' access to capital from a wide array of investors. However, for the state, this financing mechanism is not always a priority. Not every SOE is dependent on public equity investments for its funding. The state has at its disposal various alternative strategies for financing, which do not hinge on capital market investors. These strategies include leveraging land as capital, deriving profits from state monopolies in sectors like tobacco, petroleum, and banking, and utilizing tax revenues. Therefore, SOEs have the capability to fund their operations and growth without exclusively depending on public equity investments.

When public financing becomes insignificant, the objectives behind SOEs' corporatization grow more ambiguous. Although some academics advocate for the enhancement of SOEs' corporate governance through corporatization (Qian, 1995, p. 24), the transition to a corporate structure does not guarantee improved governance. The success of such an initiative is contingent upon specific institutional frameworks, including whether the state offers implicit guarantees for SOEs or provides subsidies in times of insolvency, what degree of autonomy the state grants to these SOEs, and/or whether the SOEs undergo securitization and partial privatization. While converting SOEs into state-owned corporations might lower ownership costs, there is a potential risk of escalating regulatory costs, making them more akin to their private counterparts (Naughton, 2018). LTS sheds light on the trade-offs between different concerns when designing the legal forms of SOEs.

III The Reverse Trend

In recent times, there has been a notable shift against the promotion of independence for SOEs, reversing the previous trend. A significant change in this regard is the introduction of a requirement for the establishment of Party branches within SOEs. SOEs were mandated to amend their corporate charters to incorporate clauses related to Party-building (*dangjian clauses*). The introduction of the Party-building requirement has raised concerns among some observers because the power and responsibilities of Party organizations within SOEs remain unclear (Naughton, 2018; Lin, 2020, p. 478).

Lin and Milhaupt (2021) have categorized these provisions into ten distinct types, which encompass a range of requirements and practices. These include the incorporation of the term "Constitution of the Chinese Communist Party" into the company's documents, the provision of financial support for Party-related activities, the establishment of an official Party committee within the organization, the mandate for the chairman and Party secretary roles to be held by the same individual, the establishment of a full-time position for the deputy Party secretary, the implementation of the Party's cadre management principle for the appointment of managers and directors, the necessity for senior management to consult with the Party committee on significant decisions, and the simultaneous appointment of top executives to positions within the company and as representatives within the Party committee (Chen et al., 2023).

Some of these provisions are primarily symbolic in nature and lack substantive implications. However, certain provisions directly pertain to the personnel structure within these corporations. It is crucial to recognize that many SOEs are under state control. In fact, the Party-building requirements in the charter specifically target SOEs that are solely or predominantly owned by the state. For mixed-ownership enterprises, the government emphasizes the need for cautious implementation of Party-building practices, avoiding oversimplification or uniform application. The opinions of other shareholders, including institutional investors, should be considered.

In cases where the state already holds complete ownership of the shares, the introduction of a Party organization within SOEs has a limited impact on corporate governance. The state retains the ability to exert its power irrespective of the Party's involvement. The Party, in this context, functions as a conduit for the owners' influences, akin to how a privately owned family corporation might establish family councils or clan meetings to govern differently while retaining control. From a corporate governance standpoint, the Party's presence does not significantly impact corporate governance.

The Party-building requirement may make a difference if the Party's potential prioritization of motives beyond profit-seeking, such as regulatory objectives. For instance, the Party may mandate a state-owned electricity grid company to supply electricity to rural areas at lower costs, potentially affecting minority shareholders' interests, if any. Similarly, the Party may impose environmental protection or social responsibility requirements. Initially, even when the state was the sole owner, it could consider nonprofit motives. Nevertheless, the Party's intervention may yield different consequences if the government agency responsible for controlling the SOE primarily focuses on profit and operates within clearer guidelines. In contrast, the Party, as an opaque entity, may have various undisclosed goals. If the SOE owner prioritizes profit-seeking objectives, it may elevate regulatory costs and wield substantial power to influence government policymaking.

The reverse trend of corporatization can be understood from the perspective of LTS. Party-building fortifies the state's control over SOEs, thereby reducing regulatory costs (Gu and Yang, 2023). Party members can exert influence over corporations even without explicit legal authorization, enabling the state to exercise "residual power" not conferred by the law. Meanwhile, the Party's intervention may also increase ownership costs, which can be attributed to several factors. Firstly, the Party pursues multiple objectives, rendering the evaluation of managerial performance challenging. Party members may argue that the corporation should prioritize certain goals for the Party's interests while benefiting themselves. Secondly, the Party is not held accountable for the corporation's losses. Party members are not necessarily assessed based on the corporation's profit generation and may prioritize other political objectives that may conflict with the corporation's profit-seeking goals. Consequently, they may pursue these political goals excessively, fostering an environment conducive to corruption. This analysis explains why, thus far, the Party-building provisions adopted by private corporations have predominantly been symbolic. Meanwhile, for those SOEs that have implemented substantial Party-building provisions, they are primarily concentrated in sectors where the pursuit of diverse regulatory goals is deemed necessary.

IV The State Ownership Spectrum

This section aims to establish a spectrum of state ownership that helps explain the various organizational forms of SOEs, considering the trade-offs between regulatory costs and ownership costs.

At one end of the spectrum, we find state-owned SOEs that operate as direct government extensions. This organizational form entails the highest ownership costs, as the firm lacks autonomy and managers simply execute government directives. It faces a "soft budget constraint," where financial discipline is weak, and managers lack strong incentives to perform well due to the absence of clear performance measurement. However, regulatory costs are minimal in this form. The state exercises complete control over the SOEs, unencumbered by predefined legal frameworks, enabling unrestricted governmental authority.

As we move toward corporatized SOEs, we observe relatively lower ownership costs and higher regulatory costs. Corporatization transforms the SOE into a profit-oriented entity, enhancing the measurability and oversight of managerial performance. The degree to which regulatory costs are reduced depends on the extent of state intervention. If the state retains a majority shareholding and the power to appoint directors, it can still steer the SOE toward state objectives, limiting the reduction in regulatory costs and the increase in ownership costs.

The interplay between ownership costs and regulatory costs is influenced by the degree of privatization following the corporatization of SOEs. Partial privatization through the sale of shares to private investors can further reduce ownership costs. These outside investors, wielding significant voting power, can impede transactions that may harm their interests. Governments may opt for partial privatization, maintaining some control, and establishing agreements with private investors to determine the number of board members the government can appoint. These public-private joint ventures occupy a middle ground in the ownership spectrum, situated between purely private and public enterprises. They are likely to experience lower ownership costs compared to SOEs due to active monitoring by private investors, while their profit-seeking incentives are higher than those of pure SOEs. These arrangements emerge as governments seek to mitigate ownership costs while retaining some level of market control.

The balance between ownership costs and regulatory costs can also be adjusted through various institutional arrangements within corporatized SOEs. The government may retain appointment rights for a few board members who represent its interests. Furthermore, the inclusion of an independent director, not affiliated with the government, may be mandated to represent the interests of public consumers. Other examples include mandatory production and disclosure of important information by SOEs, as well as their attachment to an existing ministry (Vernon, 1984, p. 41). Reinforcing Party control enhances the state's authority over the SOE, increasing ownership costs while reducing regulatory costs. These arrangements enable regulators to maintain partial control despite the corporatization and asset partitioning process, reducing regulatory costs and improving coordination between the state and SOEs.

The trade-off between ownership costs and regulatory costs can also be influenced by the structure of the government department responsible for exercising shareholder's rights. If the state establishes specific channels through which regulators can exert influence on the decision-making processes of SOEs, regulatory costs can be reduced. Alternatively, shareholders' rights can be exercised by a separate entity, such as the SASAC, while the regulator maintains control through legal means. In this scenario, regulatory costs would likely be higher as the regulator would be bound by legal constraints.

One example that illustrates the different arrangements of the state's control over SOEs in China is the governance of Chinese state-owned insurance companies. A significant distinction between state-owned insurance companies and other insurance companies lies in the appointment and removal powers pertaining to their senior managers. Initially, in 1998, the Central Financial Committee held the authority to appoint senior managers of state-owned insurance companies. Following the dissolution of this committee in 2003, the appointment powers were transferred to the Insurance Regulatory Commission, the regulatory body overseeing all insurance companies. It was not until 2012 that the Organizational Committee of the Party assumed the appointment rights for entities such as PICC, PLICC, and China Taiping Life Insurance from the Insurance Regulatory Commission. Thus, from 2003 to 2012, the state-owned insurance companies are effectively regulator owned.

Such an arrangement naturally facilitates insurance regulation, as the interests of the insurance regulator and the companies are aligned. Prior to 2010, the Chinese Insurance Regulatory Commission (CIRC) primarily employed command-and-control regulations, commonly known as prescribed regulations. These regulations aimed to actively supervise and monitor the conduct of insurance companies. However, the effectiveness of these methods came into question as it was discovered that many lower-level employees were violating regulations without the knowledge or awareness of their managers. Consequently, the CIRC had to allocate significant resources to monitor the behavior of a large number of employees within each insurance company. Nevertheless, the regulation of central insurance enterprises by the CIRC exhibited certain differences before 2010. Additional requirements were imposed on state-owned insurance companies, transferring some of the regulatory burdens to the SOEs themselves. These companies were mandated to establish internal regulations that defined administrative penalties for SOE managers, such as warnings, demerits, and demotions, in cases where the SOE incurred losses. As a result, senior managers, including department managers or local branch leaders, could be held accountable for penalties, regardless of whether they were directly responsible for the decisions that caused the loss. This system incentivized senior managers to closely monitor the behavior of junior employees, helping to prevent such instances from arising. In this manner, the CIRC delegated a portion of its regulatory function to state-owned insurance companies.

At the opposite end of the spectrum, we find securitized SOEs, where the majority of shares are held by public investors, effectively transforming the state into a financial investor. The government can interfere through the internal voting process. In these cases, the state's control still displays the characteristics of state ownership, as the state could exercise the voting rights at its discretion, thereby retaining some residual control over these enterprises and also bearing the economic consequences of their decisions. In this scenario, regulatory costs may still be lower compared to fully private enterprises, as the state considers its own interests in the firm and avoids taking actions that could significantly harm the corporation.

Another arrangement observed in certain European countries is the implementation of a golden share, whereby the government retains certain decision-making powers. Some Chinese scholars have suggested adopting similar arrangements of golden shares in China (Deng, 2015). With golden shares, the state can only exercise control over certain significant decisions, leaving the daily operations to the managers of the corporations. Since clearly defining the state's control in advance faces the incompleteness problem, this approach increases regulatory costs while reducing ownership costs. LTS provides a theoretical framework for understanding the trade-offs involved in selecting legal forms within the spectrum of state ownership.

V Policy Implications

This chapter proposes several policy recommendations. Firstly, it challenges the notion that all SOEs should conform to the modern corporate mode. There is a prevailing belief that the government should relinquish control and bolster the autonomy of all SOEs. OECD guidelines for corporate governance of SOEs, for instance, caution against undue government interference in these entities (OECD, p. 18). However, proponents of corporatization often presume that government control through legal means is superior to direct ownership, without substantiating why. This chapter emphasizes that using legal mechanisms is not inherently better and is often accompanied by social costs arising from relational friction due to clearly demarcated boundaries between the government and firms. The choice between legal and ownership control should depend on their respective costs. While quantifying these costs may be challenging, it is not impossible. China should adopt a differentiated approach for profit-driven SOEs and public-focused SOEs in different sectors, implementing distinct regulations for each. The primary purpose of public-oriented SOEs is to strengthen the state's oversight of business activities, so emphasizing their corporatization is misguided.

Currently, China has predominantly focused on ownership through its mixed-ownership reform strategy. The state maintains control and utilizes command and control measures of the SOEs when necessary. The decision to establish a socialist market economy by the Central Committee of the CPC emphasizes that the appropriate level of state-owned equity in companies should vary based on industry and equity dispersion. In sectors where control is deemed necessary, the state retains a controlling position. In other sectors, it assumes a passive investor role, holding a block of shares when control requirements are minimal. However, the concept of mixed ownership encompasses a broad range of institutional arrangements that have not been fully acknowledged. This chapter suggests that China could develop distinct corporate-level regulations and adjust the organizational arrangements to complement the mixed-ownership regime.

More specifically, China should consider distinguishing different types of SOEs based on the level of regulatory costs. SOEs in sectors where regulatory costs are low should be mainly governed by corporate law. The state should refrain from providing implicit support to profit-seeking SOEs and from burdening them with policy requirements. The internal governance of profit-seeking SOEs should also adhere to corporate law, with the board of directors serving as the authoritative body of the corporation. Without concerning about the state control, adopting the corporate form can significantly reduce ownership costs without a corresponding increase in regulatory costs. With the state's primary goal being profit maximization, it does not necessarily need to retain control rights and can instead function as a strategic investor. Limited liability and entity shielding play crucial roles in facilitating share transferability and reducing information costs. Additionally, selecting managers from the market rather than exclusively from within the bureaucratic system can be beneficial. Meanwhile, SOEs operating in an environment where regulatory costs are high can be governed by special laws and regulations. The state has a variety of options, including establishing Party organizations within these enterprises and placing the managers directly under the regulators to better channel the regulator's orders.

Applying the same corporate law to different types of SOEs and private companies can have unintended consequences, particularly in terms of protecting minority shareholders (Pargendler, 2012, p. 504; Clarke and Howson, 2012, p. 240). To address this issue, it would be beneficial to establish distinct corporate form arrangements for different types of SOEs and private companies, without affecting the ordinary corporate form for private enterprises. This would allow for tailored regulations that take into account the unique characteristics and objectives of each entity, ensuring appropriate protection for minority shareholders. By recognizing the different needs and considerations of various types of companies, the legal framework can be better aligned with the interests of all stakeholders involved.

Conclusion: Measures to Reduce Regulatory Costs and Reform of State-Owned Enterprises

While state ownership has historically been perceived as a solution to *market failures*, this book asserts that it is more appropriate to regard it as a response to *legal failures*. *Legal failures* impact both the demand and supply of SOEs. The incompleteness of law deters private investment, thus elevating the demand for the products and services offered by SOEs. Simultaneously, it impairs the state's capacity to exert control through legal means, necessitating state ownership. SOEs may gain prevalence in instances where the regulatory costs associated with law are substantial, despite the generally higher ownership costs.

LTS views privatization as fundamentally a process of legalization rather than liberalization. Privatization does not always mean the state's withdrawal from private sectors; in many cases, it is accompanied by expanded or stricter regulatory oversight. Privatization is thus better understood as a transformation of the state's means of control from ownership to law. The transition from state ownership to legal governance and the subsequent easing of regulatory constraints (i.e., market liberalization) are not invariably linked and can occur independently. Currently, many calls for privatization fail to recognize this distinction and essentially reflect a "legal centrist view" (Ellickson, 1991, p. 4), which presumes the superiority of a clear legal demarcation between the public power of the government and private property of enterprises. This view overlooks the potential social costs of developing sophisticated legal and regulatory institutions in developing countries such as China. While clearly defining the scope of public power and private property of enterprises undeniably promotes stability and predictability for investors, it also incurs relational friction due to the incompleteness of the law (Masten, 2011). Promoting private enterprises and limiting the role of SOEs without first developing the necessary legal institutions to clearly demarcate the boundaries between the state and the enterprise would likely lead to underinvestment or undermine regulatory objectives.

The explanatory theory offered in this book generates important implications, which will be considered in this Conclusion chapter. The major implication of LTS is that states with a large number of SOEs should aim to reduce regulatory costs if they hope to further reform the SOEs and promote economic efficiency. This chapter explores several potential strategies for achieving this objective. A thorough examination of measures that may reduce regulatory costs provides valuable guidance to policymakers. More importantly, it reinforces the explanatory aspects of the theory developed in this book, as these measures themselves face considerable difficulties and challenges, underscoring the complexities of reducing regulatory costs and privatizing SOEs in China.

Section I of this chapter will examine the potential role of courts in adjudicating disputes between the government and the enterprise within a regulatory relationship and consider how they may mitigate regulatory costs by restraining opportunistic behavior. Subsequently, the section will delve into the deliberation of how courts should employ legal doctrines to adjudicate conflicts arising between governmental entities and enterprises. These analyses are important because while regulation undoubtedly incurs costs, if these costs can be easily reduced, they cannot be recognized as a lasting influence on China's ownership regime. In fact, one may even believe that the prevalence of SOEs causes higher regulatory costs rather than the reverse and that after the privatization of SOEs, the state could be more motivated to develop institutions that reduce regulatory costs. To address this concern, Section I will be devoted to examining some of the mechanisms through which courts may reduce regulatory costs and illustrating why reducing regulatory costs may encounter certain difficulties.

Section II of this chapter will then consider how the state could enhance its control over private enterprises through various means, hence facilitating the reform of SOEs and promotion of the private sector from the supply side. This section will also consider the limitations of the state's control and reiterate the advantages of state ownership in maintaining that control.

These two sections resonate with the overarching themes of this book – examining the evolution of SOEs through both demand and supply perspectives. On the demand side, whether SOEs are needed to fill the gap left by private enterprises depends on how well courts and other institutions can curb opportunistic behavior of the government. On the supply side, whether the state is willing to reform SOEs or promote private investment depends on its ability to maintain control of private enterprises.

I Measures to Curb Opportunistic Behavior

As illustrated in this book, a major source of regulatory costs is the opportunistic behavior of either the government or the enterprise. Because of the incompleteness of the law, both the government and the enterprise may act opportunistically. This section considers several measures that may alleviate the problem of opportunistic action.

A *The Rule of Law or the Rule of Meta-Law?*

One possible approach to address the concerns raised by incomplete law is for courts to assume a role in constraining the government's actions within regulatory interactions, mirroring their role in regulating contractual dealings among private entities. Meanwhile, the court needs to allow the government to adopt policies that are legitimate and not opportunistic. This approach is not entirely the same as the general proposition to enhance the "rule of law" in China (Wang, 2015, p. 86). In recent years, some have noted that China has "turned towards law" (Zhang and Ginsburg, 2019). The state has sought to strengthen legal professionalism and heighten the status of courts, perhaps in an attempt to further boost the confidence of investors (Zhang and Ginsburg, 2019, pp. 368–369). However, simply emphasizing the importance of the courts and ensuring the legal compliance falls short of fully addressing the important problem of the incompleteness of law. For example, one of the major threats to investors' confidence in investing is the sudden change of policies that breaks the expectations of the investors. The issuance of new laws or the discretionary implementation of new policies can significantly impact existing property rights and, consequently, affect investor confidence. Yet the procedures for enacting the laws or policies may be completely consistent with the existing legal framework. If the rule of law requires not only formal compliance with the procedures and allocation of power ex ante but also the maintenance of the expectations of investors protection, it may conflict with the state's other legitimate concerns such as environmental protection.

LTS offers a slightly different implication than the call for strengthening protection of private enterprises and constraining the government with the rule of law, emphasizing the importance of curbing opportunistic behavior. It suggests that China needs to adopt "meta-laws" (Smith, 2020). According to Henry Smith, meta-laws are important because first-order laws are always incomplete and may lead to opportunistic behavior (Smith, 2020). Hence, first-order laws need to be supplemented by second-order principles that can be applied to curb opportunistic behavior (Pound, 1942; Ohnesorge, 2005, p. 108; Smith, 2020; Vermeule, 2020). These meta-laws, often possessing characteristics that might seem contradictory to the conventional understanding of the rule of law (Smith, 2020, p. 335), would involve the establishment of courts or other regulatory authorities acting as impartial arbitrators between the government and enterprises. Their role would be to prevent either side from engaging in opportunistic actions, thereby striking a delicate balance between the imperative of safeguarding investor interests and the pursuit of other state objectives. The roles of court and other regulatory institutions in curbing opportunistic actions of the government and private enterprises in the regulatory relationship resemble their roles in contract law, where scholars have noticed that courts often need to apply contract law doctrines based on whether evidence of opportunism is presented (Sabel and Simon, 2012, pp. 1275–1276; Posner, 2014, p. 97).

This analysis yields two key implications for China. The first concerns institution-building, with a focus on strengthening judicial power and enhancing the expertise of judges. This aims to create a more robust and impartial legal framework. The second implication revolves around refining the substance of the law itself, by empowering courts with greater flexibility to apply standards and principles. This would enable the judiciary to more effectively mediate the complex relationship between business enterprises and the government, fostering a legal environment that can better respond to nuanced cases and evolving challenges.

B Legal and Regulatory Institutions

The court's role in adjudicating the disputes arising out of a regulatory relationship is more crucial than the one in the contractual relationship. In Coase's world, entitlement allocation between private parties could be handled by either the court or a regulator. In contrast, under LTS, when the allocation involves the state and a private party, it must be managed through the judicial system or a relatively separate system from the administrative government. This is necessary because the administrative government is a party to such disputes and may exhibit bias in entitlement allocation. Just as transaction costs create room for governmental intervention, the presence of regulatory costs suggests the need for judicial constraints over the government (Smith, 2020, p. 328).

Another way to understand the important role of the court is to distinguish two types of incompleteness of laws. When laws governing private parties are incomplete, it may be necessary and efficient to allocate the power to a court or a regulatory authority to fill the gap (Pistor and Xu, 2002). A more difficult issue arises when the law governing the relationship between the government/regulator and the private party is incomplete. In this case, the government/regulator always has an incentive to act opportunistically. The incompleteness problem cannot be easily resolved by granting the power to the regulatory authority since it is one of the parties. A relatively impartial organization such as the judicial system needs to be engaged to resolve the dispute in order to reduce regulatory costs.

When a dispute between the government and the enterprise arises, judicial review of the government decision can be viewed as an effort to allocate the entitlement. For example, the compensation offered to private enterprises during a legal transition or a policy change. If the court holds the legal transition to be invalid (perhaps because it is not in the public interest) or grants the private enterprise extremely high compensation, it would be akin to allocating the "entitlement of legal changes" to the private enterprise. If, by contrast, the court holds the legal transition to be valid and only grants the private enterprise trivial compensation, it would be functionally equivalent to allocating the "entitlement of legal changes" to the government. If regulatory costs were zero, entitlements could be allocated easily and efficiently through ex ante rulemaking. However, in reality, the incompleteness of the law makes ex ante allocation more complex and costly. To resolve the incompleteness problem requires the development of certain institutions that could curb opportunistic actions while allowing legitimate policy changes.

To reduce regulatory costs, China could greatly benefit from the establishment of a more autonomous judicial system capable of providing robust safeguards for private enterprises. As highlighted in Chapter 3, there is empirical evidence that certain sectors receive more pronounced protection from the courts compared to others. This assessment is made within a relative context, yet there is also potential for an augmentation of the absolute protection levels. Especially in areas where comprehensive nationwide legal transitions are infrequent, reinforcing the power of the judiciary becomes pivotal. By bolstering the autonomy of the courts and safeguarding corporate property rights against undue governmental interventions, a conducive environment for the further advancement of the private sector can be fostered. This would significantly contribute to the continued growth of the private economy.

However, it is also important to recognize that developing an independent legal system in China presents a significant challenge (Peerenboom, 2002). A recent incident exemplifying this struggle is China's attempt at judicial reform. It has long been recognized that many local courts were influenced by local governments in their decisions because the local governments control their finance and personnel decisions (Chen, 2014). In 2014, the SPC endeavored to initiate a judicial reform to promote the power of local courts by assigning provincial governments the responsibility of managing personnel, finance, and property of local courts within their respective provinces. The goal was to reduce local governments' control over these courts, especially for the ones below the provincial level. However, the implementation of this reform measure faced obstacles in several provinces.

One issue that arose from the reform was the disparity in salaries for judges in affluent areas (Wang, 2021a). Before the reform, the self-selection process in these wealthy regions likely led to the recruitment of highly skilled judges with extensive expertise in law. However, with the provincial government taking control of finance allocation, the salaries of these capable judges might have been reduced, causing dissatisfaction among them. Consequently, some of these highly skilled judges could have chosen to leave their posts in response to the salary changes brought about by the reform.

Another issue stems from the significant contributions of local judicial institutions in maintaining social stability and resolving societal conflicts. In response, some local party committees and governments provided support to judicial bodies in the form of office spaces and financial subsidies. While such support may affect judicial power, it positively impacts on improving working conditions and motivating the better work performance among judicial personnel. The reform may break this connection and thus weaken the local courts' function of helping the local governments implement their policies.

Furthermore, after the reform, some local courts faced higher communication and management costs as they needed to interact with higher-level officials. The office in charge of managing them operated at a greater distance with fewer personnel, leading to delayed responses to the needs of these local courts (Chen, 2017; Wang, 2021a). The reform incident serves as a poignant reminder of the challenges involved in establishing a powerful judicial system within China's political framework. Acknowledging the complexities and challenges in developing a more powerful judicial system does not imply its impossibility. Rather, it suggests that achieving such a system is a long-term endeavor that necessitates substantial resources and sustained political commitment.

To be sure, it is not an absolute necessity for the court to act as the sole independent adjudicator that deters opportunistic actions; the government might adopt measures of self-restraint. To illustrate, in instances where the government intends to implement major policies that might negatively impact the interests of private corporations, China could impose a series of procedural constraints on the policymaking process to prevent opportunism. These can include initiating a notice-and-comment process, allowing for a grace period to adjust to the new policy, or providing financial compensation to the adversely affected private entities. Such actions would indicate that government bodies recognize the societal implications of their policy decisions and have, to some extent, incorporated these considerations into their policy formulation processes. Consequently, this approach can lead to private entities developing expectations that governmental decisions regarding significant policy shifts will be made after a careful assessment of their potential costs and benefits. This expectation may, in turn, build trust and confidence among private investors, which is of paramount importance given that law is often incomplete. These procedural measures may thus mitigate governmental opportunism to some extent even in the absence of judicial enforcement.

Additionally, independent regulatory agencies may also be developed to serve as impartial arbitrators between the executive government and regulated enterprises. They are independent both from the political branches and from the regulated enterprises (Halberstam, 2010, p. 191), although the de facto independence is contested (Vermeule, 2013). Once the links between independent agencies and the political branch are weakened, they can exercise their regulatory power without being subject to strong political pressures. Independent agencies thus serve the important function of allowing governments to make credible commitments (Gilardi, 2002; Scott, 2008, p. 44). While independent agencies are most prevalent in the United States, some European countries have also adopted independent agencies after partially privatizing SOEs (Scott, 2008, p. 42).

China has not established independent agencies, perhaps because the government is used to maintaining control with a one-party system.

However, it is still possible to design similar institutions that enhance the independence and accountability of regulators. For example, according to Article 13 of the *Guangdong Price Department Working Rules and Procedures for Cost Inspections for Government Price Regulations* (*Guangdongsheng Wujiaju Zhengfu Zhiding Jiage Chengben Jianshen Gongzuo Guicheng*), Guangdong province requires all prefectural governments to establish a small committee to inspect the costs of water utilities before they adjust water tariffs. The committee is constituted by at least two qualified specialists and other specialists in accounting or economics, who must recuse themselves if they have an interest, either directly or indirectly, related to the regulated enterprise. This committee is responsible for the cost inspection work, and might be punished if they violate regulatory rules. These innovations may enhance the independence of regulators and reduce the possibility of opportunism caused by political pressure.

C *Substance of Law*

Chapters 2–4 demonstrate that there is a substantial demand for the goods and services provided by SOEs in specific regulated sectors, such as the coal mining and infrastructure sectors. These findings can be explained by the fact that the state frequently changes laws or policies, imposing significant costs on the parties, and the boundaries between public power and private property are blurred in some sectors more than others.

How can China enhance the protection of private enterprises? One possibility is to limit the government's discretion in forcing the closure of coal mines by requiring them to use clear guidelines regarding the emission requirements. The law could stipulate that private coal mines may only be shut down if they violate certain regulatory rules that are established in advance and consistently applied, thereby limiting the discretion of local government. If the state provides clear requirements of greenhouse gas emission or environmental regulatory standards, private investors who can meet the standards can still prevail in the market given their lower agency costs. The proportion of assets held by private coal mines would not necessarily decline. China could further enhance the protection of private enterprises by mandating that courts grant substantial compensation to those affected during legal transitions. Providing robust protection through significant compensation not only elevates the cost for governments when shutting down private enterprises, thereby disincentivizing such actions, but also encourages future private investment.

However, both of these measures would constrain the flexibility of the law and increase the cost of implementing the state's policies given the incompleteness of law. It would also reduce the incentives of the private parties to anticipate policy changes and adjust their behavior accordingly. Thus, this book posits that the prevalence of SOEs is closely related to the incompleteness of law. As long as the incompleteness cannot be easily resolved, it is hard to strengthen the protection of private enterprises without hindering the state's ability to regulate the market.

While the above analysis shows the difficulties in reducing regulatory costs, efforts could still be made to enhance the legal and regulatory institutions to achieve this goal. While completely cutting off the relationship between local governments and local courts is difficult, it is possible to develop the ability of the courts to help reduce regulatory costs.

In the context of China, a significant contributor to regulatory costs stems from government opportunism. If the court could adeptly restrain such opportunistic behavior, safeguarding private property in the process, it would instill greater investor confidence. Nonetheless, as mentioned earlier, overly constricting governmental actions might impede policy flexibility. Hence, courts are tasked with discerning instances of opportunistic government actions from legitimate exercises of power in the public's interest. To achieve this, courts should adopt legal doctrines that facilitate differentiation among cases and curb opportunistic conduct.

The theory of regulatory costs offers valuable insights into the formulation of legal doctrines and their judicial application. For instance, during a legal transition, courts should assess the foreseeability of new policies at the time of investment and determine whether these policies underwent a formal rule-making process, providing stakeholders the opportunity to raise objections and offer comments. In instances where there is a significant concern over government opportunism, the court should maintain the reasonable expectation of the private enterprise. This entails providing stronger protections, either through higher compensation or by imposing additional procedural restraints, to safeguard against arbitrary changes in law that could adversely affect private investments.

The function of courts in reducing regulatory costs is similar to their function in reducing transaction costs between private parties. Scholars have long noted that courts can apply contract law doctrines to curb opportunistic behavior and hence reduce transaction costs (Muris, 1981; Sabel and Simon, 2012, pp. 1275–1276). For example, when a contractual party hopes to modify the contract, courts may review the modification with contractual doctrines. This includes the rule that enforces modification only when a new consideration is provided and whether the modification is "fair and equitable in view of circumstances not anticipated by the parties when the contract was made" (Muris, 1981, pp. 529, 539). These doctrines enable the courts to approve modifications that are necessary and mutually beneficial while deterring opportunistic actions, hence promoting transactions ex ante.

The difference is, of course, subtle and needs to be determined in specific contexts. However, it is still possible to adopt some criteria for determining when the government is acting opportunistically. This section will provide some examples of administrative law doctrines to illustrate how courts may curb opportunistic behavior and reduce regulatory costs. Administrative law remains the most important body of law governing the operation of government and the demarcation of public power and private property, which would significantly influence regulatory cost. As some scholars suggest, administrative law aims to fulfill two major functions: to prevent the abuse of regulatory power by the rule of law and to promote effective regulation (Rodriguez, 2008; Mashaw, 2010). Both of these functions reduce regulatory costs. On the one hand, administrative law seeks to protect private parties from the abuse of state power by tethering the regulatory power to the rule of law. Thus, it enhances the state's ability to make credible commitments and prevents the state from acting opportunistically. On the other hand, it also seeks to avoid imposing overly harsh constraint on governmental power, in order to prevent the opportunistic conduct by the private parties that may harm the public interest.

1 Compensation for Changes in the Law or Policies

To illustrate, consider the protection of private enterprises when a new law or policy change affects their property interests. After private investors make an investment, the state may change the law that imposes a higher burden on the enterprise or even force its closure. It should be noted that it is possible that the change is entirely in the public interest and generates net social welfare. In addition, the private investors may also be able to foresee the enactment of this new law or policy, in which case the state cannot be deemed to be acting opportunistically. In Chapter 1, I argue that the government can be viewed as acting opportunistically "when it promulgates or modifies a new law or policy, or exercises the discretion in a way that cannot be foreseen and contrary to the reasonable expectations of the private investors at the time of their investment based on the existing law, political agenda, and social norm." If the state promulgates a new law or policy that is entirely unanticipated, and the legal change reduces the net social welfare and causes a transfer of wealth from existing private enterprises to other parties, it can be viewed as opportunistic.

One way to curb the opportunistic behavior of the government is to develop a doctrine similar to regulatory taking in the United States. As Chapter 3 shows, Chinese administrative law provides compensation to private enterprises when the government promulgates a new law that negatively affects their property interests. Chinese courts currently already apply the law in different sectors differently. They could further develop a test that distinguishes opportunistic actions of the governments from necessary adjustments of the law, hence further reducing regulatory costs. While such a distinction is no doubt difficult and would need to be made in a specific context, considering certain factors can aid in the assessment.

First and foremost, the identity of the decision-making authority plays a pivotal role in determining the susceptibility to opportunistic behavior. The concern of opportunism looms particularly large when a government intentionally deviates from its commitments. By contrast, if a higher-level government introduces a novel policy that inadvertently results in the breach of a commitment made by a lower-level government, the risks of opportunism are somewhat mitigated.

For instance, when a central government introduces a fresh set of environmental regulations compelling the closure of local private enterprises, concerns over government opportunism are less pronounced. This can be attributed to the fact that the central government is more inclined to consider an array of factors when formulating such regulations. Moreover, the potential for regulatory abuse is curtailed. Central government policymaking garners heightened public attention, transpires over a protracted duration, and exhibits a greater degree of predictability. Even if policy adjustments are initiated by the central government, provided investors perceive the scope of affected enterprises to be limited, their confidence would remain relatively unscathed.

Second, the legal transition can take the form of either a new law that applies generally and consistently or a policy decision that applies specifically to one or several regulated parties. This scope and nature of the legal transition should also affect the judge's decision. Changes in the application or selective enforcement are particularly suspicious and are more likely to be an abuse of power. As long as the state does not abuse its power arbitrarily, normal policy changes would not significantly deter investment. One example that illustrates its importance is the case of *Xiamen Wan Heng Real Estate Development Co., Ltd. v. Xiamen Urban Planning Commission (Xiamen shi Wanheng Fangdichan Kaifa Youxian Gongsi su Xiamenshi Guihua Weiyuanhui)*. Between 1994 and 2001, the Xiamen Urban Planning Commission issued construction permits a project to construct a commercial property. In 1995, a temporary permit for the underground part was granted to Xiamen Puda Company. Despite its temporary nature, it was executed according to strict guidelines. This permit held legal validity and influenced the aboveground construction's foundation. Xiamen Puda Company started underground construction based on this permit. However, the planning department later adjusted the planning indicators for the Puda Plaza project, taking into consideration the location conditions of the plot at that time and the architectural planning needs of the Xiamen University–Putuo Mountain area. These adjustments, reflected in permits from 1995 to 2001, affected the Puda Plaza project's investments and construction for Xiamen Wan Heng Company and Xiamen Puda Company. Adjustments in plot ratio and building area led to objective financial losses. Unlike a law that applies generally to all enterprises within its scope, the policy change in this case concerned only the interests of the investors in the particular property. It is hence more likely to be an opportunistic action of the government.

It should be noted that the abovementioned factors apply not only to the protection of property interests of private enterprises but also to the enforcement of contracts between the government and the enterprises. As Chapter 4 illustrates, the government sometimes decides to modify or terminate the contracts it has entered into with an enterprise. Currently, Chinese courts do not substantively review whether the modification or termination is in the public interest. However, they do offer compensation to the affected parties. Such modification or termination could be entirely legitimate, as the circumstances may change. However, since the government is one of the parties, there is a significant concern that it may be acting opportunistically. Courts can also consider the above factors to distinguish different types of modification or termination of administrative contracts. This may reduce the regulatory costs arising under such a relationship and hence promote private parties' incentives to contract with the government.

2 Judicial Review of Administrative Decisions

Apart from requiring compensation for private enterprises due to the promulgation and modification of laws and policies, courts can also curb opportunistic government actions by reviewing the exercise of discretion. In the terms of law and economics, compensation could largely be viewed as a form of "liability rules," while judge's ruling on the validity of an administrative decision resembles a "property rules" approach (Calabresi and Melamed, 1972).

Courts could focus on either the substance of the decision, its procedure, or both. Different jurisdictions have adopted different approaches. One example that illustrates the function of procedure in curbing opportunistic actions is the administrative law in the United States. In the United States, the *Administrative Procedure Act of the United States* (the APA) sets out procedural requirements that enhance the transparency of and public participation in regulatory rulemaking. Agencies are required to follow the notice-and-comment procedure, including a public hearing to ensure public participation in the decision-making process. Public participation may exert pressure on regulatory agencies by making the arguments for and against a certain regulation transparent (Rose-Ackerman and Rossi, 2000, p. 1455). Increasing public participation enhances the legitimacy of the administrative process, thus promoting support for government actions (Tyler, 2006). However, the notice-and-comment procedure sometimes exerts too much of a burden on agencies. To address this, courts sometimes allow agencies to avoid the rulemaking procedure. In doing so, the courts' approach can be viewed as an attempt to distinguish regulatory decisions that are more and less likely to be opportunistic.

The case law generally supports this view. For example, section 553 of the APA exempts interpretive rules from the notice-and-comment procedure. While the meaning of interpretive rules is left ambiguous, agencies may find it advantageous to use interpretive rules to define the meaning of regulatory rules. In *Hoctor v United States Department of Agriculture*, the agencies issued an "interpretive rule" that required Hoctor to change the fence height, based on the Animal Welfare Act, which would cost him a significant amount of money. The court argued that the requirement of fence height is itself a regulation, instead of an interpretation. The court held that to distinguish legislative and interpretive rules, it has to "separate the cases in which notice-and-comment rulemaking is required from the cases in which it is not required" (Cass et al., 2006). Judge Posner argued that if the rules are interpreted in a way that would affect the rights of many people, and agencies would have received many comments had they followed the notice-and-comment procedure, then these interpretive rules constitute substantive rulemaking (Cass et al., 2006). He expressed concern that agencies might exploit the ambiguity of interpretive rules to make significant decisions unilaterally, without public input, which could lead to opportunistic and potentially unfair outcomes.

Procedural constraints play a crucial role in curbing opportunism by enabling courts to uphold the principle of legality as administrative decisions grow increasingly complex (Vermeule, 2020, p. 366). This complexity often arises from the inherent incompleteness of law, necessitating delegation to administrative agencies because the legislature cannot anticipate every potential circumstance. Principles focused on process strike an essential balance between allowing the government the freedom to exercise discretion and avoiding the risks of opportunism, while also imposing overly restrictive controls.

Courts may also review the substance of the administrative decision. In Germany, for instance, courts sometimes rely on the proportionality principle to review discretionary decisions made by the government (Schwarze, 1992). The court would examine whether the use of discretion is suitable, necessary, and proportional to its objective (Schwarze, 1992), which would balance the public interest of the state with the private interest of the regulated parties. When the involved rights are fundamental rights, the court would adopt a stricter examination of the exercise of discretionary power. Although the primary rationale behind the proportionality principle is to safeguard fundamental rights, it could also curb the potential government opportunism by emphasizing the evaluation of alternative measures that could achieve the same governmental goals at lower costs (Schwarze, 1992).

Chinese courts could adopt doctrines that are functionally similar to curb opportunistic government discretion. They could consider various factors to determine if the government is acting opportunistically. These include the consistency of the law's application by the regulatory authority, unexplained changes in interpretation or administration methods, interference with the reasonable reliance interests of private parties by new regulatory rules or decisions, and the economic impact of regulatory decisions. Empirical studies show that Chinese courts have begun to apply the proportionality principle in recent years as the legal system becomes increasingly mature (Ma and Yu, 2022). In some instances, Chinese courts could impose stricter procedural requirements.

Empirical research also indicates that Chinese courts sometimes protect private property by regulating governmental decision-making procedures (Mao and Qiao, 2021). However, the procedural requirements currently imposed by Chinese courts largely take the form of rules rather than standards (Kaplow, 1992; Zeng, 2021b, 2024a). Developing a standard-based approach may enable courts to regulate opportunistic actions on a case-by-case basis.

3 Responses to Counterarguments

One may raise a counterargument to the aforementioned perspective that governments would not enact the law opportunistically, because the lawmaking process is subject to political process (Kaplow, 1986). In addition, if the political process is not effective in controlling governmental action, then the judicial system may also be incapable of controlling governmental action (Rose-Ackerman and Rossi, 2000). While this criticism appears valid in some states, it may not hold in China's context because of two observations. First, China's local governments' policy-making is not subject to the same rigorous political process as in some liberal states and hence may breed opportunism. Second, while Chinese courts are generally weak in their political power, higher-level courts may have strong power over lower-level governments, which enables them to control opportunistic behavior.

Another objection is that Chinese courts may be incapable of applying flexible standards that distinguish opportunistic actions from the legitimate exercise of rulemaking and enforcement power. There is a thick literature on the use of rules versus standards in civil law and common law jurisdiction. La Porta et al. argue that common law courts are more capable of applying flexible standards as opposed to rigid rules compared with civil law courts (La Porta et al., 2008). In addition, some studies show that equity plays a significant role in curbing opportunism (Smith, 2016, p. 328). In the United States, administrative law was developed in a way significantly influenced by equity. According to Henry Smith, there are always circumstances that cannot be fully specified in advance. Equity can address opportunism because it is applied ex post, which helps keep the regulators in line (Smith, 2016, p. 328). In countries without the tradition of equity, courts may face a greater challenge in constraining the government because they lack this mechanism to address unforeseen circumstances and curb opportunistic behavior.

However, the empirical evidence presented in Chapter 3 shows that Chinese courts are already applying the vague rule of Article 8 in different context in a way largely consistent with the proposition of LTS. There are thus reasons to believe that it is still possible for Chinese courts to gradually develop functionally equivalent legal doctrines or principles that reduce regulatory costs.

D *Comparison with Other Reform Proposals*

The implications derived from LTS diverge significantly from those proposed by existing studies. Since the inception of SOE reform in China, there have been two competing perspectives on the appropriate approach to reform. One prominent view is the property school (*chanquan pai*), which advocates for privatization as essential for the reform of SOEs. Scholars such as Wu Jinglian (1994b) argue that unclear ownership arrangements, inadequate internal governance structures, and management inefficiencies have contributed to the poor performance and stagnation of SOEs. Zhang Weiying (1995) emphasizes that ownership reform is a prerequisite for effective SOE reform. By involving non-state economic entities and allowing them to assume the role of shareholders, effective incentive mechanisms and governance structures superior to those of SOEs can be established to fundamentally address the inefficiencies of SOEs. This perspective is supported by empirical evidence indicating that private firms and privatized SOEs generally outperform SOEs (Tan and Zheng, 2004; Liu, 2000; Liu and Li, 2005; Song and Yao, 2005).

In contrast to the property school, scholars represented by Lin Yifu advocate for a market school (*shichang pai*), which emphasizes the reduction of policy burdens on SOEs and creating an environment that ensures fair competition. According to Lin et al. (1997), a fair and competitive market can generate information regarding the performance of enterprises, which enables owners to effectively supervise the behavior of managers. However, due to the current policy burdens faced by SOEs, and the lack of a fair and fully competitive market environment, it is challenging to obtain sufficient information on the performance of these enterprises. From this perspective, creating a fair and fully competitive market environment is crucial for the reform of SOEs (Lin et al., 1997).

Neither of the two schools discussed above sufficiently considers the role of law. LTS, by contrast, posits that the reform of SOEs needs to consider the incompleteness of law and the existence of regulatory costs. While LTS acknowledges that privatization can indeed enhance performance, its implications diverge from the property school of thoughts because it also recognizes the potential for high regulatory costs associated with such a transition. Just as Coase treats firms as the results of transaction costs, LTS suggests that SOEs can be viewed as a result of high regulatory costs. LTS also disagrees with the market school's notion that SOEs should be completely relieved of all policy burdens. One of the notable advantages of SOEs is their ability to bear policy burdens at lower costs. Therefore, the focus should be on refining regulations and strengthening the state's regulatory capacity through the implementation of the rule of law.

LTS shares the view with the market school and many others that China needs to establish a fair market environment that provides robust protection to private enterprises against governmental opportunism. However, it also recognizes that there is a cost of strong property protection – the hindrance of necessary policy changes. LTS emphasizes that the key of reforming SOEs is to reduce regulatory costs rather than simply to strengthen property protection. Achieving this goal necessitates a more powerful and competent legal and regulatory system capable of resisting government influence and distinguishing between opportunistic actions and legitimate exercises of control.

II Measures to Strengthen the State's Control of Private Enterprises

As noted in previous chapters, one of the major reasons for the state to maintain SOEs is to strengthen its control over business enterprises. However, alternative approaches may be adopted to strengthen the state's control over private enterprises. If the state could strengthen its control over private enterprises and enforce the law at lower costs, its motives to maintain SOEs may be attenuated. Therefore, it becomes crucial to explore how the state can enhance its oversight of private enterprises using innovative regulatory approaches, and to identify the potential challenges that could limit the success of these measures.

A The Promises and Challenges of Innovative Regulatory Measures

There is a thick literature on how regulations can be made more effective (Gilad, 2010; Baldwin et al., 2011, p. 137). A thorough review of the literature would be beyond the scope of this book and not feasible here. In this Conclusion chapter, it would be sufficient to note that regulation can be designed to resemble state ownership, achieving regulatory goals at relatively lower costs. One notable idea is the approach of responsive regulation, proposed by Ayres and Braithwaite (1992). Under this approach, regulators would adopt different types of regulatory measures in response to the conduct of regulated private enterprises. They would initially take a soft approach to persuade private enterprises to cooperate and comply with regulatory orders, escalating regulatory measures to punish wrongdoings if private enterprises attempt to evade regulation (Ayres and Braithwaite, 1992, p. 20). Responsive regulation breaks down the distinction between "internal" and "external" control over an enterprise by allowing regulators to influence managerial decisions, using their regulatory power as leverage to ensure compliance by private corporations (Ayres and Braithwaite, 1992, p. 103; Laffont and Tirole, 1993, p. 637).

In a regulatory relationship between a regulator and a private enterprise, the two parties usually have divergent interests. The private enterprises normally seek to maximize their profits by minimizing the costs of regulation. It thus may choose to evade regulations if doing so increases its profits. The regulator, on the other hand, generally pursues regulatory goals and seeks to ensure compliance. The resources spent by the private enterprises in evading regulations and those by the regulator in detecting wrongdoings are social costs created by the regulatory relationship. Due to the constraints of budget and resources, regulators often do not possess sufficient capacity to detect wrongdoings and sanction private enterprises (Braithwaite, 2006, p. 888). Private enterprises may therefore feel it worthwhile to spend resources in evading regulations. This new strategy might compel private enterprises to comply with regulatory rules and cooperate with regulators to achieve regulatory goals by making cooperation more advantageous than evasion. It would thus save private enterprises the costs created from evading the regulation and regulators the costs created from detecting these wrongdoings (Ayres and Braithwaite, 1992, p. 26).

Moreover, private enterprises may possess internal information and techniques that may better achieve efficient regulation. By engaging a variety of actors to regulate private enterprises, including the private enterprises themselves and industry associations, the government can employ the knowledge of industry insiders to design better rules and help improve the regulatory regime (Ayres and Braithwaite, 1992, p. 39). Therefore, responsive regulation reduces regulatory costs, facilitates cooperation between regulators and enterprises, and promotes effective regulation (Braithwaite, 2006, p. 887).

The transformation of external regulation into a long-term cooperative relationship, where the interests of the state and the regulated party are aligned, resembles the concept of a long-term relational contract (Priest, 1993). Transaction cost economics have identified a range of mechanisms between contracts and hierarchies to curb opportunism, including vertical integration, secured property rights, and contractual governance terms (Klein et al., 1978; Williamson, 1979, 1983; Geis, 2009, p. 118). Such a reactive strategy would best promote cooperation between regulators and the regulated party, and hence best ensure compliance with regulatory rules (Ayres and Braithwaite, 1992, p. 20).

Ayres and Braithwaite argue that responsive regulation can "transcend the regulatory debate" between scholars who believe regulation is necessary for the public interest and those who support free markets (Ayres and Braithwaite, 2006, p. 3). It may alleviate the enforcement cost of the government when dealing with private enterprises and hence facilitates the reform of SOEs. If regulators could wield equally strong informal control over private enterprises with responsive regulation, state ownership might not be necessary.

Although responsive regulation enables regulators to enhance their control over private enterprises, there are certain limitations on such control. In the context of China, responsive regulation would face certain difficulties because the punitive measures that the Chinese government holds have their limitations. Private enterprises may become bankrupt, which undermines their incentives to cooperate. When private corporations cause damage to society, the best the state can do is to shut them down. However, shareholders do not lose more than they invest in the corporation. For example, when a SIFI fails, it creates negative externalities for the whole financial system, but its shareholders do not take responsibility for the negative externalities. The state could resort to criminal sanctions, but these are typically reserved for extreme cases where its discretion is significantly limited. It is very difficult for the government to impose sufficient sanctions on the bank to deter it from taking excessive risks ex ante because the shareholders have nothing to lose when the bank becomes insolvent (Shavell, 1984, p. 360).

While the challenges posed by limited regulatory measures are common to responsive regulation, China faces particularly acute limitations. One reason is the possibility of shareholders absconding to countries with no extradition treaty with China. A recent example highlighting this issue is the collapse of several financial platforms that promote peer-to-peer lending. In such cases, shareholders take investors' money and flee to other countries, leaving investors to suffer significant losses. As of the end of 2022, China has ratified extradition treaties with only forty-five countries, and treaties with an additional fourteen countries require mutual or unilateral approval for enforcement. This underscores that shareholders of private corporations may not always bear all the costs, and the existing regulations may not be sufficient to effectively address wrongdoings.

Additionally, it is more difficult to identify enterprises in the market that will continue to exist for a long time. For the responsive regulation approach to be effective, a sustained, repeated relationship between regulators and enterprises is typically essential (North, 1990, p. 12; Ayres and Braithwaite, 1992, p. 30; Dixit, 2004, p. 16; Gilson, 2007, p. 637). In such regulatory relationships, governments and enterprises can either cooperate, thereby mutually benefiting, or act opportunistically by choosing to "defect." In a onetime interaction, both parties may encounter a "prisoners' dilemma," where defection emerges as the rational choice. To achieve a cooperative equilibrium, repeated interactions with no predetermined end are necessary (North, 1990, p. 12). If cooperation has a definite endpoint, governments and enterprises might opt to defect in the final period, which can undermine incentives to cooperate in earlier stages, ultimately preventing sustained cooperation. This reactive strategy relies on a strong relationship between the parties and ongoing long-term transactions. According to game theory, the higher the likelihood that the repeated game will continue, the more advantageous it becomes for the parties to adopt a cooperative stance. While scholars generally assume that regulators and enterprises in developed economies are inclined to form long-term relationships, such enduring partnerships may be relatively rare in developing countries like China (Ayres & Braithwaite, 1992, p. 21).

B Reliance on the Corporate Conglomerates and Foreign Investors

To mitigate these issues, regulators could identify corporations with specific ownership structures that increase the likelihood of their long-term existence. However, relying on these ownership models also comes with its own set of challenges.

1 Private Conglomerates

Relying on corporate conglomerates may also alleviate some of the concerns associated with regulatory costs. Scholars have long been interested in the efficiency of conglomerates. Additionally, they have examined the advantages and disadvantages of private conglomerates (Khanna and Yafeh, 2007; Ramachandran et al., 2013; Morck, 2011). Ronald Gilson notes that conglomerates in developing countries have an important advantage in maintaining the reputation. A successful corporation in an industry can transmit its reputation to another industry, which could give it an edge in market competition, especially in developing countries where reputation plays a significant role (Gilson and Black, 1995, p. 332; Gilson, 2007). This chapter suggests that reputation is also important when it comes to regulation. Private conglomerates that have proven successful in other industries may have a lower incentive to act opportunistically, since they have more to lose by evading regulation.

The Chinese banking industry illustrates this point well. In recent years, a significant number of private conglomerates have started to operate in the industry. By June 2017, seventeen private banks had obtained licenses from the Banking Regulatory Commission. Among them, five have shareholders who are affiliates of internet corporations, including Tencent and Alibaba, two of the largest internet giants in China. Other shareholders include Suning Commerce, affiliated with Suning Appliance, a large corporation selling home-use appliances, and SANY Heavy Industry, a heavy machine producer. Only one of the seventeen banks has a shareholder that operates in the financial industry (Lv, 2017).

In the insurance industry, China has also allowed several new insurance companies to develop. For example, one of the newly established insurance companies was the Evergrande Life Insurance, a company affiliated with the China Evergrande Group. China Evergrande Group is a prominent Chinese conglomerate with core businesses in real estate and diversification into many other sectors. It became well known after it acquired the professional soccer team based in Guangzhou in 2010, which has since won eight consecutive championships of the Chinese Football Association Super League, significantly boosting the reputation of the company. In 2015, this corporate conglomerate was granted a license to enter the insurance industry.

Private conglomerates have also entered some of the highly regulated industries with natural monopolies. One example is the telecommunications industry. The famous state-owned monopoly corporation, China United Telecommunications, recently underwent a partial privatization. A group of private investors were invited to purchase equity interests in this traditionally state-owned corporation. These investors again included several of the largest and most reputable private internet companies, including Tencent, Alibaba, Baidu, and JD.com. The telecommunications industry is heavily regulated due to its susceptibility to natural monopolies. Similarly, in the railway industry, another natural-monopoly industry, a group of private investors led by Fosun Business – a corporation affiliated with a private conglomerate that started in the pharmaceutical industry, and later expanded into insurance, financial investment, real estate, steel, and several other industries – acquired a controlling equity position in a company operating high-speed rail in Zhejiang Province (Tian, 2021). This marked the first time a private corporation had invested in the railroad industry.

However, conglomerates also incur certain social costs and are not always capable of reducing regulatory costs. First, although private conglomerates can foster a long-term relationship between the government and the enterprise, they are not necessarily the best way to organize corporations. Corporations that are good at one type of business do not necessary possess the knowledge to succeed in another industry, even if they have a lower incentive to act opportunistically. In fact, empirical evidence casts doubt on the efficiency of conglomerates (Gilson and Black, 1995, p. 332). Managers in a private conglomerate may consider building a corporate empire that strengthens their positions in a corporation rather than promotes the benefits of the shareholders.

One recent example is the failure of LeTV, one of the leading online video companies in China. LeTV was founded by Jia Yueting in 2004, and went public on the Shenzhen Stock Exchange on August 12, 2010 (Zhang, 2010a). LeTV was an empire; its businesses included video streaming, cloud computing, sports media, music, film studio, electric cars, smartphones, and VR. LeTV's footprint extended into the financial sector as well. In 2016, LeTV obtained a license to establish a microcredit company and a factoring company in Chongqing (Zhou, 2017). Statistics shows that LeTV collected 45 million RMB in 2015 and 46 million RMB in 2016 from the government subsidies. However, the LeTV empire suddenly crumbled at the end of 2016 due to a serious cash crunch. The financial issue first became evident in its smartphone business (Kang, 2017). In order to enlarge its market share of the smartphone business, LeTV undersold its products, ignoring whether the price could cover its production costs. A similar problem happened in its electric car business. In November 2016, Jia sent an email to his staff in which he admitted that business over-expansion was the reason for the cash crunch (Ren, 2016). However, the reason behind the crisis seems more complicated than over-expansion. A large number of LeTV sales came from related-party transactions, raising the possibility of overstating its business operations, which could potentially constitute fraud (Qu, 2017).

More importantly, private conglomerates may not necessarily reduce risks in regulated markets. On the contrary, they may enhance the systemic risks, since, as corporations become larger, their failure may have significant social impacts. Governments may therefore need to support them when they face bankruptcy, which gives rise to a "too-big-to-fail" problem (Wilmarth, 2008). Private conglomerates may then expand to gain access to regulated industries without fully internalizing the negative consequences of the expansion, which is similar to the moral hazard problem in the financial industry.

The example of China Evergrande Group best demonstrates the risks associated with private conglomerates. The group's troubles escalated significantly in 2021 when it defaulted on several debt payments, triggering widespread concerns about its solvency. This led to a liquidity crisis and a series of missed payments to suppliers, creditors, and investors. In August 2023, Evergrande filed for bankruptcy protection in the United States, further highlighting the severity of its financial distress. According to investigations by the China Securities Regulatory Commission (CSRC), Evergrande Real Estate inflated its revenue by hundreds of billions of yuan through premature revenue recognition and other means during the period from 2019 to 2020. The scale of the financial fraud was substantial, misleading investors and severely damaging the fairness and transparency of the capital market. As a result, Evergrande and its related responsible individuals received severe penalties, including hefty fines and bans from the market. This incident suggests that large private conglomerates are not necessarily safer or more concerned about their reputation in their business operations or adherence to regulations.

Another notable example is Anbang Insurance Group. Established in 2004, Anbang is "one of the largest insurance groups in China." Its businesses include "property and casualty insurance, life insurance, health insurance, pension insurance, asset management, financial leasing, banking, insurance sales, and insurance brokerage and other financial services." Anbang has rapidly expanded in recent years. From 2004 to 2014, its registered capital grew from 0.5 billion RMB to 61.9 billion RMB. In May 2017, Caixin, a Chinese media outlet, published an influential article entitled "A Maze of Capital Leads to Anbang's Aggressive Expansion." The article argued that the capital investments made by Anbang's shareholders actually came from Anbang's subsidiaries, which could be further traced back to Anbang itself (Guo, 2015). In June 2017, Anbang issued an announcement that its CEO Wu Xiaohui was temporarily unable to continue in his role due to personal reasons. In February 2018, Wu was prosecuted for illegal fundraising and embezzlement.

According to reports, Wu faked a financial report to gain approval from CIRC to issue insurance products. After using these insurance products to raise funds, Wu withdrew this money from Anbang and used it to increase Anbang's registered capital, make overseas acquisitions, pay off corporate debts, and cover his personal consumption (Shang, 2018).

The above discussion indicates that private conglomerates are not necessarily long-term players. Moreover, these companies create systemic risks and further enhance the burden on the state to stabilize the market by taking over the debts of the corporation. The failure of Anbang could have caused social unrest since the insurance policyholders are everyday consumers. The Chinese regulators thus had no choice but to take over the assets of Anbang in March 2018. The China Insurance Security Fund (CISF) injected around 60 billion RMB into Anbang in order to protect the insurance policyholders, which amounts to 52 percent of total CISF assets (Xu, 2018).

2 Foreign Investors

Another strategy to reduce regulatory costs involves attracting foreign investors to participate in regulated industries (Haggard and Huang, 2008). Both central and local governments in China actively seek to bring reputable foreign corporations into various regulated sectors. Notably, some foreign investors entered the Chinese market even before it was fully opened to domestic private investors, presenting an intriguing political economy challenge for many scholars (Haggard and Huang, 2008).

Many foreign investment banks and commercial banks have entered the Chinese banking industry. For instance, in 2005, China began inviting foreign private investors to acquire share blocks in state-owned banks. That year, Bank of America purchased 9 percent of China Construction Bank's stocks. Similarly, Bank of China introduced Royal Bank of Scotland and Temasek as minority shareholders in the same year. In 2006, ICBC brought in several foreign financial institutions as strategic investors, including Goldman Sachs. Notably, joint-stock banks sought to introduce foreign strategic investors even earlier than state-owned banks. For example, China Everbright Bank, a joint-stock commercial bank controlled by an SOE directly under the State Council's control, invited the Asian Development Bank to hold 1.9 percent of its shares in 1996.

Another example can be found in the insurance industry. New China Life Insurance is a life insurance company cofounded by a group of SOEs and foreign investors in 1996. Later, a group of other SOEs, including the Baosteel Corporate Group and several other electricity companies, and a group of foreign insurance companies, including the Zurich Insurance Group, obtained equity interests in the corporation.

In municipal infrastructures, foreign investors have also played a significant role. Before 1998, 95 percent of all equity stocks in the water utilities industry were owned by the state. A few foreign investors, however, had entered the municipal water utilities industry. In 1992, Suez, a famous French utilities company, was the first foreign firm to invest in a water company in China. By contrast, domestic private investors were not allowed to invest in the water utilities market during this period. The existence of these foreign-invested utilities companies indicates that the state was allowing local governments to introduce private companies into public water supply at the time.

Several reasons underlie the regulators' welcoming attitude to foreign investors. First, foreign corporations have good management skills, which reduce the operation costs of these businesses. Secondly, foreign investors have invested a sunk cost in their reputation. If they act opportunistically in relation to regulatory rules, both the Chinese central and local governments may exclude them from the markets. The reputational sanction would be much stronger for foreign investors with their well-known brand names than for domestic corporations that can easily be liquidated and reincorporated to carry out new transactions.

However, granting privileges to foreign investors may not be a politically popular idea because it implies unequal treatment of domestic private investors and foreign investors. Thus, attempts to introduce foreign investors sometimes encounter political resistance. For example, several pollution accidents were reported in Qingdao, a prefecture where water utilities were operated by Qingdao Guangwei, a company with a foreign investor, Veolia (Hao, 2007). Later, when Veolia attempted to acquire a water utilities company in Xi'an, the CEO of the water utilities company expressed his objections to the central government construction department, claiming that foreign private investors would hurt the public interest by raising the water tariff and incurring unnecessary costs that would be hard to monitor. The Xi'an government ultimately did not sell equity interests in the company to Veolia (Jia, 2008). The point of this example is not to argue for or against favoring foreign investors in regulated industries, but to highlight the difficulty in identifying corporations that have the potential for long-term operation, especially in the early stages of Chinese development.

To sum up, private conglomerates and foreign investor ownership can alleviate regulatory costs to some extent, which increases the proportion of private firms in regulated industries in China. However, they also face certain limitations. To the extent that these alternative corporate ownership regimes fail to adequately address the regulators' concerns, state ownership may remain a less costly option.

Thus, while employing more innovative regulatory measures may enable the Chinese government to enforce regulatory rules at lower costs and maintains substantial control over private businesses, this influence is subject to certain constraints, contingent upon the existence of a sustained, ongoing relationship between the state and the enterprise. The government can only affect the behavior of private corporations when the ultimate "carrots" and "sticks" are strong enough. Consequently, the state can effectively regulate major corporations with a high likelihood of long-term operations, but its control over smaller and medium-sized enterprises – able to exit the market without significant repercussions – is comparatively limited.

III Closing Remarks

The analysis presented in this book suggests that the role of state ownership is significantly influenced by the effectiveness of legal and regulatory institutions in overseeing private enterprises. Accepting political or political economy theories might lead one to support the direct privatization of SOEs and limiting their activities. However, LTS posits that such privatization only addresses symptoms rather than the root causes – the high social costs associated with replacing informal mechanisms based on state ownership with a formal legal and regulatory system. LTS suggests that where law is incomplete, SOEs arise as a natural outcome either because the state is concerned about losing control or because private investors are concerned about the safety of their investments. This is not to imply that addressing symptoms is unimportant. Indeed, privatization can have complex political impacts and may diminish the influence of SOEs as an interest group on policy-making (Pargendler, 2012). However, this book emphasizes that SOE reform is fundamentally constrained by the state's ability to develop a robust legal and regulatory system.

Emphasizing the role of legal and regulatory institutions does not necessarily mean advocating for always replacing state ownership with law. Employing formal laws and regulations to govern the state-enterprise relationship is sometimes costly, while state ownership can serve as a form of less formal mechanism. To some extent, LTS aligns with criticisms against the "legal centrist view" that overemphasizes the role of law in society (Ellickson, 1991, p. 4). Despite advances in legal knowledge, effective regulation of sectors such as banking and finance still faces significant challenges. Even in countries like the United States, with its long history of financial regulation, financial crises occasionally occur. Additionally, much of the utilities sector in the United States remains owned by municipal governments (Masten, 2011). Relational friction between the state and regulated entities likely contributes to the persistence of state ownership in liberal markets. There is no reason to think that a state with relatively weak regulatory institutions like China could completely privatize similar sectors without incurring significant social costs, given that various measures to curb opportunistic behavior and strengthen the state's control of private enterprises discussed above all face limitations.

Building robust legal and regulatory institutions can promote the development of private enterprises, hence reducing the ownership costs associated with state ownership. However, this is likely to be a challenging process because it involves not simply strengthening the legal protection for private enterprises but also balancing property interests and the state's various policy goals. To develop legal institutions capable of such tasks no doubt requires substantial financial and human resources (Schafer, 2006, p. 115). As China's recent judicial reform aiming to centralize the control of local courts illustrates, enhancing the power of local courts may prove challenging and sometimes costly. Additionally, augmenting the expertise of judges and regulators can foster private investments but necessitates investing in the education of judicial and regulatory officials, offering competitive salaries to attract talented individuals, and enhancing their social status to assure their independence. Despite these challenges, there are reasons to believe that further investments in the legal system would be beneficial given the potential reduction in ownership costs and promotion of efficiency. Over recent decades, China has heavily invested in physical infrastructure like roads, bridges, and public transportation, believing in their long-term economic benefits. While these investments have supported China's economic growth, the returns on physical infrastructure will likely diminish over time. It might now be time for China to consider investing more in its legal infrastructure to better support the growth of private enterprises.

REFERENCES

ABA Committee on Corporate Laws. (1990). Other Constituencies Statutes: Potential for Confusion. *Business Law*, 45(4), 2253–2271.

Acemoglu, D., & Robinson, J. A. (2013). *Why Nations Fail: The Origins of Power, Prosperity, and Poverty*, 437–438. New York: Crown Currency.

Adams, S., & Mengistu, B. (2008). Privatization, Governance and Economic Development in Developing Countries. *Journal of Developing Societies*, 24(4), 415–438.

Ameyaw, E. E., Chan, A. P. C., & Owusu-Manu, D.-G. (2017). A Survey of Critical Success Factors for Attracting Private Sector Participation in Water Supply Projects in Developing Countries. *Journal of Facilities Management*, 15(1), 35–61.

Ang, Y. Y. (2009). *How China Escaped the Poverty Trap*. Ithaca, NY: Cornell University Press.

Aylen, J. (1987). Privatization in Developing Countries. *Lloyds Bank Review*, 163, 15–30.

Ayres, I., & Braithwaite, J. (1992). *Responsive Regulation: Transcending the Deregulation Debate*. New York: Oxford University Press.

Bai, C.-E., Lu, J., & Tao, Z. (2006a). The Multitask Theory of State Enterprise Reform: Empirical Evidence from China. *The American Economic Review*, 96(2), 353–357.

(2006b). 国有企业改制效果的实证研究 [Empirical Studies on the Effects of Reform of State-Owned Enterprises].《经济研究》 *[Economic Research]*, 41(8), 4–13.

(2009). How Does Privatization Work in China? *Journal of Comparative Economics*, 37(3): 453–470. https://doi.org/10.1016/j.jce.2008.09.006.

Bai, R. (2016). Research on Withdrawal of State-Owned Small-and Medium-Sized Enterprises and "De-Capacity" Issues under Supply-Side Structural Reform. 《经济学动态》, 7, 65, 69.

Bainbridge, S. M. (1993). In Defense of the Shareholder Wealth Maximization Norm: A Reply to Professor Green. *Washington. & Lee Law Review*, 50, 1423.

Baldwin, R., Cave, M., & Lodge, M. (2011). *Understanding Regulation: Theory, Strategy, and Practice*. New York: Oxford University Press.

Banerjee, G., & Munger, M. (2004). Move to Markets? An Empirical Analysis of Privatization in Developing Countries. *Journal of International Development*, 16, 213–240.

Barr, M. S. (2012). The Financial Crisis and the Path of Reform. *Yale Journal on Regulation*, 29(1), 91–119.

Beck, K. I. (2023). The Political Economy of State Sector Restructuring in China: Cross-Provincial Evidence 2008–2017. *Journal of Chinese Political Science*, 28, 273.

Benjamin, L. et al. (2020). Mass Digitization of Chinese Court Decisions: How to Use Text as Data in the Field of Chinese Law. *Journal of Law and Courts*, 8(2), 177–201.

Berger, A. N., Hasan, I., & Zhou, M. (2009). Bank Ownership and Efficiency in China: What Will Happen in the World's Largest Nation? *Journal of Banking & Finance*, 33(1), 113–130.

Berle, A. A., & Means, G. G. C. (1932). *The Modern Corporation and Private Property*. Piscataway, NJ: Transaction Publishers.

Biglaiser, G., & Brown, D. (2003). The Determinants of Privatization in Latin America. *Political Research Quarterly*, 56, 77–89.

Black, B., Kraakman, R., & Tarassova, A. (2000). Russian Privatization and Corporate Governance: What Went Wrong? *Stanford Law Review*, 52(6), 1731–1808.

Blanchette, J. (2021). *Confronting the Challenge of Chinese State Capitalism*. Washington, DC.: The Center for Strategic and International Studies.

Bortolotti, B., Fantini, M., & Siniscalco, D. (2004). Privatisation around the World: Evidence from Panel Data. *Journal of Public Economics*, 88(1–2), 305–332.

Bossone, B. (2000). What Makes Banks Special? A Study of Banking, Finance, and Economic Development. *Policy Research Working Paper Series*, 2408.

Braithwaite, J. (2006). Responsive Regulation and Developing Economies. *World Development*, 34(5), 884–898.

Bratton, W. W. (2001–2002). Enron and the Dark Side of Shareholder Value. *Tulane Law Review*, 76, 1275–1358.

Breen, M., & Doyle, D. (2020). The Determinants of Privatization: A Comparative Analysis of Developing Countries. In I. Geva-May, B. Guy Peters, & J. Muhleisen, eds, *Institutions and Governance in Comparative Policy Analysis Studies*, 86–105. Oxford: Routledge.

Brown, T. L., & Potoski, M. (2005). Transaction Costs and Contracting: The Practitioner Perspective. *Public Performance & Management Review*, 28(3), 326–351.

Byrd, W., & Gelb, A. (1990). Township, Village, and Private Industry in China's Economic Reform. *World Bank Policy Research Working Papers*, 38966.

Cai, Y. (2002). Relaxing the Constraints from above: Politics of Privatizing Public Enterprises in China. *Asian Journal of Political Science*, 10, 94.

Cai, Z. (蔡之兵). (2016). 地方政府去产能效果与特征：2006–2014年 [The Effectiveness and Characteristics of Overcapacity Reduction by Local Government: 2006–2014].《改革》*[Reform]*, 10, 45.

Calabresi, G., & Melamed, A. D. (1972). Property Rules, Liability Rules, and Inalienability: One View of the Cathedral. *Harvard Law Review*, 1089–1128.

Calem, P. S., & LaCour-Little, M. (2004). Risk-Based Capital Requirements for Mortgage Loans. *Journal of Banking & Finance*, 28(3), 647–672.

Campbell, C. (2021, July 13). Here's What the Crackdown on China's Big Tech Firms Is Really About. *Time*. https://time.com/6079877/china-ipo/.

Cao, Y., Qian, Y., & Weingast, B. R. (1999). From Federalism, Chinese Style to Privatization, Chinese Style. *Economics of Transition*, 7, 103.

Carnell, R. et al. (2009). *The Law of Banking and Financial Institutions*, 4th ed. Burlington, MA: Aspen Publishers.

Chaisse, J. et al. (2022). *Regulation of State-Controlled Enterprises: An Interdisciplinary and Comparative Examination*. Wiesbaden: Springer Professional.

Chan, A. P. et al., (2015). Cross-Sectional Analysis of Critical Risk Factors for PPP Water Projects in China. *Journal of Infrastructure Systems*, 21(1), 04014031.

Chang, Y., & Klerman, D. M. (2021). Settlement Around the World: Settlement Rates in the Largest Economies. *Journal of Legal Analysis*, 14(1), 80–175.

Chang, Y., & Lin, Y.-H. (2022). Do State-Owned Enterprises Have Worse Corporate Governance? An Empirical Study of Corporate Practices in China. *European Business Organization Law Review*, 23, 711.

Che, J., & Qian, Y. (1998). Insecure Property Rights and Government Ownership of Firms. *The Quarterly Journal of Economics*, 113(2), 467–496.

Chen, C. C., Guo, R.-J., & Lin, L. Y.-H. (2023). The Effect of Political Influence on Corporate Valuation: Evidence from Party-Building Reform in China. *International Review of Law and Economics*, 73, 106–120.

Chen, H. (2017, August 22). "人财物省级统管"改革的成效与完善 [The Effectiveness and Improvement of the Reform of Provincial Management of Personnel, Finance, and Materials]. 第十二届中国法学青年论坛专题报道演讲与报告 [The 12th China Law Youth Forum Special Report Speech and Report].中国法学会 [*China Law Society*]. https://www.chinalaw.org.cn/portal/article/index/id/20329.html.

(2021). Is There Really a "Nanshan Must-Win"? An Analysis Based on the Nanshan District Court's Judgment Concerning Tencent in 2020. 中国法律评论微信公众号 [*China Law Review*, WeChat Channel].

Chen, H. (陈慧颖), & Yu, N. (2010, October 19). 新华人寿痛苦转型 [New China Insurance's Painful Transformation].《新世纪》*[Century Weekly]*. http://finance.sina.com.cn/money/insurance.

Chen, L., & Tang, Y. (2014). 混合所有制改革与国有企业政策性负担：基于早期国企产权改革大数据的实证研究 [Mixed Ownership Reform and

Policy Burden of State-Owned Enterprises: An Empirical Study Based on Big Data of Early State-Owned Enterprise Property Rights Reform]. *The Economist*, 11, 13–23.

Chen, L. Y., & Frost, R. (2020, November 4). China Halts Ant Group's IPO, Throwing Ma Empire into Turmoil. *Bloomberg Law*. https://news.bloomberglaw.com/securities-law/china-stops-jack-mas-35-billion-ant-ipo-from-going-ahead.

Chen, Q., Huang, W., & Wang, S. (2021). 基于案例的我国2014–2020年PPP项目失败原因分析 [Analysis of the Reasons for the Failure of China's PPP Projects from 2014 to 2020 Based on Case Studies]. 《建筑经济》 *[Construction Economy]*, 3, 10–14.

Chen, W. (2010, January 11). 一位山西煤老板眼里的煤炭整合 [Coal Integration in the Eyes of a Shanxi Coal Boss].《经济参考报》[*Economic Reference News*]. http://www.jjckb.cn/cjxw/2010-01/11/content_201846.htm.

Chen, W. (陈卫东). (2014). 司法"去地方化"：司法体制改革的逻辑、挑战及其应对 [Judicial "De-Localization": The Logic, Challenges, and Responses of Judicial System Reform]. *Global Law Review (环球法律评论)*, 2014(1), 57–61.

(陈惟杉). (2020, November 28). 博弈永煤债：谈判场面一度激烈，被债权人质疑"早有预谋" [The Game of Yongmei Debt: The Negotiation Scene Was Once Intense, Questioned by Creditors as Premeditated].《中国新闻周刊》[*China News Week*]. https://new.qq.com/rain/a/20201128A01WF800.

Chen, Y. (陈益刊). (2016, November 28). 中央重磅文件严禁地方政府违约毁约，给PPP吃定心丸 [Central Government's Important Document Strictly Prohibits Local Governments from Defaulting on Contracts, Giving PPP a Reassurance]. 《第一财经》[*Yicai*]. http://finance.sina.com.cn/roll/2016-11-28/doc-ifxyasmv2059142.shtml.

(陈益刊). (2023, January 5). 地方仍有城投债刚兑信仰，财长刘昆再提打破兜底预期 [Local Government Debts Are Still Expected to Be Backed by Implicit Guarantees, Finance Minister Liu Kun Again Suggests Breaking the Bottom Line Expectation]. 《第一财经》[*Yicai*]. https://new.qq.com/rain/a/20201128A01WF800.

Chen, Z. (2012). Five Major Consequences of "Advance of the State, Retreat of the Private Sector". *China Nongovernmental Science Technology and Economy*, 11, 105.

Cheung, E., & Chan, A. P. (2011). Risk Factors of Public-Private Partnership Projects in China: Comparison between the Water, Power, and Transportation Sectors. *Journal of Urban Planning and Development*, 137(4), 409–415.

China Banking Regulatory Commission. (2006). 2006 Annual Report. http://zhuanti.cbrc.gov.cn/subject/subject/nianbao/chinese/zwqb.pdf.

(2010). 2010 Annual Report.

(2012). 2012 Annual Report.

(2014). 2014 Annual Report. http://zhuanti.cbrc.gov.cn/subject/subject/nianbao2014/1.pdf.

China Business News. (2012). 银监会：不对民间资本进入银行业单独设限 [Banking Regulatory Commission: Will Not Prevent Private Capital from Entering the Banking Industry]. *China Business News* (第一财经日报). http://finance.people.com.cn/bank/GB/17998200.html.

China Securities Journal. (2009). 发改委：万亿新增中央投资有四大来源 [National Development and Reform Committee: There are four major sources for the new central investment]. *China Securities Journal (*中国证券报*)*. http://news.xinhuanet.com/fortune/2009-05/22/content_11415794.htm

Choi, J. J., et al. (2016). *The Political Economy of Chinese Finance*. Cambridge, MA: Emerald Publishing.

Choudhury, B. (2008). Serving Two Masters: Incorporating Social Responsibility into the Corporate Paradigm. *University of Pennsylvania Journal of Business Law*, 11, 631–674.

Chu, Z., Liang, Q., & Jiang, H. (储著贞, 梁权熙 & 蒋海). (2012). 宏观调控, 所有权结构与商业银行信贷扩张行为 [Macroeconomic Control, Ownership Structure, and Commercial Bank Loan Expansion Behavior]. 《国际金融研究》 *[International Finance Review]*, 57(3), 57–68.

Clarke, D. C. (2003). Economic Development and the Rights Hypothesis: The China Problem. *American Journal of Comparative Law*, 51, 89.

Clarke, D. C., & Howson, N. C. (2012). Pathway to Minority Shareholder Protection: Derivative Actions in the People's Republic of China. In D. Puchniak, H. Baum, & M. Ewing-Chow, eds, *The Derivative Action in Asia: A Comparative and Functional Approach*, 243–295. Cambridge, UK: Cambridge University Press.

Clarke, D. C., et al. (2008) The Role of Law in China's Economic Development. In L. Brandt & T. Rawski, eds, *China's Great Economic Transformation*, 375–428. Cambridge: Cambridge University Press.

Clover, C., & Chon, G. (2015, January 28). Alibaba Denies Misleading Investors Over Chinese Regulator's Probe. *The Financial Times*. https://www.ft.com/content/8e6a7c70-a6dd-11e4-8a71-00144feab7de.

Coase, R. H. (1937). The Nature of the Firm. *Economica*, 4(16), 386–405.

Coffee, Jr, J. C. (2007). Law and the Market: The Impact of Enforcement. *University of Pennsylvania Law Review*, 156, 229.

Cohen, G. M. (1992). The Negligence-Opportunism Tradeoff in Contract Law. *Hofstra Law Review*, 20(4), 941–1016.

Coleman, J. L. (2001). *The Practice of Principle*. New York: Oxford University Press.

Colino, S. M. (2022), The Incursion of Antitrust into China's Platform Economy. *The Antitrust Bulletin*, 67(2), 237–258.

Crocker, K. J., & Masten, S. E. (1988). Mitigating Contractual Hazards: Unilateral Options and Contract Length. *The RAND Journal of Economics*, 19(3), 327–343.

Custos, D., & Reitz, J. (2010). Public-Private Partnerships. *The American Journal of Comparative Law*, 58, 555–584.

Dana, D. A., & Merrill, T. W. (2002), *Property: Takings 32*. Eagan, MN: Foundation Press.

Dannin, E. (2011). Crumbling Infrastructure, Crumbling Democracy: Infrastructure Privatization Contracts and Their Effects on State and Local Governance. *Northwestern Journal of Law and Social Policy*, 6(1), 46–105.

Davies, D. G. (1971). The Efficiency of Public versus Private Firms, the Case of Australia's Two Airlines. *The Journal of Law & Economics*, 14(1), 149–165.

Davis, P. J. (2013, August 30). 中国银行业坏账处理陷困局 [Chinese Banking Industry Stalemated in Handling Bad Debts].《金融时报》[*Financial Times*]. http://www.ftchinese.com/story/001052227?full=y.

Demsetz, H. (1974). Toward a Theory of Property Rights. In C. Gopalakrishnan, ed, *Classic Papers in Natural Resource Economics*, 163–177. London: Palgrave Macmillan.

Deng, F. (邓峰). (2015, December 8). 国企改革的理论困局和道路展望 [Reform of State-Owned Enterprises: The Theoretical Dilemma and The Way Forward]. https://www.aisixiang.com/data/94860.html.

Dinc, I. S., & Gupta, N. (2011). The Decision to Privatize: Finance and Politics. *The Journal of Finance*, 66(1), 241–269.

Dixit, A. K. (2004). *Lawlessness and Economics: Alternative Modes of Governance*. Princeton, NJ: Princeton University Press.

Djankov, S. et al. (2003). The New Comparative Economics. *Journal of Comparative Economics*, 31(4), 595–619.

Dong, Y. (董映颉). (2009, September 11). 地方政府设置内外资水企悬殊利润率 [Local Governments Allow Strikingly Different Profit Rates for Domestic and Foreign Owned Water Utility Enterprises].《华夏时报》[*China Times*]. http://news.dayoo.com/finance/200909/12/53869_10762634.htm.

Dong, Y.. & Liu, P. (2022). The Impact of State-Owned Capital Injection on the Performance of Private Enterprises – Based on the Research of Chinese Industrial Enterprises.《北京经济学》*[Beijing Economics]*, 21(3), 1925.

Drazen, A., & Easterly, W. (2001). Do Crises Induce Reform? Simple Empirical Tests of Conventional Wisdom. *Economics and Politics*, 13, 129–157.

Dyck, A. (2001). Privatization and Corporate Governance: Principles, Evidence, and Future Challenges. *The World Bank Research Observer*, 16(1), 59–84.

Eagle, D., & Christensen, S. (1995). Do Things Have to Get Worse Before They Get Better? The Privatization Issue of Freeing Internal Markets. In *Business Forum,* Winter/Spring. Guislain, Pierre, 83–116.

Eaton, S. (2015). *The Advance of the State in Contemporary China: State-Market Relations in the Reform Era*. Cambridge, UK: Cambridge University Press.

Ellickson, R. C. (1991). *Order Without Law: How Neighbors Settle Disputes*. Cambridge, MA: Harvard University Press.

Esfahani, H. S., et al. (2002). What Determines the Extent of Public Ownership? *Working Papers 0205, Economic Research Forum*, 1–35.

Estrin, S., & Pelletier, A. (2018). Privatization in Developing Countries: What Are the Lessons of Recent Experience? *The World Bank Research Observer*, 33(1), 65–102.

Fagaiwei (发改委). (2009, May 22). 发改委：万亿新增中央投资有四大来源 [National Development and Reform Committee: There Are Four Major Sources for the New Central Investment].《中国证券报》[*China Securities Journal*]. http://news.xinhuanet.com/fortune/2009-05/22/content_11415794.htm.

Feng, X. (2013).《中国民营企业生存环境报告2012》[Report on the Business Environment of Private Enterprises in China 2012]. Beijing: China Economic Press.

Financial Crisis Inquiry Commission. (2011). The Financial Crisis Inquiry Report: Final Report of the National Commission on the Causes of the Financial and Economic Crisis in the United States. Government Printing Office, 1–663.

Fischel, W. A., & Shapiro, P. (1988). Takings, Insurance, and Michelman: Comments on Economic Interpretations of "Just Compensation" Law. *The Journal of Legal Studies*, 17(2), 269–293.

(2013). Takings, Insurance, and Michelman: Comments on Economic Interpretations of "Just Compensation" Law. In R. A. Epstein, ed, *Constitutional Protection of Private Property and Freedom of Contract*, 381–405. Oxford: Routledge.

Foss, N. J., et al. (2000). *The Theory of the Firm. Encyclopedia of Law and Economics, Vol. III of the Regulation of Contracts*. New York: Springer.

Fox, G. (2007). The Real Coase Theorems. *Cato Journal*, 27, 373–396.

Freeman, J. (2000). The Contracting State. *Florida State University Law Review*, 28(1), 155–214.

(2003). Extending Public Law Norms Through Privatization. *Harvard Law Review*, 116(5), 1285–1352.

Friedman, M. (1966). The Methodology of Positive Economics. In *Essays in Positive Economics*, 3–16, 30–43. Chicago, IL: University of Chicago Press.

Fu, T. (付涛). (2011).《水价二十讲》[*Twenty Lectures on Water Price*]. Beijing: China Architecture Publishing.

Gao, H., & Zhou, W. (2022). Emerging Approaches to Regulating State-Owned Enterprises: The Comprehensive and Progressive Agreement for Trans-Pacific Partnership (CPTPP) and Post-CPTPP Free Trade Agreements. In L. Bartels, T. Cottier, T. Broude, & A. K. Bjorklund, eds, *Between*

Market Economy and State Capitalism: China's State-Owned Enterprises and the World Trading System, 127–153. Cambridge, UK: Cambridge University Press.

Gates, G., Ewing, J., Russell, K., & Watkins, D. (2017). How Volkswagen's 'Defeat Devices' Worked. *The New York Times*. https://www.nytimes.com/interactive/2015/business/international/vw-diesel-emissions-scandal-explained.html.

Geis, G. S. (2009). The Space Between Markets and Hierarchies. *Virginia Law Review*, 95(1), 99–153.

(2010). An Empirical Examination of Business Outsourcing Transactions. *Virginia Law Review*, 96(2), 241–300.

Gerard, F., Rokkanen, M., & Rothe, C. (2020). Bounds on Treatment Effects in Regression Discontinuity Designs with a Manipulated Running Variable. *Quantitative Economics*, 11(3), 839–870.

Gilad, S. (2010). It Runs in the Family: Meta-Regulation and Its Siblings. *Regulation & Governance*, 4(4), 485–506.

Gilardi, F. (2002). Policy Credibility and Delegation to Independent Regulatory Agencies: A Comparative Empirical Analysis. *Journal of European Public Policy*, 9(6), 873–893.

Gilson, R. J. (2007). Controlling Family Shareholders in Developing Countries: Anchoring Relational Exchange. *Stanford Law Review*, 60(2), 633–655.

Gilson, R. J., & Black, B. (1995) *The Law and Finance of Corporate Acquisitions*, 2nd ed. Eagan, MN: Foundation Press.

Gilson, R. J., & Milhaupt, C. J. (2011). Economically Benevolent Dictators: Lessons for Developing Democracies. *The American Journal of Comparative Law*, 59, 227.

Goldberg, I. (2023, November 18). China's Heavy Economic Legacy of State Ownership and Central Planning. *The Diplomat*. https://thediplomat.com/2023/11/chinas-heavy-economic-legacy-of-state-ownership-and-central-planning/.

Grossman, S. J., et al. (1986). The Costs and Benefits of Ownership: A Theory of Vertical and Lateral Integration. *Journal of Political Economy*, 94(4), 691–719.

Gu, Y., & Yang, Z. (2023). The More Red the Greener? How the Communist Party of China's Party Organizations Influences Corporate Green Innovation. *Finance Research Letters*, 55, 103860.

Gunningham, N., Kagan, R. A., & Thornton, D., (2004). Social License and Environmental Protection: Why Business Go Beyond Compliance, *Law & Social Inquiry*, 29(2), 307–341.

Guo, G. (2009). China's Local Political Budget Cycles, *American Journal of Political Science*, 53(3), 621–632.

Guo, K., & Yao, Y. (2004). The Causes of State-Owned Enterprises' Reform: A Test of Five Hypotheses. *The Journal of World Economy*, 316, 3–13.

Guo, T. (2015, February 2). A Maze of Capital Leads to Anbang's Aggressive Expansion, *Caixin*. http://weekly.caixin.com/2015-01-30/100780098.html.

Guoxinban (国新办). (2015, June 26). 国新办关于"鼓励民间资本进入银行业"专题新闻发布会开场通报 [State Council Information Office Opening Statement on the Public Release About Encouraging Private Capital to Enter the Banking Industry].《中国网》[*China.com.cn*]. http://www.china.com.cn/zhibo/zhuanti/ch-xinwen/2015-06/26/content_35917439.htm.

Haggard, S., & Huang, Y. (2008). The Political Economy of Private-Sector Development in China. In L. Brandt & T. S. Rawski, eds, *China's Great Economic Transformation*, 337–374. Cambridge, UK: Cambridge University Press.

Halberstam, D. (2010). The Promise of Comparative Administrative Law: A Constitutional Perspective on Independent Agencies. In S. Rose-Ackerman & P. L. Lindseth, eds, *Comparative Administrative Law*, 191. Cheltenham, UK: Edward Elgar Publishing.

Hamdani, A., & Kamar, E. (2012). Hidden Government Influence over Privatized Banks. *Theoretical Inquiries in Law*, 13(2), 567–596.

Hammami, M., Ruhashyankiko, J.-F., & Yehoue, E. B. (2006). Determinants of Public-Private Partnerships in Infrastructure. *IMF Working Papers*, 99, 1–39.

Han, X. (韩晓东). (2009, May 22). 发改委：万亿新增中央投资有四大来源 [National Development and Reform Committee: There Are Four Major Sources for the New Central Investment].《中国证券报》[*China Securities Daily*]. https://finance.cctv.com/20090522/100688.shtml.

Han, Z., & Dai, M. (2008). 中国民营化的财政动因 [Fiscal Motives of China's Privatization].《经济研究》*[Economic Research]*, 2, 56–67.

Hanna, T. M. (2018). *Our Common Wealth: The Return of Public Ownership in the United States*. Manchester, UK: Manchester University Press. https://www.manchesterhive.com/downloadpdf/9781526133786/9781526133786.pdf.

Hansmann, H. (1987). Economic Theories of Nonprofit Organization. In W. W. Powell & R. Steinberg, eds, *The Nonprofit Sector: A Research Handbook*, 27–42. Stanford, CA: Stanford University Press.

(1988). Ownership of the Firm. *Journal of Law, Economics, & Organization*, 4(2), 267–304.

Hansmann, H., & Kraakman, R. (2000). The Essential Role of Organizational Law. *The Yale Law Journal*, 110(3), 387–440.

Hansmann, H. B. (1980). The Role of Nonprofit Enterprise. *Yale Law Journal*, 89(5), 835–901.

Hao, Y. (2007, November 2). 威立雅卷入自来水管道排污风波 [Veola Involved in Scandals of Sewage Distribution through Tap Water Pipelines). *China Business Newspaper*. http://finance.sina.com.cn/g/20071104/13434135878.shtml.

Hao, Y., & Gong, L. (2017). Mixed State-Owned and Private Equity Participation and Corporate Performance Improvement. *Economic Research Journal*, 52(3), 122–135.

Hart, O. (2003). Incomplete Contracts and Public Ownership: Remarks, and an Application to Public-Private Partnerships. *Economic Journal*, 113(486), C69–C76.

Hart, O., & Moore, J. (1990). Property Rights and the Nature of the Firm. *Journal of Political Economy*, 98(6), 1119–1158.

Hart, O., Shleifer, A., & Vishny, R. W. (1997). The Proper Scope of Government: Theory and an Application to Prisons. *The Quarterly Journal of Economics*, 112(4), 1127–1161.

Hausman, C., & Rapson, D. S. (2018). Regression Discontinuity in Time: Considerations for Empirical Applications. *Annual Review of Resource Economics*, 10, 533–552.

He, H. (何海波) (2016). 从全国数据看新《行政诉讼法》实施成效 [From the National Data to See the Effectiveness of the Implementation of the New Administrative Litigation Law].《中国法律评论》*[China Law Review]*, 3, 145–149.

He, X., & Su, Y. (2013). Do the 'Haves' Come Out Ahead in Shanghai Courts? *Journal of Empirical Legal Studies*, 10(1), 120–145.

Hemming, E., & Unnithan, N. P. (1996). Determinants of privatization levels in developing countries. *Social Science Quarterly*, 77(2), 434–444.

Hill, C., & Painter, R. (2009). Berle's Vision Beyond Shareholder Interests: Why Investment Bankers Should Have (Some) Personal Liability. *Seattle University Law Review*, 33(4), 1173–1199.

Hills, Jr, R. M., & Qiao, S. (2017). Binding Leviathan: Credible Commitment in an Authoritarian Regime. *Minnesota Law Review*, 102(112), 1591–1617.

Hou, Y. (2019). *The Private Sector in Public Office: Selective Property Rights in China*. Cambridge, UK: Cambridge University Press.

Howson, N. C. (2017). China's Corporatization without Privatization and the Late Nineteenth Century Roots of a Stubborn Path Dependency. *Vanderbilt Journal of Transnational Law*, 50, 961–1006.

Hsueh, R. (2017). *China's Regulatory State: A New Strategy for Globalization*. Ithaca, NY: Cornell University Press.

Hu, Y., Song, M., & Zhang, J. (2006). 中国国有企业民营化绩效研究 [Studies on the Effects of Privatized State-Owned Enterprises].《经济研究》*[Economic Research]*, 7, 49–60.

Huang, J. (黄金老). (2013). 实行贷款限额控制的必然性及其优化措施 [The Necessity of Lending Amount Control and Its Possible Improvement].《金融发展评论》*[Financial Development Review]*, 6(1), 006.

Huang, W., & Ma, S. (黄卫根, 马世昌). (2018, May 23). 国资委192号文指导下央企规范参与PPP项目问题研究 [Research on Issues of Central Enterprises' Participation in PPP Projects under the Guidance of Document No. 192 of SASAC].《人民论坛网》. http://www.rmlt.com.cn/2018/0523/519553.shtml.

Huang, Y. (2008). Just How Capitalist is China? *MIT Sloan Research Paper*, No. 4699-08, 1–57.

International Monetary Fund (IMF), Fiscal Affairs Department. (2020). *Fiscal Monitor, April 2020: Policies to Support People during the COVID-19 Pandemic*. Washington, DC: International Monetary Fund.

Janssen, R., et al. (2016). Why Local Governments Rarely Use PPPs in Their Road Development Projects: Understanding the Barriers. *International Journal of Managing Projects in Business*, 9(1), 33–52.

Jia, H. (2008, July 18). 西安自来水公司反对威立雅收购国有资产 [Xi'an Water Utilities Oppose Veolia Purchasing State Assets]. *21st Century Economic News*. http://finance.sina.com.cn/g/20080718/02235104705.shtml.

Jiang, C. (江春霞). (2016). 交通基础设施PPP项目失败诱因及启示——基于25个PPP典型案例的分析 [Causes and Insights of Failure of Transportation Infrastructure PPP Projects: Analysis Based on 25 Typical PPP Cases].《北京交通大学学报(社会科学版)》 *[Journal of Beijing Jiaotong University (Social Science Edition)]*, 15(3), 50–58.

Jiang, D. (蒋丹). (2014). 国企为何需要行政化的治理——一种被忽略的效率性解释 [Why Does State-Owned Enterprise Need Governmental Governance: An Overlooked Efficiency Explanation].《现代法学》 *[Modern Law Science]*, 5, 14–28.

Joskow, P. L. (1987). Contract Duration and Relationship-Specific Investments: Empirical Evidence from Coal Markets. *The American Economic Review*, 77(1), 168–185.

(1988). Asset Specificity and the Structure of Vertical Relationships: Empirical Evidence. *The Journal of Law, Economics, and Organization*, 4(1), 95–117.

(1994). Vertical Integration and Long-term Contracts: The Case of Coal-Burning Electric Generating Plants. *The Journal of Law, Economics, and Organization*, 1(1), 33–80.

Kang, J. (2017, July 10). The Fail of LeTV Empire. *Communication Industry Newspaper*.

Kapczynski, A., & Michaels, J. (2024). Administering a democratic industrial policy. *Harvard Law & Policy Review*, 18(2), 279–344

Kaplow, L. (1986). An Economic Analysis of Legal Transition. *Harvard Law Review*, 99(3), 509–617.

(1992). Rules versus Standards: An Economic Analysis. *Duke Law Journal*, 42, 557.

Kaufman, G. G. (1996). Bank Failures, Systemic Risk, and Bank Regulation. *Cato Journal*, 16(1), 19–45.

Keleman, R. D., & Sibbett, E. C. (2004). The Globalization of American Law. *International Organization*, 58(1), 103–136.

Kessides, I. N. (2004). *Reforming Infrastructure: Privatization, Regulation, and Competition. Policy Research Report*. Washington, DC: World Bank and Oxford University Press.

Khanna, T., & Yafeh, Y. (2007). Business Groups in Emerging Markets: Paragons or Parasites? *Journal of Economic Literature*, 45(2), 331–372.

Klein, B., Crawford, R. G., & Alchian, A. A. (1978). Vertical Integration, Appropriable Rents, and the Competitive Contracting Process. *The Journal of Law and Economics*, 21(2), 297–326.

Kornai, J. (1986). The Soft Budget Constraint. *Kyklos*, 39(1), 3–30.

Kowalski, P., et al. (2013). State-Owned Enterprises: Trade Effects and Policy Implications. *OECD Trade Policy Working Papers*, No. 147.

La Porta, R., Lopez-de-Silanes, F., & Shleifer, A. (2002). Government Ownership of Banks. *The Journal of Finance*, 57(1), 265–301.

(2008). The Economic Consequences of Legal Origins. *Journal of Economic Literature*, 46(2), 285–332.

La Porta, R., Lopez-de-Silanes, F., Shleifer, A., & Vishny, R. (1998). Law and Finance. *Journal of Political Economy*, 106, 1113–1155.

Laffont, J.-J., & Tirole, J. (1992). Should Governments Commit? *European Economic Review*, 36(2–3), 345–353.

Laffont, J. J., & Tirole, J. (1993), *A Theory of Incentives in Procurement and Regulation*. Cambridge, MA: The MIT Press.

Lan, X. (2021). *Staying Inside: Chinese Governments and Economic Development.* Shanghai: Shanghai People's Press.

Levy, B., & Spiller, P. T. (1994). The Institutional Foundations of Regulatory Commitment: A Comparative Analysis of Telecommunications Regulation. *Journal of Law, Economics, & Organization*, 10(2), 201–246.

Li, J. (李军慧). (2009, June 26). 中再集团人事权移交中投监管层理清责任 [Appointment Rights of China Re-Insurance Handed Over to China Investment, the Regulator Clarified its Duty]. 《华夏时报》 [*China Times*]. http://www.chinatimes.cc/article/5933.html.

(2017). The Power Logic of Justice in China. *The American Journal of Comparative Law*, 65(1), 95–144.

Li, P., & Shen, Y. (2010). 媒体的公司治理作用：中国的经验证据 [The Corporate Governance Function of the Media: Empirical Evidence from China]. 《经济研究》*[Economic Research]*, 4, 4–13.

Li, S., & Xia, J. (2008). The Roles and Performance of State Firms and Non-State Firms in China's Economic Transition. *World Development*, 36(1), 39–54.

Li, Y. (2022). Court Structure, Judicial Independence, and the Attraction of Foreign Investment: Evidence from Judicial Recentralization in China. https://ssrn.com/abstract=3994808

Li, Y., & Zhang, X. (2008). 中国国有企业民营化前后的绩效对比分析 [A Comparative Study on Corporate Performance before and after Privatization of Chinese State-Owned Enterprises]. *Nankai Economic Studies*, (4), 97–107.

Liao, M. (廖岷). (2010). 关于信贷增长的几点看法 [Several Opinions on the Growth of Lending]. 《金融与保险》 [*Finance and Insurance*]. http://202.119.108.161:93/modules/showContent.aspx?title=&Word=&DocGUID=408355bbec764e1bae6b3f8b7d20fec2.

Liebman, B., Stern, R., Wu, X., & Roberts, M. (2023). Rolling Back Transparency in China's Courts. *Columbia Law Review*, 123, 2407.

Liebman, B. L. (2011). *A Return to Populist Legality? Historical Legacies and Legal Reform*. Cambridge, MA: Harvard University Press.

Liebman, B. L., & Milhaupt, C. J. (2016). *Regulating the Invisible Hand? The Institutional Implications of Chinese State Capitalism*. New York: Oxford University Press.

Lin, J. (林劲标). (2020a). 特许经营权重复许可的效力认定及归责 [Recognition of Effectiveness and Attribution of Repeated Licenses of Concessions].《人民司法》*[People's Judicature]*, 8, 95–98.

Lin, J. Y., Cai, F., & Li, Z. (1998). Competition, Policy Burdens, and State-Owned Enterprise Reform. *The American Economic Review*, 88(2), 422–427.

Lin, L.-W. (2020b). Mandatory Corporate Social Responsibility? Legislative Innovation and Judicial Application in China. *The American Journal of Comparative Law*, 68, 576.

Lin, L. Y.-H. (2020c). Institutionalizing Political Influence in Business: Party-Building and Insider Control in Chinese State-Owned Enterprises. *Vermont Law Review*, 45, 441–480.

Lin, L. Y.-H., & Milhaupt, C. J. (2021). Party Building or Noisy Signaling? The Contours of Political Conformity in Chinese Corporate Governance. *The Journal of Legal Studies*, 50(1), 187–217.

Lin, Y., Cai, F., & Li, Z. (1997). 现代企业制度的内涵与国有企业改革方向 [The Essentials of Modern Enterprise Institutions and the Direction of the Reform on State-Owned Enterprises].《经济研究》*[Economic Research]*, 3, 3–10.

Liscow, Z. (2018). Is Efficiency Biased? *University of Chicago Law Review*, 85(7), 1649–1718.

Listokin, Y. (2019). A Theoretical Framework for Law and Macroeconomics. *American Law and Economics Review*, 21(1), 46-80.

Liu, R. (刘瑞明). (2013). 中国的国有企业效率：一个文献综述 [The Efficiency of China's State-Owned Enterprises: A Literature Review].《世界经济》*[The Journal of World Economy]*, 11, 136–139.

(2019). *How State-Owned Enterprises Drag on Economic Growth: Theory and Evidence from China*. Shanghai: Truth & Wisdom Press.

Liu, T., Zhao, T., & Wang, S. (2016). 基于案例的我国PPP项目再谈判情况研究 [Case-Based Study on the Renegotiation of PPP Projects in China].《建筑经济》*[Construction Economics]*, 9, 31–34.

Liu, X. (刘小玄). (2000). 中国工业企业的所有制结构对效率差异的影响——1995年全国工业企业普查数据的实证分析 [The Impact of Ownership Structure on Efficiency Differences in Chinese Industrial Enterprises: An Empirical Analysis of the 1995 National Industrial Census Data]. *Economic Research (经济研究)*, (2), 17–25.

Liu, X. (刘小玄), & Li, L. (李利英). (2005). 企业产权变革的效率分析 [An Analysis of Enterprise Property-Rights Reform: Efficiency Perspective]. *Social Sciences in China (中国社会科学)*, (2), 4–16.

et al. (2021). *Catch-Up and Radical Innovation in Chinese State-Owned Enterprises: Exploring Large Infrastructure Projects*. Cheltenham, UK: Edward Elgar Publishing.

Lu, L., & Zhang, A. L. (2021). Regulating Fintech Corporations Amidst Covid-19 Pandemic: An Analysis of Ant Group (Alipay)'s Suspension of IPO and Business Restructuring. *Company Lawyer*, 42(10), 341–343.

Luo, D., & Liu, X. (2009). Political Relations, Barriers to Entry and Firm Performance—Empirical Evidence from Chinese Private Listed Companies. 《管理世界》, 5, 97–106.

Lv, D. (吕东). (2017, January 1). 二批民营银行股东旗：不乏互联网基因股东 [The Second Group of Private Bank Licensees Includes Many Internet Companies]. 《证券日报》 [*Securities Daily*].

Ma, C., & Yu, X. (2022). The Application of the Principle of Proportionality in Administrative Adjudication. *Journal of Shandong University (Philosophy and Social Sciences Edition)*, 4, 58–68.

Ma, Y. (2012). Coal Restructuring: State-Owned Enterprises in Name but Not in Reality, Private Enterprises in Reality but Not in Name.《中国经济导报》.

Macaulay, S. (1963). Non-Contractual Relations in Business: A Preliminary Study. *American Sociological Review*, 28, 55–67.

Macey, J. R. (1991). An Economic Analysis of the Various Rationales for Making Shareholders the Exclusive Beneficiaries of Corporate Fiduciary Duties. *Stetson Law Review*, 21, 23–44.

(1999). Fiduciary Duties as Residual Claims: Obligations to Nonshareholder Constituencies from a Theory of the Firm Perspective. *Cornell Law Review*, 84(5), 1266–1281.

Macey, J. R., & Miller, G. P. (1988). Bank Failures, Risk Monitoring, and the Market for Bank Control. *Columbia Law Review*, 88(6), 1153–1226.

Mankiw, N. G. (2009). Smart Taxes: An Open Invitation to Join the Pigou Club. *Eastern Economic Journal*, 35, 14–23.

Mao, W., & Qiao, S. (2021). Legal Doctrine and Judicial Review of Eminent Domain in China. *Law & Society Inquiry, University of Hong Kong Faculty of Law Research Paper No.* 2020/050, 1–34.

Mashaw, J. L. (2010). Explaining Administrative Law: Reflections on Federal Administrative Law in Nineteenth-Century America. In S. Rose-Ackerman & P. L. Lindseth, eds, *Comparative Administrative Law*, Chapter 2, 44. Cheltenham: Edward Elgar Publishing.

Masten, S. E. (2011). Public Utility Ownership in 19th-Century America: The "Aberrant" Case of Water. *The Journal of Law, Economics, & Organization*, 27(3), 604–654.

et al. (1991). The Costs of Organization. *The Journal of Law and Economics*, 27(2), 403–417.

Maurer, N., & Sharma, T. (2001). Enforcing Property Rights Through Reputation: Mexico's Early Industrialization, 1878–1913. *The Journal of Economic History*, 61(4), 950–973.

McCrary, J. (2008). Manipulation of the Running Variable in the Regression Discontinuity Design: A Density Test. *Journal of Econometrics*, 142(2), 698–714.

Megginson, W. L., & Netter, J. M. (2001). From State to Market: A Survey of Empirical Studies on Privatization. *Journal of Economic Literature*, 39(2), 321–389.

Megginson, W. L., & Sutter, N. L. (2006). Privatisation in Developing Countries. *Corporate Governance: An International Review*, 14(4), 234–265.

Michelman, F. I. (1967). Property, Utility and Fairness: Comments on the Ethical Foundations of "Just Compensation" Law. *Harvard Law Review*, 80(6), 1165–1258.

Milhaupt, C. J. (1998). Property Rights in Firms. *Virginia Law Review*, 64(6), 1145–1194.

Milhaupt, C. J., & Lin, L. (2013). We Are the (National) Champions: Understanding the Mechanisms of State Capitalism in China. *Stanford Law Review*, 65(4), 697–759.

Milhaupt, C. J., & Zheng, W. (2014). Beyond Ownership: State Capitalism and the Chinese Firm. *Georgetown Law Journal*, 103, 665.

Minow, M. (2003). Public and Private Partnerships: Accounting for the New Religion. *Harvard Law Review*, 116(5), 1229–1270.

Mitts, J. (2015). Systemic Risk and Managerial Incentives in the Dodd-Frank Orderly Liquidation Authority. *Journal of Financial Regulation*, 1(1), 51–94.

Morck, R. (2011). Finance and Governance in Developing Economies (Working Paper No. 16870). *National Bureau of Economic Research*. https://doi.org/10.3386/w16870.

Muris, T. (1981). Opportunistic Behavior and the Law of Contracts. *Minnesota Law Review*, 65, 521–590.

Nanfeng, C. (南风窗). (2009, September 14). 经济学家建议重建金融工委加强监管 [Economists Suggests that Financial Working Committee be Re-established to Enhance Regulation]. *Sina*. http://news.sina.com.cn/c/sd/2009-09-14/133418646707.shtml.

Napolitano, G. (2010). The Role of the State in (and After) the Financial Crisis: New Challenges for Administrative Law. In P. Lindseth & S. Rose-Ackerman, eds, *Comparative Administrative Law*, 569–591. Cheltenham, UK: Edward Elgar Publishing.

Naughton, B. (2018). State Enterprise Reform Today. In R. Garnaut, L. Song, & C. Fang, eds, *China's 40 Years of Reform and Development: 1978–2018*, 375. Canberra, Australia: The ANU Press.

Nellis, J. (2002). Privatization and Enterprise Reform in Transition Economies: A Retrospective Analysis. *The World Bank Operations Evaluation Department*, Working Paper 23737, 1–58.

(2003). Privatization in Latin America. *Center for Global Development, Working Paper*, 31, 1–32.

Nie, H., (聂辉华) et al. (2022, July 22). 中国城市政商关系排行榜（2017）[The Rankings of Government-Business Relations in Chinese Cities (2017)]. *National Academy of Development and Strategy, Renmin University of China.* http://nads.ruc.edu.cn/zkcg/ndyjbg/c9ad75bec3024ec0bb24e4fc6b7d3c14.htm.

Niu, Y. (牛颖惠). (2009, June 26). 国寿等四大险企正式升格副部级 [Four Major Insurance Companies Rising to the Vice-Ministerial Level].《京华时报》[*China Times*]. http://www.chinatimes.cc/article/5933.html.

North, D. C. (1990). *Institutions, Institutional Change and Economic Performance.* Cambridge, UK: Cambridge University Press.

OECD. (2015). *OECD Guidelines on Corporate Governance of State-Owned Enterprises*, 2015 ed. Paris: OECD Publishing. https://doi.org/10.1787/9789264244160-en.

OECD Development Centre. (1997). Urban Credit Co-Operatives in China. *Working Paper No. 125*, 97(86), 1–79.

Ogus, A. (2007). Regulatory Arrangements and Incentives for Opportunistic Behaviour. In T. Eger, M. G. Faure, & N. Zhang, eds, *Economic Analysis of Law in China*, 151–163. Cheltenham, UK: Edward Elgar Publishing.

Ohnesorge, J. K. (2005). The Rule of Law, Economic Development, and the Developmental States of Northeast Asia. In C. Antons, ed, *Law and Development in East and South-East Asia*, 91–127. Oxford, UK: Routledge.

Organisation for Economic Co-operation and Development. (2017). The Size and Sectoral Distribution of State-Owned Enterprises. *OECD Publishing.* https://doi.org/10.1787/9789264280663-en.

Ouyang, J. (欧阳洁). (2014, March 11). 银监会主席尚福林:民营银行破冰 试点自担风险 [Chairman Shang Fulin of the Banking Regulatory Commission: Private Banks Breaking Ice, the Pilot Banks Bearing Risks Themselves].《人民网–人民日报》[*China Daily*]. http://finance.people.com.cn/money/n/2014/0311/c42877-24597581.html.

Pargendler, M. (2012). The Unintended Consequences of State Ownership: The Brazilian Experience. *Theoretical Inquiries in Law*, 13(2), 503–524.

(2019). How Universal Is the Corporate Form? Reflections on the Dwindling of Corporate Attributes in Brazil. *Columbia Journal of Transnational Law*, 58, 1.

Pargendler, M., Musacchio A., & Lazzarinittt S. G. (2013). In Strange Company: The Puzzle of Private Investment in State-Controlled Firms. *Cornell International Law Journal*, 46(3), 569–609.

Parkin, M. (2019). *Economics*, 13th global ed. Harlow, UK: Pearson.

Peerenboom, R. (2002). *China's Long March toward Rule of Law*. Cambridge, UK: Cambridge University Press.

Pei, M. (2016). *China's Crony Capitalism: The Dynamics of Regime Decay*. Cambridge, MA: Harvard University Press.

et al. (2010). *A Survey of Commercial Litigation in Shanghai Courts*. In R. Peerenboom, ed, *Judicial Independence in China: Lessons for Global Rule of Law Promotion, 221–233*. Cambridge, UK: Cambridge University Press.

Pelzman, S. (1971). Pricing in Public and Private Enterprises: Electric Utilities in the United States. *Journal of Law and Economics*, 14(1), 109–147.

Peng, B. (2014, June 16). 中央司改办负责人解读司法体制四项先行试点总体考虑: 坚持顶层设计与实践探索相结合，积极稳妥推进 [Central Judicial Reform Office's Deputy Director Interprets the Four Pilot Projects of Judicial System Reform: Adhering to the Combination of Top-Level Design and Practical Exploration, Promoting Steadily]. *People's Daily*. http://politics.people.com.cn/n/2014/0616/c1001-25151030.html.

Peter, H. S. (2000). Law and Post-Privatization Regulation Reform: Perspectives from the U.S. Experience. In L. Manzetti, ed, *Regulatory Policy in Latin America: Post-Privatization Realities*, 24–48. Coral Gables, FL: North-South Center Press.

Pistor, K. (2013). A Legal Theory of Finance. *Journal of Comparative Economics*, 41, 315–330.

Pistor, K., & Xu, C. (2002). Incomplete Law. *New York University Journal of International Law and Politics*, 35, 931–1013.

(2005). Governing Stock Markets in Transition Economies: Lessons from China. *American Law and Economics Review*, 7(1), 184–210.

Posen, A. S. (2023, August 2). The End of China's Economic Miracle: How Beijing's Struggles Could Be an Opportunity for Washington. Foreign Affairs. September/October 2023 issue.

Posner, R. A. (1986). *Economic Analysis of Law*, 3rd ed. Boston, MA: Little, Brown.

(2013). The Concept of Regulatory Capture: A Short, Inglorious History. In D. Carpenter & D. A. Moss, eds, *Preventing Regulatory Capture: Special Interest Influence and How to Limit It*, 49–56. Cambridge, UK: Cambridge University Press.

(2014). *Economic Analysis of Law*. Burlington, MA: Aspen Publishing.

Pound, R. (1942). *Administrative Law*. Pittsburgh, PA: Fred B. Rothman and Co.

Priest, G. L. (1993). The Origins of Utility Regulation and the "Theories of Regulation" Debate. *The Journal of Law and Economics*, 36(1, Part 2), 289–323.

Putniņš, T. J. (2015). Economics of State-Owned Enterprises. *International Journal of Public Administration*, 38, 815.

Qian, H., & Liu, Y. (2019). 混合所有制，股权结构对公司绩效的影响 [The Influence of Mixed Ownership and Ownership Structure on Corporate Performance]. *Statistics & Decision*, 35(23), 185–188.

Qian, Y. (钱颖一). (1995). 企业的治理结构改革和融资结构改革 [The Reform of the Governance Structure and Finance Structure of Enterprises]. *Economic Research (经济研究)*, (1), 20–29.

(2002). A Third Perspective of the State Ownership of Enterprise: A Transitional Institutional Arrangement, *Jing Daokan*, 5, 1.

Qiao, S. (2023a). The Authoritarian Commons: Divergent Paths of Neighborhood Democratization in Three Chinese Megacities. *American Journal of Comparative Law*, 31(2), 388–443.

(2023b). Finance against Law: The Case of China. *Harvard International Law Journal*, 64(2), 431–487.

Qin, Y., et al. (2020).《PPP全流程运作实务》[PPP Full Process Operation Practice, 2nd ed.]. Beijing: China Legal Publishing House.

Qu, L. (2017, August 14). LeTV: Deconstructing Its Capital Structure Behind Crisis. *China Business Newspaper*.

Ramachandran, J., Manikandan, K. S., & Pant, A. (2013). Why Conglomerates Thrive (Outside the US), *Harvard Business Review*. https://hbr.org/2013/12/why-conglomerates-thrive-outside-the-us.

Ramamurti, R. (1999). Why Haven't Developing Countries Privatized Deeper and Faster? *World Development*, 27(1), 137–155.

(2000). A Multilevel Model of Privatization in Emerging Economies. *The Academy of Management Review*, 25(3), 525–550.

Ramo, J. C. (2004). The Beijing Consensus. *Foreign Policy Centre*. https://fpc.org.uk/publications/the-beijing-consensus/.

Reitz, J. C. (2005). Political Economy and Separation of Powers. *Transnational Law and Contemporary Problems*, 15, 579–629.

Ren, F. (任芳), & Liu, B. (刘兵). (2006, December 18). 国资委：国有经济应保持对七个行业的绝对控制力 [SASAC: State-Owned Economy Should Maintain Absolute Control over Seven Industries]. The Central People's Government of the People's Republic of China. http://www.gov.cn/govweb/ztzl/2006-12/18/content_472256.htm.

Ren, M. (2016, November 8). LeTV Cash Crunch Happens Earlier than Expected. *China Security Newspaper*.

Reuters Staff. (2019, August 5). 中国金融：截至2018年末民间资本控股的银行业金融机构超3,000家——银保监会 [China's Finance: As of the End of 2018, More than 3,000 Banking Financial Institutions Controlled by Private Capital—CBIRC]. *Reuters*. https://www.reuters.com/article/%E4%B8%AD%E5%9B%BD%E9%87%91%E8%9E%8D%EF%BC%9A%E6%88%AA%E8%87%B32018%E5%B9%B4%E6%9C%AB%E6%B0%91%E9%97%B4%E8%B5%84%E6%9C%AC%E6%8E%A7%E8%82%A1%E7%9A%84%E9%93%B6%E8%A1%8C%E4%B8%9A%E9%87%91%E8%9E%8D%E6%9C%BA%E6%9E%84%E8%B6%853%2C000%E5%AE%B6-%E9%93%B6%E4%BF%9D%E7%9B%91%E4%BC%9A-idCNL4S2512EL.

Roberts, B. M., & Saeed, M. A. (2012). Privatizations Around the World: Economic or Political Determinants? *Economics & Politics*, 24(1), 47–71.

Rodriguez, D. B. (2008). Administrative Law. In K. E. Whittington, R. D. Kelemen, & G. A. Caldeira, eds, *The Oxford Handbook of Law and Politics*, 403–419. Oxford: Oxford University Press.

Roe, M. J. (1991). A Political Theory of American Corporate Finance. *Columbia Law Review*, 91(1), 10–67.

Rose, C. M. (2000). Property and Expropriation: Themes and Variations in American Law. *Utah Law Review*, 1, 1–38.

Rose-Ackerman, S., & Rossi, J. (2000). Disentangling Deregulatory Takings. *Virginia Law Review*, 86(7), 1435–1495.

Sabel, C. F., & Simon, W. H. (2012). Contextualizing Regimes: Institutionalization as a Response to the Limits of Interpretation and Policy Engineering. *Michigan Law Review*, 110(7), 1265–1308.

Sabry, M. I. (2015). Good Governance, Institutions and Performance of Public Private Partnerships. *The International Journal of Public Sector Management*, 28(7), 566–582.

Sapienza, P. (2004). The Effects of Government Ownership on Bank Lending. *Journal of Financial Economics*, 72(2), 357–384.

Sappington, D. E., & Stiglitz, J. E. (1987). Privatization, Information and Incentives. *Journal of Policy Analysis and Management*, 6(4), 567–585.

Schafer, H.-B. (2006). Rules versus Standards in Rich and Poor Countries: Precise Legal Norms as Substitutes for Human Capital in Low-Income Countries. *Supreme Court Economic Review*, 14, 113–134.

Schizer, D. M. (2017). Energy Subsidies: Worthy Goals, Competing Priorities, and Flawed Institutional Design, *Tax Law Review*, 70, 243–304.

Schuck, P. H. (1999). Law and Post-Privatization Regulatory Reform: Perspectives from the US Experience. *Yale Law School, Program for Studies in Law, Economics and Public Policy, Working Paper*, 222. https://papers.ssrn.com/sol3/papers.cfm?abstract_id=191353.

Schultz, K. E. (2018). Public-Private Partnerships: Structuring the Revival of Fiscally Distressed Municipalities. *New York University Journal of Law & Business*, 15(1), 189–228.

Schwarcz, S. L. (2014). The Governance Structure of Shadow Banking: Rethinking Assumptions about Limited Liability. *Notre Dame Law Review*, 90, 1–30.

Schwarze, J. (1992). *European Administrative Law*. London: Sweet & Maxwell.

Scott, C. (2008). Agencification, Regulation and Judicialization: American Exceptionalism and Other Ways of Life. In T. Ginsburg & A. H. Y. Chen, eds, *Administrative Law and Governance in Asia*, 38–58. London: Routledge.

Selvarajah, P. (2010). The AIG Bailout and AIG's Prospects for Repaying Government Loans. *The Review of Banking and Financial Law*, 29, 363.

Shang, Z. (2018, April 2). The Legal Analysis on the Wu Xiaohui Case. *China United Business Newspaper.*

Shapiro, C., & Willig, R. D. (1990). Economic Rationales for the Scope of Privatization, *Princeton University Discussion Paper*, 1–33.

(2019). Economic Rationales for the Scope of Privatization. In E. Suleiman & J. Waterbury, eds, *The Political Economy of Public Sector Reform and Privatization*, 55–87. Oxford: Routledge.

Shavell, S. (1984). Liability for Harm versus Regulation of Safety. *The Journal of Legal Studies*, 13(2), 357–374.

(2011). Corrective Taxation versus Liability as a Solution to the Problem of Harmful Externalities. *The Journal of Law and Economics*, 54(S4), 249–266.

Shaviro, D. (2000). *When Rules Change: An Economic and Political Analysis of Transition Relief and Retroactivity*. Chicago, IL: The University of Chicago Press.

Sheng, H., & Zhao, N. (2013). China's State-Owned Enterprises: Nature, Performance and Reform. *Series on Chinese Economics Research*, 1, 195.

Shi, T. (施天涛), & Du, J. (杜晶). (2007). 我国公司法上关联交易的皈依及其法律规制 [A Chinese Copy of Rules on Deal of Interests Conflicts].《中国法学》*[China Legal Science]*, 6, 126–140.

Shirley, M. M., & McDonald, L. G. (1995). *Bureaucrats in Business: The Economics and Politics of Government Ownership* (Vol. 4). Washington, DC: World Bank Publications.

Shleifer, A. (1998). State versus Private Ownership. *Journal of Economic Perspectives*, 12(4), 133–150.

Shleifer, A., & Vishny, R. W. (1994). Politicians and Firms. *The Quarterly Journal of Economics*, 109(4), 995–1025.

Simon, H. A. (1957). *Administrative Behavior*. New York: Free Press.

Sina Finance. (n.d.). Company Information: SH600036. http://finance.sina.com.cn/realstock/company/sh600036/nc.shtml.

Smaoui, H., & Boubakri, N. (2004). Conditions for Success: The Importance of Legal Governance in the Privatization Process. *University of Petroleum and Minerals, Saudi Arabia. Conference Paper* (No. 219).

Smith, H. E. (2016). Equity and Administrative Behaviour. In P. G. Turner, ed, *Equity and Administration*, 326–366. Cambridge, UK: Cambridge University Press.

(2020). Equity as Meta-Law. *Yale Law Journal*, 130, 1050–1144.

Solomon, S. D., & Zaring, D. (2018). Transactional Administration. *Georgetown Law Journal*, 106(4), 1097–1138.

Song, L. (宋立刚), & Yao, Y. (姚洋). (2005). 改制对企业绩效的影响 [The Impact of Restructuring on Enterprise Performance]. *Social Sciences in China (中国社会科学)*, (2), 17–31.

State Council Information Office. (2015, June 26). 国新办关于"鼓励民间资本进入银行业"专题新闻发布会开场通报 [State Council Information Office

Opening Statement on the Public Release about Encouraging Private Capital to Enter the Banking Industry]. China.com.cn (中国网). http://www.china.com.cn/zhibo/zhuanti/ch-xinwen/2015-06/26/content_35917439.htm.

Stigler, G. J. (1971). The Theory of Economic Regulation, *Bell Journal of Economics*, 2(1), 3–21.

(1989). Two Notes on the Coase Theorem. *Yale Law Journal*, 99(3), 631–633.

Stiglitz, J. (1999a). Quis Custodiet Ipsos Custodes? *Challenge*, 42(6), 26–67.

(1999b). Whither Reform: Ten Years of the Transition. Paper Prepared for the Annual World Bank Conference on Development Economics, Washington, DC, *Annual World Bank Conference on Development Economics*, 27–56.

Stiglitz, J. E. (2013). The Economics Behind Law in a Market Economy: Alternatives to the Neoliberal Orthodoxy. In D. Kennedy and J. E. Stiglitz, eds, *Law and Economics with Chinese Characteristics: Institutions for Promoting Development in the Twenty-First Century*, 153–186. Oxford: Oxford University Press.

Su, J., et al. (2021). 我国社会资本参与基础设施PPP项目的主要顾虑研究 [Study on the Main Concerns of Social Capital Participation in Infrastructure PPP Projects in China]. 《建筑经济》*[Construction Economy]*, 8, 81–85.

Szamosszegi, A., & Kyle, C. (2011). An Analysis of State-Owned Enterprises and State Capitalism in China. *Capital Trade, Incorporated for US-China Economic and Security Review Commission*, 41, 1–105.

Tan, J. (谭劲松), & Zheng, G. (郑国坚). (2004). 产权安排、治理机制、政企关系与企业效率——以"科龙"和"美的"为例 [Property Rights Arrangements, Governance Mechanisms, Government–Enterprise Relations, and Enterprise Efficiency: A Case Study of "Kelon" and "Midea"]. *Management World (管理世界)*, (2), 104–116.

Tang, W. (唐伟杰). (2009, August 11). 人均收入高20% 专家析自来水公司亏损真实原因 [Salaries of Employees in Water Utility Companies 20% Higher than Average: The Real Reasons for the Loss of Water Utility Companies]. 《中国新闻网》 [*China News Online*]. http://www.chinanews.com/cj/cj-cyzh/news/2009/08-11/1812044.shtml.

Tecco, N. (2008). Financially Sustainable Investments in Developing Countries Water Sectors: What Conditions Could Promote Private Sector Involvement? *International Environmental Agreements: Politics, Law and Economics*, 8(2), 129–142.

The World Bank. (2013). The Global Financial Development Report: Rethinking the Role of the State in Finance. Washington, DC: World Bank Group. http://siteresources.worldbank.org/EXTGLOBALFINREPORT/Resources/8816096-1346865433023/8827078-1346865457422/GDF_2013_Report.pdf.

Tian, Y. (2021, November 21). 复星牵头投资！我国首条民营资本控股的高铁试运行 [Fosun Leads Investment! The Trial Operation of China's First

Privately-Held High-Speed Rail]. 《中国证券报》 [*China Securities Journal*]. http://finance.ce.cn/stock/gsgdbd/202111/27/t20211127_37120972.shtml.

Tirole, J. (1994). The Internal Organization of Government. *Oxford Economic Papers*, 46(1), 1–19.

Titternbrun, J. (1997). *Private versus Public Enterprise: In Search of the Economic Rationale For Privatisation*, 56–64. Cambridge, UK: Janus Publishing.

Trebilcock, M. J., & Iacobucci, E. M. (2003). Privatization and Accountability. *Harvard Law Review*, 116(5), 1422–1453.

Troesken, W., & Geddes, R. (2003). Municipalizing American Waterworks, 1897–1915. *Journal of Law, Economics, and Organization*, 19(2), 373–400.

Trubek, D. M. (1972a). Max Weber on Law and the Rise of Capitalism. *Wisconsin Law Review*, 1972, 720–753.

(1972b). Toward a Social Theory of Law: An Essay on the Study of Law and Development. *Yale Law Journal*, 82(1), 1–50.

Tyler, T. R. (2006). *Why People Obey the Law*. Princeton, NJ: Princeton University Press.

Upham, F. K. (2008). From Demsetz to Deng: Speculations on the Implications of Chinese Growth for Law and Development Theory. *NYU Journal of International Law and Politics*, 41, 551.

Vermeule, A. (2009). Our Schmittian Administrative Law. *Harvard Law Review*, 122(4), 1095–1149.

(2013). Conventions of Agency Independence. *Columbia Law Review*, 113(6), 1163–1228.

(2020). Rules, Commands, and Principles in the Administrative State. *Yale Law Journal Forum*, 130, 356–369.

Vernon, R. (1984). Linking Managers with Ministers: Dilemmas of the State-Owned Enterprise. *Journal of Policy Analysis and Management*, 4(1), 39–55.

Vickers, J., & Yarrow, G. (1991). Economic Perspectives on Privatization. *Journal of Economic Perspectives*, 5(2), 111–132.

Viscusi, W. K., Harrington, Jr, J. E., & Sappington, D. E. (2005). *Economics of Regulation and Antitrust*. Cambridge, MA: The MIT Press.

Vogel, S. K. (1996). *Freer Markets, More Rules: Regulatory Reform in Advanced Industrial Countries*. Ithaca, NY: Cornell University Press.

Wall Street. (2014, November 15). 民营银行发起人协议曝光：持股5%以上股东要兜底50万元以下个人存款 [Agreement Signed by Private Banks Promoters Exposed: Shareholders with More than 5% Shares to Pay Individual Deposits below RMB 500,000]. http://wallstreetcn.com/node/210698.

Wall Street. (2021, October 14). 中国的"雷曼时刻"不会来临 [The Lehman Moment of China Would Not Come]. http://wallstreetcn.com/node/77955.

Wang, H., et al. (2018). Commercial Investment in Public-Private Partnerships: The Impact of Contract Characteristics. *Policy and Politics*, 46(4), 589–606.

Wang, J. (2014). The Political Logics of Corporate Governance in Chinese State-Owned Enterprises. *Cornell International Law Journal*, 47(3), 631–668.

(王俊丹). (2015, July 2). 城商行IPO重启，民资享受财富盛宴 [Urban Commercial Banks IPO Reinitiated, Private Investors Getting a Big Pie]. 《21世纪经济报道》[*Twenty-first Century Business Herald*]. http://m.21jingji.com/article/20150702/bdf0fe681ff8321f488eaf6eeb325e56.html.

(王俊岭). (2023, May 31). 民营企业在企业总量中的占比达到92.3%——民营经济稳步迈向高质量 [As of the End of March, the Proportion of Private Enterprises in the Total Number of Enterprises Reached 92.3%—Private Economy Steadily Moving Towards High Quality]. 《人民日报海外版》*People's Daily Overseas Edition*, 3.

Wang, J., & Cheng-Han, T. (2020). Mixed Ownership Reform and Corporate Governance in China's State-Owned Enterprises. *Vanderbilt Journal of Transnational Law*, 53(3), 1055–1107.

Wang, J. (王俊豪), & Jin, X. (金暄暄). (2016). PPP模式下政府和民营企业的契约关系及其治理——以中国城市基础设施PPP为例 [The Contractual Relationship between the Government and Private Enterprises under the PPP Model and Its Governance—The Example of Urban Infrastructure PPP in China]. 《经济与管理研究》*[Research on Economics and Management]*, 3, 62–68.

Wang, S. (2004). Safety Production Supervision of Coal Mines: Transformation of China's Governance Model. *Comparative Study*, 13, 79.

Wang, S., & Yang, D. Y. (2021). *Policy Experimentation in China: The Political Economy of Policy Learning* (NBER Working Paper No. w29402). National Bureau of Economic Research. https://doi.org/10.3386/w29402.

Wang, X. (王锡锌). (2006). 公共决策中的大众、专家与政府 [The Public, Expertise, and Government in Public Decision-Makings]. 《中外法学》*[Peking University Law Journal]*, 4, 462.

Wang, Y. (2015). *Tying the Autocrat's Hands: The Rise of the Rule of Law in China*. Cambridge, UK: Cambridge University Press.

(2019). More Authoritarian, the More Judicial Independence? The Paradox of Court Reforms in China and Russia. *University of Pennsylvania Journal of Constitutional Law*, 22, 529.

(2021a). "Detaching" Courts from Local Politics? Assessing the Judicial Centralization Reforms in China. *The China Quarterly*, 246, 545.

(王燕平). (2021b, December 22). 今年A股IPO融资额首破5000亿创历史纪录 [This Year's A-Share IPO Financing Amount First Broke 500 Billion, a Historical Record]. 《钱江晚报》[*Qianjiang Evening News*]. https://www.chinanews.com.cn/cj/2021/12-22/9635404.shtml.

Wang, Y., & Zhao, Z. J. (2014). Motivations, Obstacles, and Resources: Determinants of Public-Private Partnership in State Toll Road Financing. *Public Performance & Management Review*, 37(4), 679–704.

Wee, S.-L. (2014, April 14). China Blames France's Veolia for Tap Water Pollution. *Reuters*. https://www.reuters.com/article/china-water-veolia-idINKBN0D20CA20140416.

Wei, Z., & Varela, O. (2003). State Equity Ownership and Firm Market Performance: Evidence from China's Newly Privatized Firms, *Global Finance Journal*, 14, 65–82.

Wen, J. (2022). State Employment as a Strategy of Autocratic Control in China. *Working Paper of the Structural Transformation of Economic Growth*, London.

Williamson, O. E. (1971). The Vertical Integration of Production: Market Failure Considerations. *American Economic Review*, 61(2), 112–123.

(1975). *Markets and Hierarchies*. New York: The Free Press.

(1979). Transaction-Cost Economics: The Governance of Contractual Relations. *The Journal of Law and Economics*, 22(2), 233–261.

(1983). Credible Commitments: Using Hostages to Support Exchange. *The American Economic Review*, 73(4), 519–540.

(1985). *The Economic Institutions of Capitalism: Firms, Markets, and Relational Contracting*. New York: The Free Press.

(1996). *The Mechanisms of Governance*. New York: Oxford University Press.

(1999). Public and Private Bureaucracies: A Transaction Cost Economics Perspectives. *Journal of Law Economics & Organization*, 15(1), 306–342.

Wilmarth, Jr, A. E. (2008). The Dark Side of Universal Banking: Financial Conglomerates and the Origins of the Subprime Financial Crisis. *Connecticut Law Review*, 41(4), 963–1050.

World Bank. (1995). *Bureaucrats in Business: The Economics and Politics of Government Ownership*. A World Bank Policy Research Report. World Bank. http://documents.worldbank.org/curated/en/197611468336015835/Bureaucrats-in-business-the-economics-and-politics-of-government-ownership.

World Bank Group. (2020). *Private Participation in Infrastructure (PPI) 2020 Annual Report*. Washington, DC: The World Bank, 1–27.

Wu, J. (1994a). Modern Enterprise and Its Reform. 《经济研究》*[Economic Research]*, 3, 10.

(吴敬琏). (1994b). 现代公司与企业改革 *[Modern Corporations and Enterprise Reform]*. Tianjin: Tianjin People's Publishing House.

(2005). *Understanding and Interpreting Chinese Economic Reform*. Knutsford, UK: Texere Publishing.

Wu, N. (吴楠). (2013, May 7). 多地开听证会拟提高水价 低水价被指在补贴富人 [Public Hearings Are to Be Convened in Many Cities to Raise Water Tariffs; Low Water Tariffs are Subsidizing the Rich].《北京晚报》 [*Beijing Evening News*]. http://finance.sina.com.cn/china/20130507/165515377126.shtml.

Wu, W., et al. (2009). The Government Background and Tax Incentives of Executives in Chinese Listed Companies. 《管理世界》*[Management World]*, 3, 134 –142.

Wu, Y. (武亚东). (2022, January 8). PPP成稳增长重要抓手：去年前11月开工项目478个 投资额近9000亿元 [PPP Has Become an Important Grasp of Stable Growth: 478 Projects Started in the First 11 Months of Last Year, with an Investment of Nearly 900 Billion RMB].《经济日报》[*Economic Daily*]. http://www.gov.cn/xinwen/2022-01/10/content_5667335.htm.

Xu, C. (2018, April 9). CISF Spends 60.8 RMB Billion Recuing Anbang. *Beijing Business Newspaper.* https://global.chinadaily.com.cn/a/201804/04/WS5ac469fea3105cdcf651643b.html.

Xu, N. (徐诺金). (2003). 关于我国民营银行的发展问题 [The Development of Private Banks in Our Country]. 《金融研究》 *[Journal of Financial Research]*, 12, 36–43.

Xu, W., Chen, J., & Xu, G. (2017). An Empirical Analysis of the Public Enforcement of Securities Law in China: Finding the Missing Piece of the Puzzle. *European Business Organization Law Review*, 18(2), 367–389. https://doi.org/10.1007/s40804–017-0070-6.

Xu, Y. (2012). *The Political Economy of State-Owned Enterprises in China and India*. Chicago, IL: The University of Chicago Press.

Xu, Z. H. (2009, September 14). 经济学家建议重建金融工委加强监管 [Economists Suggests That Financial Working Committee be Re-established to Enhance Regulation]. *Nanfeng Chuang*. https://news.sina.com.cn/c/sd/2009-09-14/133418646707.shtml.

Yair, L. (2016). A Theoretical Framework for Law and Macroeconomics. *Yale Law School, Public Law Research Paper No.* 586; *Yale Law & Economics Research Paper No.* 567.

Yang, J., Qin, H., & He, H. (2019). 裁判文书上网公开的中国实践——进展, 问题与完善 [The Chinese Practice of Publishing Judicial Documents Online: Progress, Problems, and Improvements]. *China Law Review (*中国法律评论*)*, (6), 125–147.

Yang, L. (2017). Minying Konggu Gaotie Fuxing Qianyue 462 Yi Hangshaotai Xiangmu (High Speed Rail Controlled by Private Investors, Fuxing Invested 46.2 Billion in the Hangshsaotai Project). *Xinhua Net*. http://news.xinhuanet.com/fortune/2016-09/29/c_129305918.htm.

Yang, R., et al. (2013). "准官员"的晋升机制: 来自中国央企的证据 [Promotion Mechanism of "Quasi-Officials": Evidence from Chinese State-Owned Enterprises].《管理世界》*[Management World]*, 3, 23–33.

Yang, W. (2014). The Person in Charge of the Central Judicial Reform Office Answering Questions about the Pilot Work of Judicial System Reform. *Xinhua News*. https://www.gov.cn/xinwen/2014-06/15/content_2701248.htm.

Yang, W., & Guo, F. (2020). Political Connections and Enterprise Performance of Private Enterprises in China: Impacts and Mechanisms. *International Journal of Finance and Economics*, 12(1), 1–86.

Yarrow, G. (1999). A Theory of Privatization, or Why Bureaucrats Are Still in Business? *World Development*, 27, 157–168.

Yi, F., & Li, D. (易芳, 李德庭). (2016, July 13). PPP项目中政府方出资比例影响因素初探 [Preliminary Exploration of Factors Influencing the Government's Contribution Ratio in PPP Projects]. 《君合法评》[*Junhe Law Review*]. https://www.junhe.com/law-reviews/109.

(2023). Preliminary Exploration of Factors Influencing the Government's Contribution Ratio in PPP Projects. http://www.junhe.com/law-reviews/109.

Yin, J. (尹建辉). (2012, May 28). 银监会：不对民间资本进入银行业单独设限 [Banking Regulatory Commission: Will Not Prevent Private Capital from Entering the Banking Industry]. 《第一财经日报》[*China Business News*]. http://finance.people.com.cn/bank/GB/17998200.html.

Yin, Z. (2020). 《政府和社会资本合作（PPP）实务操作指南》 [Practical Operational Guidelines for Government and Public-Private Partnership (PPP)]. Beijing: Post & Telecom Press.

Yu, A. (于安). (2017). 论政府特许经营协议 [On Government Concession Agreements]. 《行政法学研究》*[Administrative Law Review]*, 6, 1005–1078.

Yu, M., & Pan, H. (2008). Political Relations, Institutional Environment and Private Enterprise Bank Loans.《管理世界》*[Management World]*, 8, 9 –21.

Yu, N., Su, D., & Ji, M. (于宁, 苏丹丹, 季敏华). (2007, September 29). "内部人"关国亮 [Insider Guan Guoliang]. 《财经》 [*Caijing*]. http://www.caijing.com.cn/2007-05-27/100020559.html.

Yu, S. (于姝楠). (2012, March 2). 广州水价调整听证会两套方案支持人数均不过半 [Fewer than Half Support the Two Proposals for Adjustment of Water Tariffs of Guangzhou in the Hearing]. 《中国青年报》 [*China Youth Daily*]. http://finance.sina.com.cn/consume/20120302/034911496394.shtml.

Zeng, J. (2013). *State-led Privatization in China: The Politics of Economic Reform*. New York: Routledge.

Zeng, J. S. (2017a). State Ownership and Regulatory Costs: A Law and Economic Explanation for the Prevalence of State-Owned Enterprises in China. *Columbia Journal of Asian Law*, 31, 1.

(2017b). Internal and External Shareholder Liability in the Financial Industry: A Comparative Approach. *Review of Banking & Financial Law*, 37, 285.

(2019). Regulating Draconian Takeover Defenses with Soft Law: Empirical Evidence from Event Studies in China. *European Business Organization Law Review*, 20(4), 823–854..

(2021a). Entity Shielding and the Rule of "Debts-Follow-Assets" in China: An Empirical Law and Economics Analysis. *American Bankruptcy Law Journal*, 95, 1–40.

(2021b). Does Regulation of Defensive Tactics with Mandatory Rules Benefit Shareholders? Evidence from Event Studies in China. *International Review of Law and Economics*, 66, 105988.

(2023). Competing with Leviathan: Law and Government Ownership in China's Public-Private Partnership Market. *International Review of Law and Economics*, 76, 106166.

(2024). Rules versus Standards in Chinese Law on Minority Shareholder Protection: A New Taxonomy and Empirical Analysis. Working Paper, Forthcoming in *American Journal of Comparative Law*.

(2025). Law and Industrial Policy: The East Asian Experience. *Vanderbilt Journal of Transnational Law*, 57. https://papers.ssrn.com/sol3/papers.cfm?abstract_id=4745978.

Zeng, S. (2022). Environmental Policy and Compensation in China: An Empirical Analysis of Article Eight of the Chinese Administrative License Law. *Journal of Environmental Law*, 34(2), 287–305.

Zhang, C. (2023). The Global Landscape of State-Owned Enterprises: The Scale and Industry Distribution of State-Owned Enterprises in Various Economies [in Chinese]. In J. Wu, ed, *Comparison*. Beijing: CITIC Publishing Group.

Zhang, H., Huang, H., & Yan, Q. (2016). 混合所有制改革，政策性负担与国有企业绩效：基于1999–2007年工业企业数据库的实证研究 [Mixed Ownership Reform, Policy Burdens and State-Owned Enterprise Performance: An Empirical Study Based on a Database of Industrial Enterprises from 1999 to 2007].《经济学家》*[The Economist]*, 09, 32–41.

Zhang, H., et al. (2016). Mixed Ownership Reform, Policy Burden, and State-Owned Enterprise Performance: An Empirical Study Based on the Industrial Enterprise Database from 1999 to 2007. *The Economist*, 09, 32–41.

Zhang, J. (2010a, August 23). Why Some Problematic Companies Can Go Public. *China Business Newspaper*.

Zhang, J., & Zhou, L. (2008). *Competing for Growth: The Political Economy of China's Growth*. Shanghai: Shanghai Century Publishing.

et al. (2007). 中国为什么拥有了良好的基础设施 [Why Does China Enjoy So Much Better Physical Infrastructure?].《经济研究》*[Economic Research]*, 3, 4–19.

Zhang, L. (张兰). (2010b, March 19). 保监会建立案件责任追究制度 [The Insurance Regulatory Commission Establishes Case Liability Chasing System].《金融时报》[*Financial Times*]. http://finance.sina.com.cn/roll/20100319/07557593566.shtml.

Zhang, T., & Ginsburg, T. (2019). China's Turn toward Law. *Virginia Journal of International Law*, 59, 306.

Zhang, T., & Morley, J. D. (2022). The Modern State and the Rise of the Business Corporation. *Yale Law Journal*, 132, 1970.

Zhang, W. (1994), 从现代企业理论看中国国有企业的改革 [Reform of State-Owned Enterprises Based on Modern Enterprise Theory] [in Chinese].《改革与战略》*[Reform and Strategy]*, 6, 18.

(张维迎). (1995). 从现代企业理论看中国国有企业改革 [SOE Reform from the Modern Firm-Theoretical Perspective]. *Reform*, (改革) (1), 30–33.

Zhang, W., & Li, S. (1998). 地区间竞争与中国国有企业的民营化 [Interregional Competition and the Privatization of Chinese State-Owned Enterprises]. *Economic Research Journal*, (12), 13–22.

Zhang, X. (张欣). (2017). PPP 模式面临的问题及对策研究 [Research on the Problems and Countermeasures of the PPP Model].《时代金融》*[Times Finance]*, 12, 21.

et al. (2023). Counterfactual Analysis of State-Owned Enterprise Performance: A Study Based on 2004, 2008 Economic Census Data and 2015 Enterprise Data. *Contemporary Economic Research*, 331(3), 5–25.

Zhao, R., & Zhang, J. (2022). 地方司法体制改革与企业投资——来自地方法院人财物省级统管的证据 [Local Judicial System Reform and Enterprise Investment: Evidence from the Provincial Unified Management of Personnel, Finance, and Materials in Local Courts].《经济学（季刊）》*[Economics (Quarterly)]*, 2, 505.

Zheng, H., & Wang, F. (2000). 中国公司治理结构改革研究：一个理论综述 [Research on the Reform of China's Corporate Governance Structure: A Theoretical Review]. *Management World (管理世界)*, (3), 119–125.

Zheng, Y. (2017). Privatization with 'Vested Interests' in China. *Socio-Economic Review*, 17(3), 767–791. https://doi.org/10.1093/ser/mwx023.

Zheng, Y., & Huang, Y. (2018), *Market in State: The Political Economy of Domination in China*, 414–416. Cambridge, UK: Cambridge University Press.

Zhou, L. (2004). The Incentives and Cooperation of Government Officials in the Promotion Game. *Economic Studies*, 37(4), 696–727.

(周黎安). (2007). 中国地方官员的晋升锦标赛模式研究 [An Analysis of Promotion Tournament Model of Chinese Local Officials] [in Chinese]. *Journal of Economic Research*, 7, 36–50.

(2018). Bureaucratic & Economic Markets and China's Growth Story. *Chinese Journal of Sociology*, 38(2), 1–45.

Zhou, Y. (2017, August 7). Lecloud Gets Involved in Several Lawsuits: How Jia Finish Plan to Finish His Business in Chongqing. *China Business Newspaper*, A05.

Zhou, Z. (2014, August 26). 张维迎：国企全都不赚钱 利润是负的 [Zhang Weiying: All State-Owned Enterprises Are Unprofitable, and Their Profits Are Negative].《每日经济新闻》[*Daily Economic News*]. https://finance.sina.cn/china/cjpl/2014-08-26/detail-iaxixtqn6003358.d.html?from=wap.

Zhu, T. (朱天). (1998). 公司治理、国企改革与制度建设 [Corporate Governance, Reform of State-Owned Enterprises, and Institutional Building].《经济研究》*[Economic Research]*, 1, 47–51.

Zuigao Renmin Fayuan (最高人民法院) [The Supreme People's Court]. (2014).《中国法院司法改革年鉴（2014年版）》[*China Courts Judicial Reform Yearbook (2014 Edition)*], 349–377. Beijing: People's Court Press.

INDEX

Printed by Integrated Books International,
United States of America